YORUBA MEDICINE

YORUBA MEDICINE

by

ANTHONY D. BUCKLEY

CLARENDON PRESS · OXFORD

1985

Oxford University Press, Walton Street, Oxford OX2 6DP

London New York Toronto
Delhi Bombay Calcutta Madras Karachi
Kuala Lumpur Singapore Hong Kong Tokyo
Nairobi Dar es Salaam Cape Town
Melbourne Auckland
and associated companies in
Beirut Berlin Ibadan Mexico City Nicosia

Oxford is a trade mark of Oxford University Press

Published in the United States
by Oxford University Press, New York

British Library Cataloguing in Publication Data

Buckley, Anthony D.
Yoruba medicine.
1. Yorubas—Medicine   2. Folk medicine—
Nigeria, Western
I. Title
615.8' 82' 096692   R653.N6
ISBN 0–19–823254–3

Library of Congress Cataloging in Publication Data

Buckley, Anthony D.
Yoruba medicine.
Originally presented as the author's thesis
(doctoral)—University of Birmingham, 1982.
Bibliography: p.
Includes index.
1. Yorubas—Medicine.   I. Title.
DT515.45.Y67A57   1985   615.8'99'09669   84–23762
ISBN 0–19–823254–3

Set by Wyvern Typesetting Limited, Bristol

Printed in Great Britain
at the University Press, Oxford
by David Stanford
Printer to the University

To Kathleen and Linda

Acknowledgements

This study arises out of a Ph.D. thesis presented in the Department of Sociology and the Centre of West African Studies at the University of Birmingham in 1982. I received considerable help over many years, and I wish to acknowledge this with gratitude.

The SSRC provided funds which enabled me to spend one year at the University of Birmingham at the Centre of West African Studies. The Leverhulme Trust gave me a generous grant to travel to Nigeria and to support me while I was there. This was supplemented by an additional award from the Esperanza Trust. Later I received a two-year research studentship from Queen's University of Belfast. I wish to express my thanks to these bodies for their generosity.

On a more directly academic, and also personal level, my thanks are due to many people, only some of whom I may list here. I was fortunate in having early in my career two gifted teachers, Dr Harold Turner and Dr R. E. Bradbury. In different ways, their ideas continue to exercise great influence over me and my work. I benefited greatly from the stimulating influence of the Centre of West African Studies at the University of Birmingham, its staff and students. Later, I was fortunate in being able to participate in the lively intellectual atmosphere of the University of Ibadan. Professor Okediji of the Department of Sociology and Professor Armstrong of the Institute of African Studies were especially helpful. I was given an office at the Institute and found the staff there to be most kind and generous with their support and assistance. I am grateful to Professor Peter Guttkind, Professor Robin Horton, Dr Gavin Williams, Dr Robert Home, Dr Peter McKenzie and to many others for helpful and stimulating discussion.

It will become clear to the reader of my text that my thanks are especially due to my informants and to others whose help I solicited when in Nigeria. These include Mrs Ajayi, and Messrs Popoola, Awotunde, Bolaji, Mabo, and Adeniji, but there are many others. These will, I trust, forgive me if I express special thanks to the three men whose assistance was especially important when I was in Nigeria. Mr Adebawọ and Mr Fatoogun, were close associates of mine for many months, during which time my admiration and affection grew. It was a pleasure and a privilege to meet them. The other was Mr J. A. Ayandokun, who for two years was an almost constant companion in the role of field assistant and translator. His contribution to this work is incalculable.

Since returning to the United Kingdom, and with the support of Professor Meyer Fortes, I obtained a place at the Queen's University of Belfast where I was helped considerably by Professor John Blacking as well as by Dr James Moody and others, both staff and students in the Department of Anthropology.

My present employer, the trustees and director of the Ulster Folk and Transport Museum, and Dr Alan Gailey have done much to enable me to complete this work. I wish to thank Mrs Fionnuala Prosser for our most helpful conversations. Mrs Elizabeth Martin was kind enough to read through the text and to make careful and well-judged editorial comments. Mrs Claire Gallacher typed the by no means easy text and I wish to thank her for her care and cheerfulness.

I shall now make special mention of those people who have sustained me throughout this enterprise. Dr Elizabeth Tonkin became supervisor following the early and tragic death of R. E. Bradbury. Despite the physical distance which almost always separated us, she has exercised the greatest care and patience in this supervision. I have found her helpful advice, encouragement, and criticism to be always supportive. She has been to me an admirable teacher. For this and for her friendship, I am most grateful.

I wish finally to mention my family. My mother, Mrs Kathleen Milner, has helped me in countless ways, supporting me from the beginning and giving much help with the early drafts. My wife, Linda Buckley, has undergone many trials for the sake of this book, giving both emotional and intellectual support. For this I am for ever indebted.

To all of these people and to many others whom I have not been able to mention I wish to express my heartfelt thanks.

Contents

1
Introduction

(a) An encounter with Yoruba medicine

The Yoruba of Western Nigeria are well known to anthropologists as a people possessing a rich cultural tradition with a
highly-developed indigenous religion. Although the Yoruba
live primarily from agriculture, theirs is an urban culture based
upon the town as the fundamental settlement. Regions vary
(P. C. Lloyd 1962; Goddard 1965), but a Yoruba farmer typically regards his village or farmhouse as a provisional or even
temporary dwelling, and he finds his real home with his
patrilineal kinsmen in the family compound in the town. It is in
the town that the household, the palace, the town government,
the markets, and most of the religious shrines are located, and it
is the town which provides the geographical focus for Yoruba
cultural life.

Traditional medicine, which is only one of a number of
systems of medicinal techniques nowadays practised in
Yorubaland, forms part of the rich cultural tradition of a
Yoruba town. Although it should in many respects be regarded
as distinct from the mainstream of Yoruba traditional religion,
medicine, like many other aspects of Yoruba life, is inextricably
intertwined with it.

There are healers in Yorubaland who diverge from this
central tradition (MacLean 1964, 1978b; Oyẹbọla 1981). The
most obvious group of these are the healers trained in the
traditions of Western Europe. These include the doctors and
nurses based mainly in the hospitals and clinics, as well as the
pharmacists and those others who, with varying degrees of
formal training, dispense the medicines produced by European
manufacturers. Among these too can be listed the 'quack'
healers who sell medicines of often doubtful, sometimes downright fraudulent, medicinal value which purport to be founded
in western medical tradition (Beier 1956).

In addition, there is a specifically Christian mode of healing
practised in the indigenous *alá.dúrà* churches (Aina *c.*1932;
Mitchell 1963, 1965, 1968, 1970; Mitchell and Turner 1968;
Peel 1965, 1966, 1967; Turnbull 1959; H. W. Turner 1965,
1967a, 1967b, 1967c, 1969, 1970, 1977). Many of these eschew
all forms of medicine, traditional and modern. Others are more
lenient, but all place great reliance upon the healing power of
Christian prayer. Of lesser importance are the two types of
healer who operate within a specifically Muslim tradition. The
first of these use the medicinal practices whose roots lie in the
Koran. Some of these healers are Yoruba, and some are
members of other tribes resident in the area. The second group
of Muslim healers are the Hausa surgeons reputedly skilful in
bone-setting.

When I began two years of field-work in October 1969, I
determined to concentrate my activity upon those healers who
were within the central Yoruba tradition. It was rapidly
discovered that almost all Yoruba men knew at least a little
about traditional medicine (*oògùn*). University students at
Ibadan cured malaria by brewing barks and leaves instead of
spending their meagre resources upon western medicines.
Most household compounds contained at least one man who
was reputed to be well versed in traditional medicine. There
were also professional herbalists (*oníṣeègùn*) who were more
knowledgeable about the craft but the difference between these
and the other men was one of degree. Many men treated disease
and sold medicines as a sideline to their other occupations.
Farmers and more especially hunters whose work brought
them into contact with the forest were particularly well-
informed about the medicinal properties of plants.

Women on the other hand seemed to know relatively little
about medicine. They sometimes possessed some knowledge of
cures for minor ailments—particularly those of children—but
they seldom pretended to know more than a little. The reason
generally given for this was that medicines could be spoiled by
the presence of a menstruating woman, and that there was
therefore little point in a woman taking too much interest in the
subject. The only female *oníṣeègùn* I knew was a woman beyond
the age of childbearing.

Women however did predominate in one field of medicinal

activity, namely in the collection and sale of medicinal ingredients. There were large daily markets at Ọja Dugbè and Ọjaaba in Ibadan, as well as smaller ones elsewhere (particularly at Ọjabode), where women and a few men sold unprepared medicinal ingredients. Ingredients, it was said, were not affected by menstruation and could therefore be handled by women. Since these women were intimately familiar with the plants and animals they handled, they undoubtedly did know much about medicine, but they tended to limit their medicinal practice to the sale of ingredients. Sometimes, too, they offered advice, recommending cures to their friends, and occasionally they would sell someone a recipe.

My original, rather naïve intention was to establish close relationships with a large number of herbalists so that as a participant observer it might be possible to observe the treatment of clients and discuss the nature of medicines with each healer. Accordingly, contact was made with a number of herbalists living in Ibadan and I attempted to befriend them. They were told in general terms that I was interested to learn about medicine. Their responses to this varied from bemusement to indignation. It was absurd that I, a stranger, could hope to discuss such a subject with them and expect to gain any knowledge which approximated to the truth. The problem was that the contents of medicines were closely guarded secrets. A person might learn these medicines, but only if he was prepared to pay. Frequently, I would be proudly shown a powder said to cure some ailment; but should I ask the nature of this powder, I would be met by an embarrassed silence followed by a curt demand for money. Nor were the sums discussed small. Twenty, thirty, a hundred pounds were the sums first mentioned and no amount of bargaining could bring the price down to a figure remotely within the range of my pocket. I paid nothing so I learned nothing. Clearly this was no way to conduct my research.

It became apparent that I would have to pay for information, but this could not be done on an informal basis. A better possibility seemed to occur in the form of apprenticeship. I would pay a lump sum, in much the same manner as would an indigenous apprentice (Lloyd 1953), and would thus learn my trade from a master. This solution had much to commend it. After the initial payment, I was required to pay little extra and I would have an established position in a Yoruba home from which it would be possible to observe medicinal practices and become familiar with Yoruba daily life.

This I resolved to do, and I was soon a fully-paid-up apprentice herbalist. There was one snag. My research studentship was for two years; my apprenticeship was for four. My master with great subtlety and tact declined actually to teach me anything about his craft. I discovered that apprentices are expected to learn slowly, so very slowly that in the early stages of my apprenticeship I should learn little, if anything.

Good use was made of this time, however, in this herbalist's compound. I learned some basic Yoruba; I observed the daily routine of a Yoruba household; I became familiar with the rudiments of folklore. As my master was the leader of a guild (egbẹ́) of herbalists (Oyebọla 1981), there was a steady stream of healers through his compound and it was possible to discuss medicine with them in a general way. I talked at length to market women who sold ingredients for medicine, and they gave me information about the curative powers of plants and animals. They occasionally told me recipes for complete medicines.

It emerged that one could discuss medicine as long as the subject was not approached too directly. There were two central questions which I began to find interesting: the way that specific medicines were supposed to cure illness, and the contents of the medicines. To raise these subjects in discussion was to invite embarrassment, hostility, or a demand for a vast sum of money, but there were other topics which did not provoke such resentment. By avoiding the subject of medicines as such, and by discussing matters only indirectly related to it, it was possible to induce informants eventually to volunteer information.

Meanwhile, my position as apprentice was becoming untenable. I had learned nothing of value from my master and it became clear that I would never learn anything substantial from him. I was not permitted to witness his interviews with clients, nor would he tell me the secrets of his medicines. What was more, I concluded that our relatively informal relationship did not permit me to question him in depth about even the less touchy subjects. In consequence of all this, our relationship became strained and, sensing that he feared I might try to poison him, I donated a half-bottle of gin and left.

There were now three considerations. First, any relationships which I might henceforth have with herbalists should be such that I could question them in depth. I must force the pace. Second, it had become clear that it was necessary to study herbalists as individuals. Not only did different herbalists use quite different medicines from each other; they seemed to have no consensus about the causes of any given illness. Third, since it seemed to be impossible to ask direct questions about the contents of medicine it would be necessary to develop very close relationships in the hope that, as the herbalists grew to know me, they would volunteer the information I required. These considerations could be fulfilled only by using formal interviews with a few informants over a long period of time, using prepared questions.

In deciding upon this course of action, I was conscious that I was making a crucial decision. Much of the research which has been published on the subject of traditional healing both before and since the commencement of my field-work has been concerned with specifically sociological aspects of healing. By devoting my time to the study of the ideas of few herbalists, interviewed in the main away from the interaction of healer and patient, my ability to look at the sociology of healing would be seriously impeded. I was choosing to study only a limited social reality—that of specific healers. I was turning my attention away from the patients and away from social interaction. Such questions as the 'sick role', or the role of kin and others close to the patient (Giapassi and Kurtz 1975; MacLean 1976) would be peripheral to my task. Nor would I be able thoroughly to investigate the interrelationship between the patient's place in social structure and his choice of healer or indeed his preferred explanation of illness (Beals 1976; Elinson and Guttmacher 1971; Feierman 1979; Foster 1979; Frankenberg and Leeson 1976; Glick 1967; Riley 1980; Uyanga 1979). Quite apart from these specific worries, traditional social anthropology has always and correctly stressed the importance of seeing life as it happens, of assessing a total situation and of discovering the views of as many people as possible within that situation (cf. Strickland and Schlesinger 1969). My approach would remove the herbalist from his everyday situation and require him to talk about illnesses, medicines, and plants as abstract concepts in a context divorced from his practical life. I would find myself studying less Yoruba medicinal practice as such, and more my informants' description of their medical practices.

But herbal medicine was clearly the most important of the oníṣeègùn's practice, and to hope to discuss this in the immediate context of healing and a specific cure was unrealistic. It would require a herbalist to answer direct questions about specific medicines and this appeared to be too much to ask. Later, in my last few weeks in Nigeria, when I had built up a close and friendly relationship with my informants who had kindly given me countless recipes for medicines, I made the mistake of asking one of them what a specific cure contained. Perhaps because he knew that my time was now severely limited, and that my lack of politeness was therefore excusable, he gave me the reply I wanted. This was not before he had given me a very 'dirty' look to indicate that I should not presume too far on his good nature. Even after payment of a fee, and after a long association during which we had indicated mutual respect, knowledge was his to give, not mine to demand.

Despite its obvious limitations, confining my field research in the manner of an East (Akiga 1939) or Griaule (1965) to a few expert informants had its own peculiar advantages. There is generally in studies of medicinal systems a failure to give adequate weight to indigenous knowledge of the medicines themselves. Ngubane places her finger upon a general problem when she admits to such a weakness in her own study of Zulu medicine. 'In order to acquire a comprehensive knowledge in this field', she writes, 'I would have had to be apprenticed to an ethno-medical practitioner for some time' (1976). The simple fact is that many of the pharmacopoeia and aetiologies of illness to be found in Africa, and probably elsewhere in the third world, are too complicated to be combined, at least in the first instance, with a more sociological approach, however desirable this might be as a long-term aim.

I have been able to console myself that others have investigated many of the aspects of Yoruba medicine which I was unable to study, among them Asuni (1962, 1979); Leighton, Lambo, Hughes, Leighton, Murphey, and Macklin (1963); Lambo (1956, 1965); MacLean (1964, 1965a, 1965b, 1971, 1976, 1978a, 1978b); Orubuloye (1979), Oyebola (1980a, 1980b, 1981) and Pierce (1980), and that my work complements their varied efforts. And I am also glad that I did not adopt the methodology of Fabrega and Manning (1972) who took around a questionnaire to discover popular beliefs about the power of herbs.

When I did eventually manage to sit in on several sessions between herbalist and patient, my approach was to some extent vindicated. I did not attempt to inquire into the nature of the specific cure which was used on each occasion, but in diagnosis, the herbalist searched for the symptoms which we had already discussed in interviews. Whilst I am aware that a more direct observation of diagnosis could have been very useful for a fuller understanding of Yoruba ideas about illness, I am also conscious that direct observation could have played only a minor role in the sort of study that I had chosen.

Among the handful of informants I consulted, I shall here discuss only two. The first, Babalǫla Fatoogun, is a *babaláwo*, or priest of the *Ifá* cult, who lives near Oṣogbo. The relationship between *Ifá* and medicine will be considered later. Here it may be simply noted that as a *babaláwo*, Fatoogun is required to have learned by heart a massive body of verses and incantations which embrace most, and in principle cover all, facets of Yoruba life, including medicine. Fatoogun has had little formal schooling, he speaks no English, and at this time had only recently begun to write in Yoruba. He started to learn *Ifá* from his father when he was about nine years old, but four years later he was sent to study for eleven years under another *babaláwo*. In some ways, Fatoogun is a typical *babálawo*, quiet, unassuming, with a formidable memory for verses. More than this, however, he is gifted with philosophic insight and great subtlety. Within his own framework, he has a superb intellect, and takes a delight in exploring the ideas of his culture.

In contrast is Mr Adebawǫ, a rumbustious, good-humoured man, who is primarily a craftsman with little interest in those philosophical matters which do not affect his craft. He claims allegiance to the Church Missionary Society, but with the easygoing syncretism of the Yoruba (Schwab 1952, 829–31) he is also a *babaláwo*, though he seldom practises as such, and is a member of the Reformed *Ogbóni* Fraternity. These activities, however, are subordinate to his main concern which is the craft of medicine. Adebawǫ was born in Ijębu in a town called Ode Ogbolu, but he travelled first to the North of Nigeria and then to India with the army during the Second World War. He can read and write Yoruba and is quite fluent in spoken English. His knowledge of medicine comes from his family for he was born into a lineage of *Ifá* priests. He has been living for many years in Ibadan, but when he first arrived he was a tailor. Upon the advice of his elders he began to practise medicine in a small way, starting by treating small children suffering from convulsions (*gìrì*). According to his own account, he became so successful, that he was able to give up his tailor's trade, and devote himself exclusively to medicine, in which profession he now regards himself as both successful and prosperous. His travels do not seem to have affected him deeply, though he was impressed by the fact that in India there were cults rather similar to the *òrìṣà* cults of the Yoruba. Perhaps also his contact with the British army led him to experience European medicine at first hand, for he regards his own craft as complementary to that of European-trained doctors and he has no compunction, in certain cases, in sending his own patients to the local hospitals. In this and in his general familiarity with European medicine, Adebawǫ does not however differ significantly from other Yoruba herbalists. Whatever slight knowledge of European medicine he might possess, Adebawǫ's medicinal thought owes little or nothing to non-Yoruba influence. By disposition he is given to a jovial and robust scepticism, but he has a lively mind, is deeply serious about his trade, and knows it thoroughly.

In addition to these two informants, I also had a third, Mr Awotunde, a *babaláwo* from Oṣogbo with whom I had a close relationship for several months. I also had occasional conversations with Mrs Ajayi, an old lady herbalist from Ibadan and with a number of other informants.

By the time I had settled down with my main informants it had become clear that the major part of Yoruba medicinal practice consisted in the administration of herbal medicines to cure illnesses. Arising from this, two central questions were of interest: the first concerned the manner in which my informants understood the nature of the illnesses themselves and how they were caused; the second was the composition of the medicines and their relationships to the illnesses which they were intended to cure. Except in so far as it proved difficult to discuss illness without discussing medicine, there was no serious problem in finding out about the causation of illnesses —a list of Yoruba names of illnesses was accordingly constructed and I asked obvious questions. The difficult area was medicine.

I was fortunate in discovering in an Ibadan market a book by a Yoruba herbalist called Agosu from Ibadan. Many herbalists in recent years have begun to commit their medicinal knowledge to paper, either to help them remember it or to preserve the information for future generations. Occasionally these are published. The publication of medicinal recipes runs contrary to the general pattern of secrecy to be found in Yoruba medicinal practice. It reflects in part the growth of Islam, and to a lesser extent that of Christianity among the Yoruba. Both of these traditions encourage their followers to act for the benefit of humanity. People who have no pressing reason to keep their medicines secret may therefore achieve some prestige as philanthropists by publishing them, though they are unlikely to do so while they are still practising medicine. It was in terms of Muslim philanthropy that the existence of such books was explained to me. This particular book was found fortuitously, and despite great effort, it proved impossible to discover another like it. I was assured nevertheless that other such books existed. All it contained was a multitude of recipes for medicines of different types; and it gave me a basis to begin questioning.

Experience showed me that it was possible to ask informants about the power of ingredients, but not about their recipes. Thus if one of Agosu's medicines, say, to cure 'black menstruation' (àṣẹ́ dúdú), included the tail feathers of a parrot (ìkóódẹ), I could ask the question, 'What is the power of the parrot's tail feathers to cure black menstruation?' (Kílagbára ìkóódẹ wo àṣẹ́ dúdú?) This, together with the question, 'What causes black menstruation?' (Kínìdí àṣẹ́ dúdú?) could lead to something of an understanding of the illness and its cure.

This approach had its advantages but a major difficulty was that my informants' medicines were not at all identical with those of Agosu. A frequent response was that the ingredient in question did not in fact cure the illness I had indicated. Moreover, informants repeated, time after time, that no illness could be cured by a single ingredient alone, but only by a completed medicine.

My inquiry therefore had to edge gingerly towards the discovery of the recipes for medicine which belonged to my informants themselves. Discussion began to be based upon two central questions: 'What is the power of x in medicine?' (*Kílagbára x nínú oògùn?*) followed by, where necessary, 'What is the power of x in *this* medicine?' or 'What is the power of x to cure this illness?' (*Kílagbára x nínú oògùn.yí?* or *kílagbára x wo àrùn.yí?*). In these questions I took great care to ask about the *ingredients* of medicines and not the medicines themselves. I was, however, indirectly inquiring about ingredients in my herbalist's own medicines and I had at last escaped from Agosu's collection of recipes, about which my informants could scarcely be expected to make more than intelligent guesses.

One unintended result of this departure was that the interviews began to follow a path dictated by my informants. Instead of adopting the more logical procedure of asking first about the illness, then its cure, and finally about the relevance of each ingredient in the cure of the disease, which would have allowed me to keep a strict control over the number of illnesses and medicines to be discussed, I was now asking first about the powers of specific ingredients. Inevitably the list of illnesses and types of medicines grew to a large number in a very short time. It was now possible to relate the ingredients of the medicines to the illnesses which they were intended to combat, tackling the cause of the illness as it arose in the discussion.

For about a month after this, my research became a discussion of the powers of specific ingredients in relation to their intended purpose in medicine. Then, as my informants grew to know and respect me, they began to volunteer their knowledge of medicinal recipes. From the first, Fatoogun was more forthcoming in this than Adebawọ. Many of the medicines which Adebawọ told me in the early days were deliberately left incomplete. Later he began to confide in me more and more, and indeed he went out of his way to be helpful. As the months passed, discussion returned to the subject of the incomplete recipes, and, without impolite prompting from me, my informant would mention the ingredients which he had omitted.

There are two major areas which are not at all thoroughly discussed in this thesis. These are the important subjects of 'bad medicine' and of witchcraft. I was constantly aware that bad medicine was regarded as an important cause of illness and other misfortunes as too, though less frequently, was witchcraft. Although my informants, and especially Adebawọ, were quite familiar with the subject, they tended to evade my questions. Adebawọ explained to me that bad medicine was illegal, and that to transmit knowledge about it was to break the law. The weakness of my information on this topic is a direct result of having used the formal interview as my prime research method. A more sociological approach in the tradition of the mainstream literature on sorcery and witchcraft (e.g. Beattie 1963; Douglas 1963, 1967b, 1970; Evans Pritchard 1937; Forge 1970; Gray 1963; Holy 1976; Huntingford 1963; Jahoda 1966; Jones 1970; Levine 1963; Lewis 1970; Marwick 1967; Middleton 1963) employing participant observation and the assiduous piecing together of gossip would have revealed much more.

The interviews were conducted throughout in the Yoruba language, but since the subject matter required careful interpretation, the interviews were recorded and translated separately. More difficult passages, especially incantations and stories, were transcribed and translated word by word. A more proper procedure would have been to transcribe the whole of the interviews in Yoruba but this would have been too time-consuming. Little attempt was made to follow up each point as it was made in the course of an interview. I found that both I and my interpreter were wont to misunderstand the comments of my informants upon first hearing, and that we both tended to hear only what we wanted to hear. *Ad hoc* discussions therefore tended to be at cross-purposes and were best left alone.

In all of this I had the help of Mr Akintunde Ayandokun, a young man of great tact and understanding whose ability as an interpreter and field assistant considerably helped all of my endeavours. Though all my interviews were conducted through Mr Ayandokun, I did not feel that very much was lost thereby. On the contrary, my questioning gained, through his sympathetic intervention, a subtlety which it might not otherwise have had. In addition, because he was taking such an obvious and intelligent interest in our discussions, his presence seemed to encourage my informants to explore finer points which they might have otherwise felt were beyond my pedestrian Yoruba.

(b) A cognitive approach to Yoruba medicine

As my field notes became more copious, it was obvious that I must adopt a coherent theoretical approach to my material if I were to understand it properly. Naturally enough, there was a level at which I could claim to understand most of what my informants told me. Individuals, if they are amicable enough, can invariably communicate with each other at some level or other, however distant their points of view. But there were some ideas which were completely meaningless to me. Unfortunately these seemed to emerge at crucial points in our discussions or when my informants were at their most thoughtful. To understand these apparently incomprehensible profundities, it was necessary to develop a perspective which would incorporate and explain both these and the other statements which were more immediately accessible to my European common sense.

In seeking such a perspective, several considerations seemed important. The first was that the practice of Yoruba medicine could not be regarded as having a transcendent unity of its own. Each herbalist had his own distinctive knowledge of what caused and what cured an illness, and to pretend that such differences did not exist was to ignore the facts. Nevertheless, it was important to discover what assumptions were shared by these individualistic herbalists. It was further apparent that the bits and pieces of information which were given to me by my informants did possess some sort of unity. They were the product of rational thought, and it was a form of rationality shared by my informants but not yet by me. A final consideration was that, when I did encounter non-rational elements in my informants' statements, it should be possible to discern how such non-rationality could seem plausible to these eminently sensible men.

Let me begin by pointing to two facets in human experience. On the one hand, man is confronted by a plethora of fleeting impressions. Each glimpse, each sound, is only a fragment, an isolated moment in a world of isolated moments. He sees an object, and as he glances away, the object is gone; a tree moves, and in each instant it becomes a different perception. No two men have the same vision of the same object at the same time and no object remains the same for one man. Mere sensuous perception can never provide man with more than a chaos of indeterminate images, a flurry of colour, of sound, of smell.

Yet, on the other hand, few people regard the world as either indeterminate or chaotic. I know that this is my table, that this is my pen, and that there are clouds in the sky. I know too that if I leave the room, then when I return, the room will be much the same as when I left it. Sensuousness is my guarantee that the world is real, that defined objects exist, but it is but a portion of my experience. The second facet of my experience is therefore the order which I project and discover in it. Individual human experience begins and ends with sensuous images, but by a process of categorization a man may remove from these images their particular quality. The table is no longer a blur of colour, but a table, an instance of the category of table which exists in my act of perception and in its expression when I communicate. By the same movement, the wholly abstract category has become concrete in sensuous experience and in practical life.

This ordering of the world, even in the process of description, does not take place merely at one level. It exists through the operation of semantic and syntactical rules, whereby a resemblance is posited between patterns of distinctions between sounds and patterns of distinctions between objects. But there is another mode of organization which, though usually dependent upon language for its articulation, is of a quite different type from language itself. This second set of principles may be described as the organizing principles of encyclopaedic knowledge. They provide the means whereby specific items of knowledge about the world are organized into a meaningful pattern.

It is possible to assume that there is inherent in the world a structured order which is distinct from that which people habitually impose upon it in their descriptions. Such a view, as Hegel explains (e.g. 1970, 204), depends upon the location of universal principles in a realm which lies beyond both subject and object, spirit and nature in the Idea. But the question of whether nature in itself possesses a hidden, God-given structure has little importance here. Both anthropologists and the people they seek to understand are cast into a sea of particular sensuous impressions, and each transcends this particularity only by means of the patterning which emanates from his own individual cognitive activity. The anthropologist's task is therefore to comprehend his informants as individuals whose task in turn is to perceive, understand and act in the world in which they live, seeing it not as a plethora of sensuousness, but as an ordered pattern of related, determinate, concrete objects.

The process whereby particular sensuous impressions are transformed into a world of determinate objects organized according to structured principles must be regarded as the activity of the individual, for it is only the individual who can think and act, see, speak, or hear. Barth argues the point well that the eradication of the Hegelian Idea leaves behind not a Feuerbachian 'Humanity', but Stirner's 'Ego' (Barth 1957, xxviii–xxix). To stop at that point however is unsatisfactory, for it may not be assumed that the individual undertakes his massive task alone. Though it is only through his own cognitive activity that a person is able to grasp the world as a place full of related determinate objects, this activity is controlled and guided, supported and contradicted by others who communicate their vision of the world to him. By the time a person reaches adulthood, he may feel that he shares in the cognitive principles of his fellow men to a considerable degree. Indeed, it is by believing that he shares in other people's vision of the world, that he comes to think that the world has an objective pattern independent of his own individual consciousness (Berger 1967, 16–17). So it is also that people are able to act meaningfully together, for as Engels showed long ago, it is in common activity that language itself becomes necessary (Engels 1876, 83).

Although this is to be a study of 'cognitive anthropology' or even of 'ethnoscience', these terms are not here being used in the narrowly confining sense of ethnographic semantics. Of course it is true that language is an important means whereby the world is given order. It is however simply invalid to claim, that ethnographic semantics 'deals with describing a culture as a system of meanings which the people of one group "know" and use in their relation with each other' (Black 1969, 165). The description of the semantic distinctions made within a community is not an adequate description of its (ethno-) science. Nobody would undertake the componential analysis of Einstein's or Newton's vocabulary in order to discover what these men thought about relativity or thermodynamics. And a dictionary of New Testament Greek, however well-constructed, is no substitute for the Bible as a tool for understanding Christianity.

It seems to me plausible to suggest that the distinctions between semantic terms which are made in a community do reflect, if not absolutely, distinctions which are made in their perception of objects in the world. But to describe adequately a people's scientific knowledge, its ethnoscience, it would seem necessary to step beyond semantics towards the understanding. Science, whether that of the West or that of Africa is, after all, a structure of synthetic knowledge and is quite different from the purely analytical structure of semantic distinctions (cf. Sperber 1974, 99 ff.). It is notable that the most impressive semantically oriented studies of folk medicine (e.g. Frake 1961; Fabrega, Metzger, and Williams 1970) are the ones which inadvertently step beyond their ostensible methodology. For if there are shared semantic paradigms (Tyler 1969) which give order to the relations between specific types of objects and specific sounds, there are also paradigms which govern encyclopaedic knowledge. And these will be the main focus for this volume.

Paradigms of encyclopaedic knowledge (though he does not use this latter expression) are the concern of Thomas Kuhn's celebrated book *The Structure of Scientific Revolutions* (1962). This is a study of the history of western science, but his approach would seem to be fruitful in anthropology. Barnes (1969) and Willis (1972, 1978) have discussed this and so also has Ardener (1978). Ardener's concept of the 'template' (1970), developed as 'p' and 's' structures (1971, 1978), includes a historical dimension which places it somewhat beyond the scope of my immediate purpose.

Kuhn defines 'paradigm' as the 'universally recognised scientific achievements that for a time provide model problems and solutions to a community of practitioners' (Kuhn 1962, x). Typical examples of such paradigms are the Ptolemaic and Copernican pictures of the cosmos; Newton's physics and optics; and Franklin's electrical theories. Such ideas were frequently established only after controversy and dissention within the relevant community of scientists but once established, they remained unchallenged for a long period of time. In the period following the establishment of a paradigm, the science ceases to be revolutionary; earlier doubts and controversies are forgotten and the community settles down to 'normal science'.

'Normal science' is a concept dependent on the idea of the paradigm. Progress made in such an era, accidental discoveries apart, is the product of a conservative 'mopping up' around the paradigm. Normal science seems to be 'an attempt to force nature into the preformed and relatively inflexible box that the paradigm supplies' (Kuhn 1962, 24).

An important characteristic of the Kuhnian paradigm is its imperfection, its failure to embrace all known phenomena. What is more, the existence of facts which contradict the paradigm only sometimes leads to its abandonment. Even where the paradigm is generally recognized to be grossly unsatisfactory, it may still be used as the basis for normal research (Kuhn 1962, 81). The paradigm is the 'error' of which Bacon speaks[1] which generates truth first by absorbing to itself new phenomena and subsequently by showing a capacity to throw out insoluble problems, calling forth a new paradigm with redefined problems and new potential solutions (Kuhn 1962, 18).

One effect of Kuhn's formulation, is to cause us to exercise great caution in employing the distinction, long established in anthropology, between rational and non-rational modes of thought. In general, Europeans find themselves sceptical, even scornful, of a man who claims to have concocted a medicine from plants and animals to protect him against bullets, or equally of a man who uses impregnated soap to wash away his bad luck. In the past such medicines have been characterized by epithets such as 'magical', 'ritual', or even, for some reason, 'mystical'. The difficulty here arises because there are undoubtedly some healing techniques used in African cultures—including the Yoruba—which seem to contradict both scientific knowledge and common sense. In such cases, however, the question which arises is the one raised by Stuchlik: whose science and whose common sense is thus contradicted? (Stuchlik 1976).

Nadel's discussion of Nupe medicine, for example (1954, 133–4) rests upon a distinction between 'non-rational' and 'rational' categories of medicine. Because he admits that procedures which are non-rational in intention may sometimes in fact be efficacious, and because, conversely, 'they may act with rational intent but insufficient or faulty knowledge . . . and hence strike us as irrational or "magical" ', he offers us a fourfold classification of Nupe medicine based first of all upon the rational and non-rational intentions of the Nupe themselves, and secondly upon the 'objective' effectiveness or ineffectiveness of the remedy.

The grounds upon which he makes this distinction between 'professedly mystical' and 'professedly rational intent' are a motley collection indeed. He distinguishes them on the basis of 'their secrecy or otherwise; their commercial or non-commercial; public or private character; the diverse ways in which the knowledge of *cigbe* (medicine) is transmitted; and the different kinds of artifacts put in it' (Nadel 1954, 133–4). Nadel has thus distinguished 'rational' from 'non-rational' medicines on the basis of his own European common sense, informed by anthropological theory, without taking into account of what constitutes the common sense or the scientific knowledge of the Nupe healers themselves.

Several factors may be considered here. The first is the fairly obvious one that Yoruba medicines are constructed on the basis of the knowledge of Yoruba herbalists and that distinctions, say between rational and non-rational or herbal and magical medicines, which are not used within the paradigms of Yoruba encyclopaedic knowledge are not relevant. Second, although Yoruba herbalists have what might be termed a specialist or expert form of encyclopaedic knowledge, this

expert knowledge must in some manner be compatible with
their common-sense encyclopaedic knowledge. Third, it is my
contention, yet to be demonstrated, that by far the greater part
of a Yoruba healer's specialist knowledge is immediately compatible with the principles which govern his own common-
sense understanding of the world—and indeed that of other
Yoruba people whom I met. But fourth, there are some Yoruba
medicines which embody principles of organization which are
not immediately compatible with the paradigm of Yoruba
common sense. These types of medicines use a type of knowledge which is recognized to be qualitatively different from
common-sense encyclopaedic knowledge. This is the type of
knowledge which Sperber refers to as being 'in quotes'.

Sperber (1974, 99) argues that symbolic knowledge is knowledge 'in quotes'. Items of encyclopaedic knowledge are subject
to criticism from other synthetic statements about the world—
they are subject to rational and empirical criticism. 'Knowledge', however, is allowed into the encyclopaedia while yet
being insulated from such critical scrutiny. In this he is
following (presumably) the discussion of logical types by
Bateson (1973) which has also been taken up with characteristic perception and vigour by Goffman (1974). Sperber's
argument loses some of its force because of his use of the term
symbolic. For it is clear that even for him 'knowledge' includes
items which are scarcely to be considered figurative. He argues
for example that the expression $e = mc^2$ is not part of his own
encyclopaedic knowledge, for he is not a physicist and he has no
means of assessing its validity. The statement '$e = mc^2$' is valid,
however, does form a part of his encyclopaedic knowledge
presumably because it is a part of this knowledge that the
scientific statements of Einstein, of which this is one, are
valid.

The important point to be made here is that 'knowledge'—
and there are many different types of 'knowledge'—enters the
encyclopaedia because of a meta-knowledge. My hypothesis is
that the limited amount of Yoruba medicinal practice which
does not directly accord with the paradigms of common-sense
encyclopaedic knowledge is carefully delineated as a special
form of knowledge—knowledge in quotes. And in such cases it
is the meta-knowledge—the knowledge about the 'knowl-

edge'—which is compatible with the paradigm (see Goffman 1974, 247 ff.; Sperber 1974, 351 ff.).

By thus redefining the problem of symbolic knowledge, Sperber has rescued anthropology from an unnecessarily ethnocentric view of 'magic'. It is part of the task of the present study to dispel the remnants of Ackerknecht's view that 'primitive' medicine is magical medicine (Ackerknecht 1942, 397–8). But oddly, Sperber's argument will lead this discussion towards the Malinowskian view of Homans (1941) that 'magic' occurs at the limit of empirical knowledge 'where certainty of accomplishment breaks down'.

The inadequacy of empirical encyclopaedic knowledge for certain tasks can indeed give rise to magical techniques based on knowledge which is not compatible with paradigms of common sense. However this is only possible where such non-encyclopaedic knowledge can somehow be made part of the encyclopaedia. Any knowledge which contradicts the paradigm of common sense must be regarded as inherently absurd or mistaken by those who share the paradigm. An important task, therefore, in the study of 'magic' is to demonstrate how such 'non-rational' techniques may be used by rational people; or more precisely, how knowledge which contradicts the informant's own normal criteria of truth and reasonableness, may be admitted into his encyclopaedia of common-sense knowledge.

Kuhn has shown in his study of paradigm changes in the history of European science that new paradigms do not generally arise directly from the problem-solving of the normal science which is tied to the old paradigm. The step from one paradigm to another involves more than rational argument; it requires a leap of faith, or in Kuhn's words, a 'conversion experience'. The reason for this is that within certain limits (Kuhn 1962, 148–50) the paradigm provides the grounds for rational discussion of the scientific problems which are themselves defined by the paradigm. Scientists who disagree about paradigms are restricted in their communication because they do not share common ground.

The scorn which may sometimes be experienced by Europeans in relation to African medicine does not arise primarily from their technological superiority. A Yoruba who accepts the validity of Yoruba medicinal principles may for example exhibit scepticism about a medicine which claims to protect people against bullets—and he might demand proof that it works. A European on the contrary would not generally demand such proof. European scepticism arises from the *unreasonableness* of even attempting to construct such a medicine.

There are no absolute standards of reason which say that a medicine cannot be constructed to protect somebody from bullets. Because such an attempt is contrary to the rationality of present-day European paradigms, it need not be supposed that it is *per se* non-rational or irrational behaviour. Rather, it should be understood that each paradigm contains its own internal rationale and that there is no transcendent rationality which we know to be lying outside the expressions of the individual that embody them.

The matter however cannot be left there, for it is an undoubted fact that however many traditional Yoruba medicines may be shown to be effective, there are many others which, if subjected to the rigours of scientific investigation, would be shown to be worthless for the purpose for which they are used. Horton has argued (1967, 155) that the failure of traditional African systems of thought perpetually to seek to overthrow themselves is a sign that they are not in truth scientific.

Kuhn (1962, 145), taking Popper to task in this very issue, argues that paradigms are seldom, if ever, discarded merely because they are contradicted by observed fact. Indeed, he argues that it is this very contradiction between paradigm and evidence which makes a theory a vehicle for the problem-solving which is the normal activity of scientists. Paradoxically, Kuhn's refutation of Popper and hence of much of Horton (1967, part 2) aids the more general case espoused by Horton (1968) for 'neo-Tylorianism'. African thought is more akin to science than even Horton is willing to admit.

European scepticism of African ideas is mirrored by African scepticism of European thought. When I suggested to Adebawọ that malaria (*ibà*) was caused by mosquito bites, he chuckled gently and replied:–

ADEBAWọ. *Ibà* is caused by standing in the hot sun. I get bitten by mosquitoes many times each day (he shows me the bites) but I only get *ibà* twice a year. If you don't believe that the sun causes *ibà*, try standing in the sun for an afternoon and see what happens.[2]

Just as we would not expect western scientists to abandon their theory of malaria on the basis of Adebawọ's simple objection, nor should we expect Yoruba herbalists to abandon their theories merely because we can present them with a few inconvenient facts.

The paradigm is a basis, however unsatisfactory, for problem-solving and for the development of knowledge. Whether or not it is contradicted by known facts, the paradigm provides the means for the solution of the problems created by such facts. But it is only in unusual circumstances that the anomalous facts lead to the overthrow of the paradigm.

The main task is, then, to identify the herbalists' paradigms. But it is only in unusual circumstances that the anomalous facts underlying structure of thought within which men define and solve problems. It is not normally an object of thought. The paradigm is given expression in ideas about other things; it is not usually expressed in itself.

In Kuhn's study of the history of science, he is able to identify specific historical characters, academic 'heroes' in almost an Hegelian sense, whose work gave the first systematic expression to new paradigmatic ideas. A synchronic study such as this does not have the same advantage. In the absence of written texts, it may not be reasonably expected that a single expression of the present paradigm will be found which at some stage in the past, provided an historic copy-book for the countless ideas which have succeeded it.

This is not however at all necessary, for it is not in the constant returning of present-day thinkers to the texts of the past that a paradigm finds expression, but in the restatement and reinterpretation of these works in subsequent generations. The paradigm is to be found only in its articulation, and the work of a Kuhnian 'great scientist', however important historically, is merely one of its expressions. The paradigm may thus be discovered as easily from the work of his successors as from the great man himself.

My technique will be to select a number of characteristic

images, offered by my informants, which exhibit a clearly defined structure. Some of these will be symbolic for by no means all symbolism is incompatible with the paradigms of encyclopaedic knowledge. Where these images are symbolic, it will be argued that they have the function of evoking other patterns in the Yoruba universe which have a similar structure. Other images that will be examined are not especially symbolic but merely happen to be relevant to an understanding of Yoruba medicine. The images will be labelled Image 1, Image 2, and so forth, and it will be shown that they all have an underlying similarity of structure. Each image will be regarded as a specific articulation of an underlying paradigm—a paradigm, however, which exists only in its specific articulations.

The paradigm, and the images related to it, will be expressed as a structure of contrasted pairs. Because care has been taken to distinguish encyclopaedic from semantic paradigms, the criticisms made by Burridge (1967) of Lévi-Strauss have been bypassed. Burridge complained that Lévi-Strauss confused the concepts of contrary and contradiction, so that it was not at all clear when a contradiction could be regarded merely as a complementary opposition (1967, 94). It will become clear in the course of this thesis that encyclopaedic knowledge contains ideal structures which may be expressed in the form of complementary pairs of opposed concepts. These ideal structures however are vulnerable for they can be contradicted. Contradiction therefore is quite distinct from opposition.

The use of contrasts here owes much to the influence of writers in humoral medicine mainly among American peoples (Cosminsky 1977; Foster 1979; Harwood 1971; Logan 1973; Madsen 1955; Mazes 1968; Nash 1967; Rubel 1960) as well as to writers on the left and right hand (below p. 117). It is nevertheless only a device for presenting data in a clear manner. I do not regard this method as the only possible means of presentation. The question of the psychological validity of any given manner of presenting the structure of encyclopaedic knowledge is, it must be presumed, subject to the same objections and difficulties as were raised in relation to componential analysis in the collection of essays by Tyler (ed.) (1969).

Although discussion of symbolism will form an important

part of this essay, this is not a study of 'symbolic classification'. The emphasis will be upon the encyclopaedic knowledge which my informants expressed to me and the manner in which this knowledge is organized.

The next chapter will be a consideration of some of the basic ideas which my informants expressed about the nature of illness and medicine. From it will emerge Image 1, an abstract picture of the causes and cures for simple illnesses. Image 2, the structure of the female human body and of the cosmos, will be discussed in the third chapter. In this and in the following chapters the relationship between coloured elements in the body will be considered. It will be shown that my informants have an ideal picture of what constitutes a healthy body, and regard illness as a disruption of this ideal pattern. The final three chapters are more concerned with symbolism. In Chapter 6 will be discussed the relationship between illness and the gods *Ifá* and *Ṣọ̀npọ̀nnọ́*. Chapter 7 is devoted to the subject of medicinal incantation. Finally it will be suggested that there is a correlation between certain themes arising in Yoruba medicine and the social institutions of the Yoruba. In order not to confuse the argument unduly by including too much empirical data in the text there are a number of appendices at the end of the book. Recipes for medicines are set out in the manner that they were given to me by my informants, that is, beginning with a list of ingredients. Where known, the English or botanical name is also given together with the Yoruba name. Regrettably, the efforts of an over-enthusiastic office-cleaner destroyed my collection of pressed leaves, and it has therefore been necessary to rely upon Abraham's brilliant dictionary (1958) for purposes of identification. The Yoruba orthography will be that of Bamgboṣe (1965, 1966b). It is readily comprehensible to those who are familiar with other Yoruba orthographies, but it has the slightly unusual feature that the assimilated low tone is indicated by a dot (e.g. *Ọlọ́.run*).

Here, then, is an exploration of the ideas of some Yoruba herbalists on the subject of illness and medicine. Because Yoruba herbalists, like Yoruba wood carvers (Chappel 1972), disagree on important issues, it will be indicated as far as possible where I believe that specific ideas are typical or untypical of those of other herbalists. In the last resort however, it will be better to accept that each Yoruba herbalist has his own ideas about medicine and that these are peculiar to him alone.

What is suggested here is that underlying the diversity of Yoruba medicinal knowledge—and, indeed, underlying the overwhelming diversity to be found in Yoruba culture generally—is a simple framework of structured concepts. This structure provides not only the basis for ideas which Yoruba herbalists share. It also is the basis for their very individuality.

Endnotes

[1] 'Truth emerges more readily from error than from confusion' (Francis Bacon, *Novum Organum*).

[2] Fatoogun rather less explicitly expressed the same scepticism of this well-known and widely disbelieved western theory of the cause of malaria (below p. 81).

2

Germs and worms, or is gonorrhoea really good for you?

This chapter will deal with only the simplest descriptions of illnesses and their causes—the ones that raise the fewest theoretical difficulties. What will emerge will be a formula, a pattern used by my informants to define the nature of a fairly wide range of illnesses and to suggest likely cures. Because it seems to fulfil this function, this pattern might properly be described as a 'paradigm' in Kuhn's sense of the term. But because it accounts for only a part of my informants' ideas on the subject of illness and medicine I shall here refer to it merely as 'Image 1'. The grander term 'paradigm' will be used more sparingly to refer to the pattern formed by the amalgamation of this and other such images.

(a) Arùn (illness and disease)

The Yoruba term *àrùn*, which will be glossed as either *illness* or *disease* seems to have two related but distinct meanings. The gloss *illness* will here be used to refer to *àrùn* in the sense of a set of identifiable symptoms or an affliction of the body. Each illness has its own name but illnesses are classified according to the type of person and according to the part of the body which is affected. The first of these criteria distinguish illnesses of men (*àrùn ọkùnrin*), illnesses of women (*àrùn obìnrin*), and children's illnesses (*àrùn ọmọdé*). The second distinguishes skin illnesses (*àrùn ara*, lit. illnesses of the body), illness of the blood (*àrùn ẹ̀jẹ̀*), illnesses of the bones (*àrùn eegun*) and so on corresponding to the different named parts of the body.

The term *àrùn* will be given the gloss 'disease' where it refers, not to a group of symptoms, but to a cause of illness. Illnesses are said to be caused by several different factors including the hostile activity of witches, bad medicine and the god

Ṣònpònnó, but the main causes of illness (àrùn) are *diseases* (àrùn) which are substances in the body.

This distinction of the two senses of the term àrùn corresponds to the usage of my informants. Barrenness (àgọn), for example, is for them an illness(àrùn) but it may be caused by many different things. It may be caused by bad medicine or witchcraft or it may be caused by one of several diseases (àrùn). Each disease has its own name—and most of the important ones will be examined in due course—but there is a loose subdivision of diseases into two groups, the germ (kòkòrò) and the worm (arọn). In most instances my informants were able to tell me whether a specific disease was a germ or a worm, but the distinction had little effect upon the therapy which they used and it was not at all uncommon to find both the terms germ (kòkòrò) and worm (arọn) used interchangeably to refer to the same disease, even within the same conversation.

The term arọn refers to these creatures which in English would be called 'worms' within the human body. *Kòkòrò* can in its most general sense be translated as 'insect'. Flies, mosquitoes, ants, etc. are all *kòkòrò*. When this term refers to a disease, however, I prefer to use the gloss 'germ' since the kòkòrò in the body are usually thought to be too small to be visible and are therefore closer to the English concept of 'germ' than to 'insect'.

Yoruba herbalists—and here I speak generally and not just of my main informants—have a germ theory and a worm theory of illness which, though there are major differences, is close to that of Pasteur. It does not of course follow from this that Yoruba medicinal thought is in any way derived from that of Europe although it is of course impossible to be sure. Wallace (1958) shows that the Iroquois of the seventeenth century had theories of dreams which are rather similar in general outline to those of Freud and Jung and yet he clearly does not think the Iroquois provided the inspiration for modern psychology. At first I was tempted to suspect that the herbalists I met had merely borrowed germ theory from Europe perhaps through the media of the schools, hospitals, and radio. If this is indeed the case, then this theory has been thoroughly integrated into the broader pattern of Yoruba thought. My view now is that Yoruba germ theory is in fact a wholly indigenous development which, though it finds reinforcement in the ideas of Pasteur, has but scant origins in the influence of Europe.

(b) Some simple illnesses

The illnesses which I am seeking to reduce to the pattern of Image 1, are those which are caused by diseases, and they constitute the overwhelming majority of illnesses known to the Yoruba. Some of these raise issues of some considerable theoretical complexity which will be considered in later chapters, and for the moment we shall concentrate our attention upon those which do not stray too far from Image 1 itself.

I shall first of all consider illnesses which my informants were able to discuss in terms which exhibited the main structural features of Image 1. Illnesses which my informants found less interesting were inevitably covered in less depth, but these may also be shown to have the same general structure.

(i) Atòsí (gonorrhoea)

Abraham translates the word *àtòsí* by the medical term 'gonorrhoea' (Abraham 1958, tọ A(7)(d)) as indeed did all the people I asked who had the slightest smattering of English. We find superficially that this is a reasonable translation.

ADEBAWQ. *Atòsí* comes mainly from women. If the menstruation of a woman does not flow as well as it is expected to and if a man has sexual intercourse with her, this can cause *àtòsí*. If a man is not well and he has intercourse with a woman this can also cause *àtòsí*. *Atòsí* is a bad disease. If a man has no sexual intercourse with a woman at all he cannot be affected by *àtòsí*. If the womb of a woman is not clear (*kò mọ́*), there is disease in it; if a man has sexual intercourse with such a woman he will be affected by *àtòsí*. *Atòsí* is a type of illness that appears on the third day after it has affected the man (i.e. two days after the event). First the top of his penis will give him a bad pain. On the fourth day pus (*èétu*) will come from the penis and the man will find it difficult to urinate. *Atòsí* can prevent him from having children. This is because the germs (*kòkòrò*) have eaten up the semen bag (*ilé ọmọ*)[1] and the person may urinate blood.

Adebawọ elaborated this when I made a further inquiry.

BUCKLEY. What is the disease that prevents a person urinating?
ADEBAWQ. This is a very bad illness which can kill a person. The Yoruba (i.e. those who speak the dialect of *Qyọ*) call it *òsé*. This can block the urine but

the person will be able to defecate; alternatively it can block the faeces and the person will still be able to urinate. It may also block them both. The cause of this illness is when a person is affected by too much disease such as *àtòsí* and if a man affected by *àtòsí* impregnates a woman the disease can affect the child. This is why we find parents complaining that a newly-born baby is unable to defecate or urinate. I have not learned much about this medicine (*oògùn òsé*) but I have cured it with *oògùn ìyàgbé* (purge) and *oògùn àtòsí* (medicine for gonorrhoea).

Fatoogun's understanding of *átòsí* does not significantly contradict that of Adebawo though it will later be shown how both men see beyond this preliminary account. He distinguished six types of *àtòsí* which can quickly be listed in Figure 1. Fortunately they do not complicate the discussion unduly:

àtòsí ògbòdò	That which has just affected the patient.
àtòsí olódun méta	lit. the owner of three years, chronic *àtòsí*.
àtòsí olóyun	lit. the owner of pus.
àtòsí eléró	where the urine flows continuously in small droplets.
àtòsí egbe	Where the scrotum is swollen, blood is urinated, and a white substance flows from the penis.
àtòsí alájere	(*ajere* = colander) where the disease so perforates the penis that urine comes out of holes in the side. Before this urination will be painful and the penis will swell.

FIGURE 1. Fatoogun's six types of *Atòsí*

In making these distinctions, Fatoogun does not deny that there is but one essential illness called *àtòsí*; he merely wishes to show the different forms in which it becomes manifest. In the following extract, however, he gave the discussion a significant but subtle twist.

BUCKLEY. What causes *àtòsí*?

FATOOGUN. It (*àtòsí*) can be got from a woman, but there are many ways in which a person can be affected by a woman. *Atòsí* is present in every person. *It helps to increase semen in men.* (My emphasis.) But when a man gets *àtòsí* from a woman, this will increase the one already in his body and it will become an illness.

This remark, moreover, was repeated by Adebawo without

prompting from me when, tired at the end of an interview, in
the midst of other expansive ramblings, he said:

ADEBAWỌ. There is nobody without àtọ̀sí; it is connected to the bearing of
children. But if there is too much in the body it is dangerous.

In other words the disease àtọ̀sí, in moderation, is good for you.

(ii) Jẹ̀díjẹ̀dí (piles?)

Closely related to àtọ̀sí is the worm (arọ̀n) called jẹ̀díjẹ̀dí (jẹ + ìdí,
lit. eat bottom). In explaining a medicine, Fatoogun made a
chance remark:

FATOOGUN. The thing that helps àtọ̀sí is none other than jẹ̀díjẹ̀dí.

This opinion was reinforced by Adebawọ when he said something rather similar.

ADEBAWỌ. Anyone who is a eunuch cannot be affected by jẹ̀díjẹ̀dí or átọ̀sí.

One need have little medical knowledge to imagine why a
eunuch is unlikely to contract gonorrhoea, but why is it linked
with the disease jẹ̀díjẹ̀dí?

Abraham's dictionary translates the word jẹ̀díjẹ̀dí quite
reasonably as haemorrhoids or piles (Abraham 1958, jẹ̀díjẹ̀dí), and
indeed many English-speaking Yorubas familiar with these
terms would agree with him. But while such a translation is not
incorrect, neither is it accurate, since it ignores the large
constellation of ideas which surround both the Yoruba and
European concepts.

Here are two fairly full accounts of this disease:

FATOOGUN. When there is too much jẹ̀díjẹ̀dí in the body, the person will feel it
in the anus (ihò ìdí) because this is where the worms work. They also cause
otútù (fever) and headache (orí fífọ́). It is the most important cause of
women failing to conceive. When semen gets into the womb, jẹ̀díjẹ̀dí rushes
to the place and drinks (mu) the semen so that the pregnancy is unsuccessful. Once jẹ̀díjẹ̀dí has walked through the semen in the womb, the semen
will not be modified to become a child. Jẹ̀díjẹ̀dí can also cause bellyache (inú
rírun). This type of bellyache is different from that caused by worms (arọ̀n)[2]
and from that caused by black blood (ẹ̀jẹ̀ dúdú)[3] and by a swollen scrotum
(ìpá).[4] The type of bellyache caused by jẹ̀díjẹ̀dí is when they (the worms)
gather together in the belly and then disperse. They get together and then
disperse again. This is why the pain is at about three minute intervals.
Thus it is called inú wẹ́rẹ́-wẹ́rẹ́[5] or inú jẹ̀díjẹ̀dí. As the jẹ̀díjẹ̀dí disperse they will

go into a different part of the body where they may cause injury such as in
the blood.

ADEBAWQ. *Jèdíjèdí* is a bad disease. It can prevent a man's penis becoming
erect. Eating sweet (*dùn*) things, sugar, or honey for example, is the cause of
jèdíjèdí. These sweet things are very dangerous, especially for someone who
has been affected by *àtòsí* in the past, or for a person whose mother became
pregnant when his father was affected by *àtòsí*. *Jèdíjèdí* usually affects such
people.

Jèdíjèdí usually begins with bellyache (*inú rírun*) and dysentery (*ìgbé òrìn*).
The person affected can defecate about six times in a period of two hours;
he will also become weak due to stomach-ache. Too much milk, tomatoes,
Ovaltine etc. are the causes of *jèdíjèdí*. If this disease is in the body for too
long, it can push the anus out, and it usually takes a long time before we can
push it back in. The person will have to take medicine for it and we must
also treat the anus. If we don't do this, then it cannot be cured immediately.
He must not drink strong wine or sugar unless he wants to die. Anyone who
does not like sweet things cannot be affected by *jèdíjèdí*. I was affected by
jèdíjèdí once but I drove it away, and from that time I have never heard of
anything like *jèdíjèdí*. When I suffered from this I passed blood out with my
excreta for a full three years.

There is not in this anything that Fatoogun would disagree
with. Both men believe that blood in the faeces (*ìgbé òrìn, ìgbé èjè*
or *tápà*) are caused by *jèdíjèdí*. Fatoogun shows this in reply to
my question:

BUCKLEY. What causes *tápà*?

FATOOGUN. It is common amongst the *Tápà* people[6] which is why it is called
tápà. It is known as *ìgbé òrìn* and is caused by mucus (*ikun*) in the stomach
and by *jèdíjèdí*. *Jèdíjèdí* will block the way through which the excreta passes
with mucus so that if the person wants to defecate, it is mucus that will
come out together with only very small faeces (*ìgbé*). This will give the
person pain in his back and he will lose his appetite.

If someone eats sugar it can cause this illness—and also if you eat too
many groundnuts (*èpà*). It will give the person pains in the neck and in the
sides of the body. It can make the person pass blood with his excreta.

The belief that *tápà* is caused by eating 'sweet' things is
reinforced by Adebawọ.

ADEBAWQ. If a person eats too many sweet things, this causes *ìgbé òrìn*. and
if a person has been affected by *àtòsí*, *ìgbé òrìn* will also affect him—things
like sugar, milk, and bread. This illness is not very common among
Europeans because they usually take care about the sort of food they eat.

They can take a cup of tea[7] with only one or two cubes of sugar but we tend to use eight to ten cubes of sugar in one cup of tea.

In a later interview, Adebawǫ developed this theme.

ADEBAWǪ. *Tápà* is a very dangerous illness and it can cause illnesses that can never be cured. It can prevent a man from having sexual intercourse. When using medicine to cure *tápà* you must not eat sweet things. Anyone affected by *tápà* has a limit to the number of children that he can have. Anyone affected by *tápà* cannot have an erection in his penis. *Tápà* can also cause the anus to be pushed out. . . . *Tápà* can also stop the flow of menstruation.

Fatoogun and Adebawǫ have raised two main points so far. The first is that the worm *jèdíjèdí*, like *àtǫsí*, is encouraged to develop by the eating of sweet (*dùn*) foods and by alcohol. Correspondingly it will be seen later that it is cured by the eating of bitter and sour ingredients in medicine. The second is that *jèdíjèdí* is closely related to disorders of the genitals. Both men believe that menstrual difficulties and female infertility are so caused, and that *jèdíjèdí* is also a cause of *tápà* which in the long run can render a man impotent. While nowhere have I come across the suggestion that *àtǫsí* and *jèdíjèdí* are the same disease, it is clear that both our informants regard *jèdíjèdí* as a potential source of afflictions similar to those caused by *àtǫsí*. Hence it is believed that affliction by one can encourage the development of the illnesses by the other.

I have so far given a fairly full account of the effects of *jèdíjèdí* upon the body. For reasons of clarity, however, a significant part of Fatoogun's statement was omitted. His account continues:

FATOOGUN. *Jèdíjèdí* have their own separate bag (*àpò*) in the body where God created them. When this bag is full to the brim, some of the *jèdíjèdí* fall out and go all over the body to cause injuries. These *jèdíjèdí* affect any part of the body that they can come into contact with. They suck the blood. This can be seen because the affected part will become lean.

I asked Fatoogun where *jèdíjèdí* was to be found in the body of a healthy person. He said:

FATOOGUN. *Jèdíjèdí* is always in the body. They have their bag (*àpò*) just near the bag of semen; in a women it is near the bag of menstruation (*àṣẹ́*).

Nor is this idea peculiar to Fatoogun. An old lady herbalist Mrs Ajayi in Ibadan once told me the same thing.

BUCKLEY. What causes *jẹ̀díjẹ̀dí*?

MRS AJAYI. God has created it in the belly.

BUCKLEY. Why is it that not everybody suffers from *jẹ̀díjẹ̀dí*?

MRS AJAYI. *Jẹ̀díjẹ̀dí* affects everybody. If a person is not affected by *jẹ̀díjẹ̀dí* that person will not have any power.

BUCKLEY. Why is it that some people suffer from *jẹ̀díjẹ̀dí*?

MRS AJAYI. This is because there are too many *jẹ̀díjẹ̀dí* in the body of those people. If a child does not have *jẹ̀díjẹ̀dí*, his penis will not be able to stand erect; or if it is a girl, she will not be able to menstruate.

Once more we have the same formula: a disease—this time a worm—is beneficial until it becomes too strong.

(iii) Image 1—preliminary discussion

Even at this stage a pattern is starting to emerge. From Fatoogun's account of *jẹ̀díjẹ̀dí* and *àtọ̀sí* a structured image of simple illnesses may be abstracted.

Such illnesses are caused by diseases which have their proper place in the body. Normally, the diseases contribute to the body's health, each one, at least in principle, having a defined role. However, the diseases may become 'too much' or 'too powerful' in the body. This arises when a person indulges in too much sweet food, too much sexual activity or too much alcohol. Fatoogun regards the diseases as being contained in 'bags' (*àpò*) in the body. When they become 'too much' they overflow their bag and cause illness.

The importance of the part of this framework of beliefs which concerns the beneficial properties of diseases to the herbalists themselves should not be overstated. Herbalists are concerned with the fact that excesses of sweet food, wine, and sexuality can cause illness, and they mention the benefits of diseases only in passing. Adebawọ in particular was most reluctant to attribute beneficial aspects to diseases other than *àtọ̀sí* (gonorrhoea), and Fatoogun denied that worms which suck the blood were in any sense beneficial. Nevertheless, in the discussion of diseases which follows, it is clear that there are generally considered to be benefits to be derived from the existence of diseases in the body, and that diseases are not, as in European thought, invasions of germs from outside the body, but rather substances placed by God within the body from birth. It will be part of the task of this study to explain how Yoruba herbalists find it reasonable to attribute both good and evil effects to diseases, but also to be accounted for is the apparent lack of interest in the benefits of diseases which my informants undoubtedly showed.

Now that the bones of Image 1 are laid out, it is possible quickly to give my informants' account of other illnesses which are rather similar. The reason that many of the comments given here are so brief is that the information given by my informants tended to be rather repetitious, and they were often keen to push on to topics which they found more interesting.

(c) Other simple illnesses

(i) Aròn inú (worm in the belly)

This worm is the commonest cause of simple bellyache. There are many different kinds of bellyache, and it has already been shown that one, the roving kind, is caused by jẹ́díjẹ̀dí. Aròn inú (sometimes called simply aròn) is the cause of most of the minor aches and pains in the belly. It is also one of the few worms which almost everyone regards as having a beneficial role in the body. Their function is to break up (fọ́) or grind (lọ̀) the food which enters the belly.

FATOOGUN. God created the worm in the body from the beginning. When one worm dies it will give birth to young ones, and these will become adults. It is essential for these worms to be in the body; they help to break up the food which has been eaten. They are red in colour. Some of them can have a red head and tail; some may be red at the head and white at the tail.

In conversations which I had both with my prime informants and with others, I found that the typical form of bellyache caused by aròn inú is a pain immediately below the chest, sometimes accompanied or preceded by rumblings in the belly (inú kíkùn). Western doctors inform me that many Yoruba people attend their clinics complaining simply that their bellies are making a noise, and this in itself is believed to be a danger signal that pain from aròn inú is on its way.

The usefulness of these worms is enshrined in a Yoruba greeting. I discovered this greeting in Abraham (1958, aròn

1 (c)), but I have myself used it in social situations and have been understood. The greeting in question is *'arọ̀n rere kó gbàá'* (may good worms get it), and it is a way of saying 'bon appetit' to someone who is eating. Like other Yoruba diseases, *arọ̀n inú* are beneficial when they remain hidden and are considered harmful only when they begin to show themselves.

(ii) *Jàṣéjàṣẹ́ (jẹ + àṣẹ́ + eats menstruation)*

Yet another kind of bellyache is caused in women by the germ which eats menstrual blood.

FATOOGUN. This is a type of germ (*kòkòrò*) like *jẹ̀díjẹ̀dí*. They live in the place where the menstruation (*àṣẹ́*) is located. These germs suck the blood and thus the woman will not be able to menstruate. If a medicine is prepared for the woman she will be able to expel these germs. They will also be found in the faeces of the woman and they will be as red as blood.

ADEBAWỌ. This worm is very difficult for a woman to expel completely. All we do is to give the woman a medicine that will drive away the worm so that the woman can conceive.

In another interview, Adebawọ said:

ADEBAWỌ. The disease that causes miscarriage (*àsoògbó*) when the pregnancy is two months old is called *jàṣéjàṣẹ́*. This woman will always complain about stomach ache. This is caused by the worm that eats menstruation in her womb.[8] After some time the menstruation will be flowing. This disease is also known as *yọnúyọnú*.

(iii) *Arọ̀n aboyún (worm of pregnant woman)*

Another worm which can be troublesome according to Fatoogun is the worm *arọ̀n aboyún*.

FATOOGUN. When the child is becoming bigger in the belly it will press the worms in the place where they stay. These worms will be trying to find another suitable place; they may get to the stomach (*ikùn*) and this will cause bellyache for the pregnant woman. This woman may expel the worm together with her faeces (i.e. if she takes the appropriate medicine).

Here again the disease which can be so troublesome has its beneficial side, as Fatoogun says:

FATOOGUN. These worms also help the child in the womb to turn in reaction to the movement of the worms. In this way the woman will know that the child is turning in her womb (i.e. so that the child may be born head downwards).

(iv) *Orí fífó* (headache)

Herbalists generally divide headaches (*orí fífó*; *orí + fíí + fó*) into a number of categories. What is normally simply given the name *orí fífó* appears to be the common headache. This according to Fatoogun:

FATOOGUN. . . . is usually caused by a worm (*aròn*) called *aròn orí* (worm of the head). It is a type of insect (*kòkòrò*) that God has created together with the flesh of the body. When this insect moves about in the head it causes a headache. The headache is as though someone is using an axe to cut his head. During this, hot water will come from the eyes. He will feel sleepy but be unable to sleep and he will feel cold. Two further types of headache are described by Fatoogun. These are *ọdẹ orí* and *orí wájú*.

FATOOGUN. *Ọdẹ orí* is caused by insects or worms in the head which bore holes from the head into the ears. They thus find their way into the open air. This enables air to get into the head from which it cannot then escape. These insects or worms will try to find the place where the hole is and make the head make a noise like rain. The medicine will kill the insects and seal up the holes. This type of headache (*orí fífó*) creates a noise in the ears *wọrọwọrọ* (the type of noise) or the head will be making a noise like boiling water.

Adebawọ distinguishes *ọdẹ orí* by the following characteristics:

ADEBAWỌ. The one called *ọdẹ orí* is the worst type of *orí*. This can make a person become mad. It is difficult to cure and there are many medicines for it: we can wash it; we can cut incisions in it. Some people affected by this disease think that someone has used hair from their heads or used their head tie (*gèlè*) in (bad) medicine to cause this. This is not true. We can prepare an infusion (*àgbo*) for the person to wash with: we can prepare some medicine to be rubbed on the head.

Ijẹbu people call this type of disease *àtoríwá* (that which comes from the head) and anybody affected by the disease cannot avoid holding a handkerchief to his face to wipe away the mucus (*ikun*). Some people can even blow out insects (*kòkòrò*) from the nose. We know that *ọdẹ orí* is affecting someone when he complains that his ears are making an unnecessary noise or if he hears the sound of ringing bells.

That the two men are talking about the same condition is made clear in the following statement by Fatoogun:

FATOOGUN. (*Orí wájú* is the type of headache that) affects the forehead (*orí wájú*). The cause is the type of worm that goes to the ears (i.e. as in *ọdẹ orí*)— but in this case it goes to the eyes to fight. This type of worm is also called *aròn ojú* (worm of the eyes). This kind of headache affects the eyes and forehead. He will complain about pain in the nose which hurts to such an extent that mucus will come from the nostrils.

It may be felt at this stage that the disease *ọdẹ orí* together with, in Fatoogun's characterization, the related disease *wájú orí*, is similar to the condition which in English is called 'sinusitis'. Care should be taken about drawing this simple conclusion, for Fatoogun does not distinguish between this manifestation of the worm and another which European thought would regard as totally different.

FATOOGUN. If the worm has come into the eye people can see it in the patient's eye and the eye will be swollen.

Moreover both informants believe that *ọdẹ orí* can lead to madness.

FATOOGUN. When someone has used medicine to cause this type of headache it can develop into madness. This type of *ọdẹ orí* which is called *ìsàsí*.[9]

Adebawọ thinks similarly. The following question was put to him:

BUCKLEY. Is it true that *orí fífọ́* can lead to madness?

ADEBAWọ. I have already told you this; that it can lead to madness. This is not the ordinary *orí fífọ́* but only *ọdẹ orí*. A person affected by *ọdẹ orí* will be thinking both good and evil things and he will not be able to sleep. From this it can result in madness. Those who are affected by ordinary *orí fífọ́* who become mad are those whose hair has been used in medicine against them. They can use the hair of the person in many kinds of medicine—one may be put under the anvil on which the blacksmith beats out his iron. Every time the blacksmith beats the anvil the person will be shouting out '*yé; yé*'.

There is one other major form of *orí fífọ́*, translated by Abraham (*fọ́* 2, c, iii) as migraine, called *túúlu*. This according to Fatoogun is:

FATOOGUN. . . . caused by an insect called *kòkòròfọrífọrí* (lit. insect which breaks the head). The insect will eat away the inside of the head. The type of headache is called *orí túúlu*. It is localized in one spot and that is how we can identify it.

(v) *Arọ̀n ìrọ* (hernia)

I asked Mr Adebawọ about *arọ̀n ìrọ*. He said:

ADEBAWỌ. This is a dangerous worm which can kill a man. Anyone who is affected by this disease will have one of his testicles (*kórópọ̀n*) outside his body while one is inside. This place (he touches his groin) will swell up. It will cause bellyache (*inú rírun*) which can kill the person if it is not cured.

This worm was also given the names *arọ̀n ìpákè* and *arọ̀n abẹ́*.

FATOOGUN. *Arọ̀n ìrọ* is also known as *kùúnú*.[10] These are the worms that cause this *ìrọ* and they live in the scrotum (*ẹ̀pọn*). They will make the testicles become big. If they prepare medicine for the person affected by *ìrọ* it must kill these worms—if not it will not cure the *kùúnú* . . . There are also the ones that live in the bag of semen (*àtọ̀*) which are called *arọ̀n jàtọ̀-jàtọ̀* (*jẹ* + *àtọ̀*: eats semen). These are the worms that cause *kùúnú*. It can also be called *ìpá*.[11]

There is no inherent difference between *ìpá* and *ìpá.kè* (*ìpá* + *òkè*— the *ìpá* of higher up) except that one affects the crotch while the other, as the name suggests, is painful further up the belly.

At another time, Fatoogun seemed to suggest that *kùsínúkùsó.de* is a name given to a minor form of *ìpá.kè*. In addition it is clear that even though *ìpá.kè* might be diagnosed by a western doctor as hernia, his own understanding of the condition is different from the western one. Asked the question 'What is *kùsínúkùsó.de*?' (= *ìpá.kè*) he replied:

FATOOGUN. This is an illness got from women (i.e. through sexual intercourse). The belly of anyone affected by this will always be rumbling (*kù*) and the person will always be suffering from bellyache (*inú rírun*). It also affects women—the one found in women is called *ìpá.bò* (*ìpá* + *òbò*—*ìpá* of the vagina). If it is not cured quickly in a man it can result in *ìpá.kè*.

BUCKLEY. What causes it?

FATOOGUN. If a woman is having sexual intercourse with several men this (i.e. the *kùsínúkùsó.de*) will meet the *àtọ̀sí* in the body of the man and will become *kùsínú*. I know that there is always *àtọ̀sí* in the body to allow us to produce children. Anybody who has intercourse with that woman will become affected by the disease.

We have already noted that Adebawọ believes that *jẹ̀díjẹ̀dí* is most likely to affect someone who has suffered from *àtọ̀sí* (gonorrhoea). Fatoogun here sees the worm *kùsínúkùsó.de* (*arọ̀n ìrọ*) working in conjunction with *àtọ̀sí*. In this case however *àtọ̀sí* is not manifest as an illness but (until it comes upon the worm transmitted from the body of the woman) is playing a beneficial role in the healthy body of the man.

What is interesting also is that, while a man may develop the illness through contact with a woman of easy virtue, there is no suggestion that promiscuous sexual conduct on the part of a man might lead him to pass the disease back to a woman. Nor does it seem to be the quality of any of the woman's sexual partners that determines her capacity to give a man *arọ̀n ìrọ*, but the sheer number of them.

(vi) *Arọ̀n àyà* (worms in the chest)

In the chest (*àyà*) is to be found a worm called *arọ̀n àyà*, which causes a sharp pain.

FATOOGUN. The chest will ache rather like bellyache (*inú rírun*) so that the person will be clutching the chest in pain.

Elsewhere he said:

FATOOGUN. This is the worm that can be found in the chest. There is a light skin that separates the liver (*ẹ̀dọ̀*) and the stomach (*ikùn*) from the chest and it is here that the worm lives. Whenever this worm moves about in the chest it usually results in chest pains. This worm does not come into the stomach; it lives permanently in the chest.

BUCKLEY. How big is this worm?

FATOOGUN. This worm is a thin one, just a bit thicker than a broom twig,[12] but it is not as long as a broom. The mouth is just like a needle's point. It lives on blood.

(vii) *Akokoro* (toothache)

My main informants made the following statements:

FATOOGUN. These germs (*kòkòrò*) grow with human beings; they feed on the blood at the bottom of the teeth.

ADEBAWỌ. *Akokoro* is a pain in the teeth; the germs which cause this like to eat sweet things like sugar and honey. If you eat too many sweet things the germs will grow and fight the bottom of the teeth. Also there are some people who do not like to use a chewing stick or a toothbrush. These people will be affected by *àkokoro*.

(viii) *Jẹ̀wójẹ̀wọ́ (jẹ + ìwọ́ = eats navel)*

FATOOGUN. There is a disease that affects small children and it affects the navel (*ìdodo*). Any child affected by this will be always crying. If you look into the navel you will find that there is something moving around in it. This disease moves inside the fat (*ọ̀rá*). If medicine is prepared for the child this disease will be expelled with the faeces.

BUCKLEY. What causes it?

FATOOGUN. They give birth to *jẹ̀wójẹ̀wọ́* together with the child. It is at the time the child begins to suck the breast that the disease will develop.

ADEBAWỌ. There is a disease called *jẹ̀wójẹ̀wọ́*. This disease can kill a child without the child having any other illness. It makes the child cry; if the mother puts her breast to the child's mouth he will stop crying but he will be sucking the breast greedily. If the mother does not take care of the child in good time, the child can die while he is sucking. Some people may be thinking that it is *gìrì* (convulsions) but *gìrì* cannot affect a child between one and thirty days old. If we inspect the navel of the child it will protrude and it will be shiny. Some worms will be moving on the surface of the navel.

(ix) *Ogòdò* and *táǹpara ẹsẹ̀*

All the illnesses so far considered have a fairly simple nature. Their symptoms were attributable to diseases in the body and, though I was able to find out about them, they aroused little enthusiasm in my informants. The last of the illnesses to be considered here were more interesting both to myself and to my informants. *Ogòdò* and *táǹpara ẹsẹ̀* (Fatoogun calls this *dáǹpara ẹsẹ̀*) are closely related illnesses and are believed to be commonly found among the Ijẹbu Yoruba—of whom Adebawọ was one.

ADEBAWỌ. This is a very bad disease, and there are some people who call it *àrùn ijẹbu* (the Ijẹbu disease) just as they call some money *owó ìjẹbu* (counterfeit money, lit. Ijẹbu money). This is because it is very common in Ijẹbu. This disease is brought about by not taking care of one's body. Nowadays the disease is called *kòkòrò* (germs). It can affect any part of the body, the cheeks, the forehead. It will eat any part of the body which is affected. In the olden days they usually removed the person affected by this disease from where the people live because it can spread. It is a disease of the olden days and is not found anywhere today. It usually affects those who do not wash their bodies or who do not take care of their clothing. There was a song in Ijẹbu sung by the *oníjùjú* (*Jùjú* musicians are those who perform a popular traditionally based form of music).

Arùn mẹ́ta ló ńbá.jẹ̀bú jà ò
Arùn mẹ́ta ló ńbá.jẹ̀bú jà ò
Ogòdò nímú
lala lẹ́rẹ̀kẹ
Níbi ká ṣowó ká má.lè nóọ.

There are three diseases which affect the Ijẹbu
There are three diseases which affect the Ijẹbu
Ogòdò in the nose
Dried saliva on the cheek
Making money and being unable to spend it.

People of Ijẹbu are notorious for making counterfeit coins, *owó ìjẹ̀bu* (lit. Ijẹbu money), and also for expertise in medicine for making men rich. Adebawọ, like other Ijẹbu sometimes exhibited a shamefaced pride in this dubious reputation. However, he seemed rather anxious, having drawn our attention to it, to discount the Ijẹbu connection with the unpleasant illness somewhat unedifyingly mentioned in the song above.

ADEBAWỌ. These diseases, however, cannot only be found in Ijẹbu nowadays because we find it in other towns like Ṣaki, Barapa and Ekiti. (At this point there was an interruption in the conversation.) *Ogòdò* is brought about by not taking care of the body. For example in olden days people had their bath once in a year. Nowadays if a man does not wash for three days he will not be healthy unless he should go and take a bath. There are some people affected by a disease called *isáká*, but if they should take a bath every day the disease will leave them.

Like *ògòdò* is another disease called *itápara*, *táṅpara ẹsẹ̀* or *dáṅpara ẹsẹ̀*.

ADEBAWỌ. This is a disease of the sole of the foot and it comes from the body. If you cut it with a razor blade you will see white things on it. There is a medicine in which we have to cut it and then apply the medicine to it. This disease is just like *ògòdò*—we (i.e. the Ijẹbu) call it *ògòdò ẹsẹ̀* (*ògòdò* of the foot) while the other one is called *ògòdò ara* (*ògòdò* of the body). Anybody affected by it will not be able to walk properly and their shoes will be worn out in no time because they will be dragging their feet on the ground.

Where Adebawọ regards these two illnesses as being caused by the same disease, Fatoogun thinks them to be distinct.

BUCKLEY. What is *táṅpara ẹsẹ̀*?
FATOOGUN. We call it *dáṅpara*. It dwells in the body and in the foot. If it is too

much in the foot of the person he will not be able to walk barefoot because it
will be very painful. The germ usually sucks the blood around it and the
area where the germs live will be dried up. If he steps on small stones it will
be very painful. That is why they say '*Ẹni dánpara ó.telẹ̀ ó tàka*' (the person
with *dánpara* steps on the ground and snaps his fingers (in annoyance)), for
it will be very painful. . . . This *dánpara* is always in the foot of everybody.
There are people whose flesh is stronger than the germ so that the *dánpara*
will not be able to affect the person. *Dánpara* has been created with the foot.

When discussing the other illness of this pair, Fatoogun also
mentions the connection with the Yoruba sub-group of Ijẹbu.
Typically, his account adds a subtle element.

FATOOGUN. This illness *ògòdò* is common among the Ijẹbu and can affect any
part of the body especially the nose (*imú*). It can cut the nose off. It is a type
of germ that causes this illness. It was in Ijẹbu that this disease entered the
earth when it left Ifẹ. That is why it is so common in Ijẹbu. Thus the saying:
ara tó bá wu ògòdò nií fimú ìjẹbu dá (*ògòdò* uses the nose of the Ijẹbu to make
whatever style it likes)—(rough translation).

So far we have looked only at the diseases which have a hiding
place in the body. Fatoogun's account of *Ogòdò* presents us with
a most interesting transformation of this idea: '*Ogòdò* entered
the earth in Ijẹbu when it left Ifẹ'. This is a curious formulation
but it is not completely unusual. There are many mythical
accounts which tell of gods who left the town of Ile Ifẹ, the
geographical centre of the Yoruba cosmos where the world was
created, and there are several accounts which tell of gods who
descended into the earth. Ṣòngó, the thunder god, descended
into the earth at Koso near Ọyọ at the site of his present shrine
(Ellis 1894, 50–6). *Ifá* entered the earth in Ifẹ itself. In such
cases the god is understood to be present, offering protection to
his worshippers by virtue of being hidden in the earth. When,
however, he emerges from his hiding place his presence can
wreak havoc upon the population. Here a formulation commonly used to define the relationship of men to the gods is used
in the context of a disease. *Ogòdò* is not hidden in the body like
the other diseases we have considered. It is hidden in the earth.
Whether it provides any benefit to the people of Ijẹbu is not
made clear, but it explains how the Ijẹbu people are peculiarly
susceptible to its disadvantages. This transformation of Image 1
also introduces an important analogy in Yoruba thought to

which we will return. The earth in certain contexts is analogous
to the body. Like the body, the earth has the capacity to hide
diseases.

(d) Types of medicine

The discussion of Image 1 and of the understanding of illness
for which it provides a basis is still barely complete. It has been
shown that diseases are sometimes regarded as being hidden in
bags in the body or at any rate that they exist in the body and
that they can be made to develop, overflow their bag and cause
illness. This happens as a result of too much sweet food, too
much sexual intercourse, and too much alcohol. The complete
picture may be achieved by looking at the medicines which cure
these simple illnesses.

Yoruba medicines are generally classified according to their
intended use. Thus *oògùn jèdíjèdí* is the medicine which will cure
jèdíjèdí; *oògùn má.gùn* is the medicine that a man will use to kill or
injure someone who has sexual intercourse with the man's wife;
oògùn ibà is the medicine to cure fever; *oògùn ìsòyè* is a medicine to
improve the memory. There is also a broad classification of
medicines with 'good' and 'bad' (*oògùn rere* and *oògùn burúku*).
Finally, medicines are classified according to the method of
their construction.

In practice, actual medicines are constructed in a multitude
of different ways as explained in each recipe, but roughly
speaking, nearly all medicines correspond to one of the following ideal types, each one named by a Yoruba term.

(i) Agúnmu (pounded medicine)

The normal method for preparing *agúnmu* (*a + gún + mu* = that
which is pounded and taken) is to take fresh ingredients and to
pound them in a mortar. They are then removed from the
mortar and placed on a basketwork tray where they stand in the
sun to dry. Finally they are ground to a powder on a flat
grinding-stone.

This type of medicine is always eaten. It may be licked from
the left hand[13] or mixed in a liquid such as water, an alcoholic
drink, or 'hot *èkọ*'.[14] Sometimes the *agúnmu* is 'used to take hot
èkọ' (*a ó.fi mu èkọ gbígbónọ́*). This means that the *agúnmu* is

moulded in the hand and used to scoop up *èkọ* in the normal Yoruba manner of eating.

(ii) *Ẹ̀tù* (burnt medicine)

Ẹtù is a black powder prepared by placing ingredients into a pot with no additional liquid and slowly heating them over a fire. The process is a lengthy one and can be rather arduous since the pot needs constant stirring and a considerable amount of smoke may result as water is driven off. In recipes one is instructed '*a ó.jóo*', which I have always translated as 'burn it'. In this context the word'*jó*' denotes this slow charring process which takes place inside the pot. Where it is intended that the ingredients should be actually set on fire or burned in some other way I have always made this clear in the recipe.

Ẹtù is usually used in one of two ways. It is taken internally, by licking it from the palm of the left hand or by mixing it with a liquid and drinking it. It is also rubbed into incisions (*gbẹ́rẹ́*) cut in a specified part of the body. The incisions are often cut with a razor blade or knife, the *ètù* is rubbed in and the wound may be covered to stop the bleeding and to keep the medicine inside.

(iii) *Agbo* (infusion)

Agbo (*à* + *gbo*, that which is squeezed) is an infusion made usually but not always from vegetable ingredients. In one kind of *àgbo*, *àgbo tútù* (fresh or cold *àgbo*), the fresh ingredients may be squeezed (*gbo*) by hand in water or more occasionally in some other liquid or they may be placed in the liquid and left for a long time before the *àgbo* is used. Alternatively hot *àgbo* (*àgbo gbígbóná*) is prepared by cooking the ingredients in water or in some other liquid and generally using the liquid while it is hot. *Agbo* is usually drunk by the patient but it is sometimes used to wash all or a part of the body.

(iv) *Asèjẹ* (medicinal food)

Asèjẹ (*à* + *sè* + *jẹ*, that which is cooked and eaten) is prepared in the manner normally employed in the cooking of food. The recipe usually contains only one or two medicinal ingredients. The remainder, usually referred to by herbalists only in outline, are included in the recipes only to give the structure of a complete Yoruba meal.

The main ingredients are cooked in a mixture of palm-oil and water and are mixed with ground-up seeds, pepper, and salt. This soup (*ọbẹ*) is eaten by scooping it up with a small wad of cooked yam or cassava, using the fingers of the right hand. It is accompanied by small pieces of fried meat or fish served on a separate dish.

This form of meal differs only slightly from the most typical form of Yoruba food. Apart from the fact that it includes ingredients selected because of their medicinal properties, the main difference between *àsèjẹ* and ordinary food lies in the strictly traditional nature of the former. Whereas in most Yoruba food, the pepper which is used is the red chilli pepper (*ata*), this is usually replaced in medicinal soup by the black pepper *iyèré* which is said to have existed in Yorubaland from time immemorial. Similarly, where normal food can include a wide range of ground-up dried seeds as well as onions and tomatoes, medicinal soup usually confines itself to the seeds of the locust bean tree (*ìgbá*) which are called *irú*. These seeds are also regarded as an ancient type of food.

(v) *Ọṣẹ* (medicinal soap)

Soap is made locally in Nigeria and, though I was told of several different kinds, the sort that is used most commonly by the Yoruba is the black soap made from palm-kernel oil (*àdín*). It has normal everyday uses in the washing of clothes and of the body—most Yoruba wash their whole bodies 'thoroughly at least once a day—but soap is sometimes used in medicine. The medicinal ingredients are usually pounded in a mortar together with the soap, and the soap is used to wash a specified part of the body and sometimes the whole body. I have come across a few instances where medicinal soap is also eaten.

Though herbalists are usually able to refer to or briefly describe their medicines by one of these terms, they do not always rigidly adhere to these different methods and are willing to improvise where there is sufficient reason. By whatever method a medicine is prepared it may be accompanied by a ritualistic mode of application or an incantation where appropriate.

(e) Medicines to cure simple illnesses

Medicines to cure the illnesses caused by the activity of diseases, whether germs or worms, are remarkable not for their differences but for their similarities. In Appendix A the recipes which my informants were kind enough to give me are discussed individually, but because they all exhibit a close resemblance to each other I may here summarize the principles upon which they are constructed.

Ingredients are always selected because they have the power *(agbára)* to cure or assist in the cure of the illness. In most cases the power is manifest in the flavour and smell of the chosen ingredients. In addition, certain ingredients are known to possess purgative and diuretic properties which also determine their usefulness. I shall later show that other features are also significant but these are not relevant to the immediate discussion.

(i) Flavours

In both the preparation of medicine and the preparation of food, it is the flavour of ingredients which primarily determines their use. Yoruba people commonly distinguish the following flavours which can be glossed as follows: *ó dùn* (it is sweet); *ó korò* (it is bitter); *ó kọn* (it is sour) and *ó ta* (it is peppery).

In one set of contexts there is an effective distinction between *dùn* (sweet) and the other flavours *korò*, *kọn*, and *ta* (bitter, sour, and peppery) which corresponds closely to the English distinction between nice and nasty flavours. In another set of contexts however the same terms are employed but they refer to distinctions of flavour which correspond roughly to the terms sweet, bitter, sour, and peppery as they are used in British English.

The two sets of contexts in which flavour terms are used seem to be best distinguished in the following manner. A medicine or a meal may be regarded as a unified totality. When a meal is so considered, it will be described as '*ó dùn*' (it is sweet) if it is well-prepared and pleasant to eat, and '*ó korò*' (it is bitter), '*ó kọn*' (it is sour), or '*ó ta*' (it is peppery) if it is unpleasant. All well-prepared complete foods are considered 'sweet' *(dùn)* even though they are often made with large quantities of pepper or with sour or bitter ingredients. Complete medicines however

are seldom, if ever, described as 'sweet'. They are constructed
so that considered as a whole, they shall have one or more of the
unpleasant flavours (korò, kọn, ta).

However, both in medicine and in food, that which is eaten is
seldom composed of a single ingredient and when medicines
and foods are discussed on the level of the ingredients we find
the flavour terms used in a different way. A good many contain
ingredients which are selected precisely because they taste
bitter, sour, or peppery. Yet if a host gives a guest some soup
containing vast quantities of pepper, he will not ask his guest if
it tastes peppery (ṣó ta?) but rather if it tastes sweet (ṣó dùn?).
Should the guest reply that the soup is peppery (ó ta) the host
will be upset. Similarly with medicine. A medicine may include
one or more ingredients because they taste sweet, but the
overall composition of the medicine will make the flavour
unpleasant.

The contrast between the use of flavour terms in these two
contexts is more clear when one considers objects which are
used both as complete foods and as ingredients. Fresh cola (obì)
and bitter cola nuts (orógbó) are eaten because they taste sweet
(dùn). If the cola is bad or stale, the eater may say that it tastes
bitter (korò). When fresh, cola or bitter cola are used as
ingredients in medicine, they are never employed because of
their sweet flavour. As complete foods they are sweet (dùn), but
as ingredients they are bitter (korò). A similar apparent ambiguity applies to alligator pepper (ataare). I have seen people eat
ataare as a complete food, in much the same way as Europeans
might eat strong peppermint sweets. When so consumed, it is
because it is sweet (ó dùn). It is seldom used as an ingredient in
food, but when it is an ingredient in medicine it is used because
it is peppery (ó ta). It is this distinction between the completed
recipe and the specific ingredients which will be seen to have
great significance in the construction and use of medicines.

Complete foods may be sharply contrasted with complete
medicines to cure illness on the basis of flavour. Whereas
complete foods are sweet (dùn), complete medicines to cure
illnesses are bitter, sour, or peppery (korò, kọn, ta). To achieve
these general flavours of bitterness, sourness and pepperiness
in the complete recipe for medicine, the ingredients which are
used emphasize these flavours but ingredients of other flavours

are also included. Just as in food sweet ingredients are combined with peppery, bitter, and sour ingredients, so in medicine
peppery, bitter, and sour ingredients are combined both with
each other and with ingredients which are sweet.

The commonest type of ingredient found in medicines to cure
disease are those which are bitter or sour (*korò, kọn*). Though
these two flavours were sometimes distinguished by my informants, in practice the distinction has no importance for their use
in medicine. The epitome of bitter flavours seems to be the herb
làpálàpá, whose flavour is also compared to the two crystalline
forms of alum (*èyà ọrun dúdú* and *èyà ọrun funfun*) sold in Yoruba
markets. Where the bitterness of an ingredient corresponds
precisely to this flavour, it is often said that it will 'gather all the
disease in the body together so that it may be expelled with the
faeces'.

This picture of the disease or 'dirt' in the body being
'gathered together' puzzled me for some time. It was explained
that the action of such bitter ingredients was like that of alum
on a bucket of dirty water. Alum is much used by the Yoruba
where there is an inadequate supply of pure water. It is ground
up and sprinkled on the surface of a bucket of water. As the
alum sinks, it carries with it the dirt to the bottom of the bucket
leaving fresh water at the top. In the same way, it would seem,
bitter ingredients not only kill worms and germs. They gather
them together at the bottom of the body so that they may be
eliminated.

To an extent, pepper (*ata*), and other ingredients which are
peppery (*ta*) are included for a similar reason. Germs and
worms do not like the taste of pepper and may be killed by it;
at least they will be expected to run away from it. However,
pepper performs an additional function in medicine by enhanc-
ing the power of the other ingredients. Thus, while occasionally
pepper may itself perform the function of bitter and sour
ingredients, it is more commonly used in conjunction with
other ingredients to strengthen their power (*ó mú wọn lókun*).

The inclusion of ingredients which taste sweet in medicine to
cure illnesses caused by diseases is usually intended to attract
the disease to the medicine so that it may be induced to taste it.
Diseases like to eat sweet things, and it is by consuming sweet
things that they develop and multiply in the body. When the

worm tries to taste the sweetness in the medicine it will discover the bitterness and sourness and will either die or be expelled from the body or return to the hiding-place in the bag where it belongs.

(ii) Smells

Closely related to flavour is smell. Ingredients are used in medicine because they have a strong smell (*ó rùn ṣùù*). Worms do not like this type of smell and react to it as they do to the taste of bitter, sour, and stinging ingredients. As with sweet flavours, something which smells sweet (*ó rùn dídùn*) can be included in a medicine in order to attract the disease, though this is not common.

(iii) Purges and diuretics

Ingredients are sometimes included to allow a patient to defecate or urinate freely. This is usually expressed by my informants as 'it will allow the man to expel the disease with his faeces (or urine)'. Purgative and diuretic ingredients are usually used in conjunction with ingredients selected because of their flavour or smell and indeed many of them are themselves bitter or sour.

(iv) Construction of typical medicines for simple illnesses

The typical medicine appropriate to simple illnesses may be summarized as follows:

(a) Bitter, sour, or peppery-flavoured ingredients and/or strong-smelling ingredients which will kill the disease or drive it away from the place where it is causing injury. The disease may be driven back into its bag in the body, or it may be driven to the place where it may be expelled together with urine or faeces.

(b) Sweet-tasting, or sweet-smelling ingredients to attract the disease.

(c) Pepper to strengthen the power of the ingredients.

(d) A purgative or diuretic to help the disease on its way out of the body.[15]

Within this basic framework there is room for subtlety in the medicine's construction. Purgatives do not seem to be commonly used when the worm is affecting the extremities of the body or when it may be expelled in some other way. Thus in medicines for toothache the medicine usually takes the form of an *àgbo* (infusion) which is used to wash the germs from the mouth. The ingredients therefore are exclusively of the bitter, sour, or peppery variety. In medicines for headache (*orí fífó*) the medicine is sometimes inhaled or otherwise administered to the forehead. Where it is inhaled, the ingredients are necessarily used because of their smell. Where it is dripped into the eyes or nostrils or where it is applied as *ètù* to incisions near the eyes it may include bitter ingredients. But in no case is a purgative necessary since the disease will flow out of the eyes and nose. Diseases affecting the extremities of the body—such as *dáñpara ęsę̀*—or affecting the body just under the surface of the skin may be treated by washing or rubbing the affected place or by the use of *gbę́rę́* (incisions). Medicines which are used to cure those diseases which are diagnosed as being within the body (*inú*) are usually imbibed. When, as in the case of *arọ̀n àyà*, the disease is a long way from the anus, it seems to be sufficient to use bitter, sour, and peppery ingredients to drive it towards the anus where it will be expelled with the faeces. When the disease is lower down in the body, and therefore already in the place where it may be expelled, the medicine is more likely to include purgatives and diuretics to help it on its way.

(f) Image 1. Some concluding remarks on simple illnesses

We may now state rather more clearly the essential features of Image 1. In the body are a number of diseases. These are not inherently harmful, and indeed may be regarded as positively beneficial to the health of the body. Fatoogun portrays these diseases as living each type in its own bag in the body—and he says that one type of disease (*dáñpara ęsę̀*) is similarly hidden in the earth.

Basically, illness is caused by over-indulgence in good food, wine, and sex. When a person eats too much sweet food or drinks to excess, or when a woman (especially) has too much sexual intercourse, then the diseases proliferate in the body. When they do, they overflow their bag and cause an illness. To counteract the effects of this excess of pleasure, and to kill off and expel the excess of disease in the body, the patient must take medicines containing bitter or sour ingredients, reinforced by pepper and perhaps helped by purgatives.

It will be seen that we have here a number of contrasting pairs of items which are related to each other and which together form Image 1 (Figure 2). In the medicines in Appendix A it will be seen that no one group of medicines differs spectacularly from the others. In particular, it matters little whether the intention of the herbalist is to kill the disease, to expel it from the body into the forest or latrine, or to drive it back into its bag in the body. Adebawọ lays little emphasis on the beneficial value of diseases and seems unconcerned about the need to drive them back to the place where God created them. Perhaps for this reason his medicines make a greater use of purgatives and diuretics than those of Fatoogun. But both men use medicines which contain neither purgatives nor diuretics. Fatoogun, who does make occasional reference to driving the disease back into its bag, does not seem to alter the construction of his medicine to fit this specific intention.

health	illness
disease beneficial to body	disease harmful to body
disease hidden in bag	disease overflowing bag
disease hidden in earth	disease emerging from earth
moderate quantity of disease	excessive quantity of disease
moderation in habits	excess in habits
moderate sex	too much sex
bitter, sour (peppery) food and medicine	{ excess of sweet food { too much alcohol

FIGURE 2. Image 1

It was noted earlier that for Fatoogun, but also for Adebawọ and other herbalists, the notion that diseases were beneficial to the body was only loosely expressed. It is not that this view is the wild fantasy of a few unrepresentative men, for several herbalists have asserted with varying degrees of vagueness that diseases are beneficial. Also Prince (1966) shows that his informants share a similar point of view (below, pp. 90 ff.).

What is to be found in the recipes in the appendices is a total lack of practical significance in the idea that diseases are beneficial. If people are willing to assert in a loose manner that diseases in general or one disease in particular bring benefit to the body, they become directly concerned with the diseases only when they are excessive or have 'overflowed their bag'. Then the appropriate response is to expel, hide, or destroy them. At no time was I ever told that germs and worms should be encouraged to grow and multiply in order to improve a person's health. The possibility that illness might be caused by an absence of disease is never considered. The herbalist always assumes that where an illness is caused by a disease, it is an excess of the disease that is at fault and he will take pains to eliminate this excess.

From a practical point of view, the theory that diseases benefit a person has no relevance to the herbalist's therapy. It is wholly peripheral to his practical life and exists only as a theoretical afterthought. In this perspective, the fact that informants are vague and indeterminate in their exposition of the benefits of disease need cause no surprise. It should rather be asked why they bother to mention these benefits at all. Why do men cling to a theory of disease which in this particular aspect has little or no practical relevance either to the diagnosis or to the treatment of illness? The answer to this question must be sought in the broader context of Yoruba thought. As this study progresses it must turn to an elucidation of ideas related to Image 1 which impel people to complete their practical theory of illness and medicine with this curious non-practical elaboration.

Endnotes

[1] *Ilé ọmọ* means literally 'the home of the child' and generally refers to the womb; in this case the reference is to the origin of the semen.

[2] i.e. *arọ̀n inú* below pp. 33 ff.

[3] Below, Chapter 5.

[4] Below, pp. 37 ff.

[5] *Wẹ́rẹ́-wẹ́rẹ́* in this context means 'stealthy'—more commonly it means 'gentle' or 'slight'.

[6] i.e. the Nupe people who live to the north of the Yoruba.

[7] The Yoruba word *tíì* can also include any of the increasingly popular hot beverages such as coffee, cocoa, Bournvita, Ovaltine, etc. which can be bought in most Yoruba towns.

[8] Adebawọ here uses the term *àtọ̀* which normally means 'semen' but I

suspect that in this case he means 'menstruation'. Contrary to what I think is normal Yoruba usage Adebawọ uses the terms àtọ̀ and àṣẹ́ which usually mean respectively 'semen' and 'menstrual blood' more or less interchangeably.

9 Abraham, 1958, sà, A, 4, b, 'using magic drugs against P'. It has been seen that Adebawọ saw fit to deny that ọdẹ orí was caused by bad medicine. Prince (1964a, 87) says that ọdẹ orí causes madness.

10 Kùsínúkùsó.de (lit. rumbling inside, rumbling outside). It is often abbreviated to kùsínú or even kùúnú.

11 Abraham (1958), writes, 'ìpá A (1) hydrocele. . . . (2) ìpá kè hernia, rupture (= kú nún)'. Whatever may be said for these translations of ìpá and ìpá.kè, it is clear that Fatoogun would be more inclined to identify kùúnú with the former rather than the latter.

12 The broom most commonly used in Yorubaland is made of the rib of the palm frond; though each stick is a single strand it is not dissimilar to the European besom.

13 The significance of the left hand in medicine is discussed below, pp. 116 ff.

14 Ẹ̀kọ is a thick porridge made from fermented cornflour. It is eaten in its white blancmange-like solidity when it is called ẹ̀kọ tútù (fresh or cold ẹ̀kọ), or it is diluted with hot water to make a thin warm gruel known as ẹ̀ko gbígbónọ́ (hot ẹ̀kọ). Its flavour is rather sour (ó kọn) and unpleasant to a European palate but its main use is as food. The liquid gruel is often fed to infants for weaning.

15 In the recipes for medicines in this work these different characteristics will be abbreviated to b, sr, sw, pep, purg, and sm. (bitter, sour, sweet, peppery, purgative, and strong-smelling).

3

Colour and the human body: redness revealed[1]

The theme of the last chapter was that, for Yoruba herbalists, illness is caused by over-indulgence in food, wine, and sex, and that it may therefore be avoided by adopting moderate habits. As well as this opposition between *moderation* and *excess* there has been seen another, rather subdued opposition between the *hidden* and the *revealed*. Fatoogun saw each disease as ordinarily and healthily *concealed* within a bag in the body. When the diseases multiplied, they *overflowed* their bag and wrought havoc upon the patient. It will become clear that the opposition between the *hidden* and *revealed*, and indeed the image of overflowing, are quite fundamental to an understanding of my informants' ideas, and perhaps too an understanding of Yoruba traditional culture in general.

The three chapters which follow will consider a series of illnesses, nearly all of which are understood according to the pattern of Image 1. They are almost all illnesses which have been caused by an excess of disease in the body, and most of them are cured by the methods which have already been explained. However, among these are one or two illnesses which are not understood directly according to Image 1. And even those which have the structure of Image 1 have features which require a more profound explanation. These slightly more complicated illnesses involve relationships between elements in the body defined by their colour considered in relation to the categories of *hidden* and *revealed*.

The task of these three chapters will be to establish an image of the healthy human body, and also the inherently similar image of the cosmos, as a structure of coloured elements. The image is based upon the colour triad found elsewhere, both in Africa and outside, of *red*, *white*, and *black*. However, the significance of these colours for the Yoruba will be found to be rather different from that among other peoples (Breidenbach 1976; Turner 1963). This structure will be given the name

'Image 2'. Illness, it will be argued, is understood to be an aberration from this ideal of the healthy human body.

There is a sense in which the devastations of illness may be understood to be comparable to a descent into chaos. But this is only partly correct. For illness exists as a logical development comprehensible in relation to the structure of the healthy body. If illness is destructive, it is an *orderly* destructiveness. The logical possibilities for disrupting the ideal structure of the body are, as will be shown, legion, and by no means all of them were discussed by my informants. The chapter headings, 'redness revealed', 'red and white confounded', and 'black blood' give some indication of the direction the discussion will take. Beyond this, however, it will be shown that Image 2, the ideal structure of the body and cosmos expressed in colours, as well as the illnesses which exist in relation to this model, are homologous with Image 1 which was discussed in the last chapter.

For the Yoruba, as indeed for the people of any culture, there are many different perspectives from which an object as complicated as the body may be examined. Abimbọla (1973 a), Awolalu (1970), Dos Santos and Dos Santos (1973) and Verger (1973) each portray different Yoruba views of the human personality which largely reflect their own different interests (Fatoogun himself features in the Dos Santos' paper with a splendidly intricate piece of Yoruba philosophy). Here Yoruba ideas about the body will be presented as a structure of coloured elements. Thus will the image of the body be used to establish a relationship between the categories of hidden and revealed on the one hand and the three basic colours on the other.

(a) Yoruba colour terms

There are three 'basic' Yoruba colour terms broadly in the sense that Berlin and Kay use this expression (1969, 5-6). They may be glossed 'white', 'red', and 'black'. Of these, the term *funfun* (white) is the most narrowly defined. It refers specifically to the limited range of colours which in English are either white or colourless. The term *pupa* 'red' embraces those colours which are light in hue and which are red, yellow, or brown. The brighter shades of red, yellow, and brown can be distinguished by the term *pón*, but for all practical purposes the terms are interchangeable. *Dúdú* 'black' refers to colours which are dark, and includes black, dark brown, and most shades of blue and green.

funfun (white)	*pupa* (red)	*dúdú* (black)
white	red	black
colourless	yellow	dark brown
	brown	green
		blue

FIGURE 3. Glossary of colour terms

These limited colour terms are the ones most used in daily life and are commonly employed in religious ritual. Where more subtle distinctions are required, people fall back upon more circuitous phraseology. Green is 'the colour of leaves' *alá.wò ewé*; yellow, 'the colour of palm-oil' *alá.wò epo*. Increasingly, English terms are also used to make such fine distinctions. In certain specialist trades, notably cloth-dyeing, fine distinctions of colour can be of great importance, but for most Yoruba, and here I include religious and medicinal specialists, they are not generally used. Most strikingly, I have found, in discussing colours with highly literate, English-speaking Yoruba, that considerable difficulty is often experienced in making a semantic distinction between colours such as 'green' and 'blue' using English colour terms.

(b) Image 2. The human body and cosmos: colours hidden and revealed

(i) Conception and birth—the young child

The human body may be regarded as an expression of some of the most fundamental categories of Yoruba thought. It is at once both the most familiar of all the objects known to man, and yet it is the most mysterious, containing a complexity of which we can only be dimly aware. It therefore embraces what I have come to regard as the central distinction in Yoruba thought between the hidden and the revealed.

All the herbalists I spoke to agreed that a child conceived in

the womb (*ilé ọmọ*) is the union of the blood (*èjẹ̀*) of menstruation (*àṣẹ́*) and semen (*àtọ̀*). According to Fatoogun the blood
and semen are bound together with a 'rope' (*okùn ọmọ*).

FATOOGUN. *Okùn ọmọ* is the place where the remnants of the menstruation
(*ìṣẹ́kù àléjò*) is to be found. The semen goes to the same place. It is from this
rope that God (*Olódùmarè*) creates the child and it is the remnant of the
menstruation that holds together the semen and the menstruation. God
creates the pattern of the child from it.

If we interpret this idea as a structured pattern of colours, we
may express it diagramatically (Figure 4) as the union of red
blood and white semen hidden inside the body of the woman by
her black skin, where they remain until the time of birth.

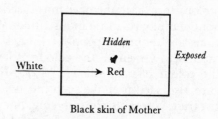

Black skin of Mother

FIGURE 4. Healthy conception

This duality of red and white continues after birth in the
healthy child (Figure 5) with the existence of blood inside his
body and the water which flows outwards as urine.

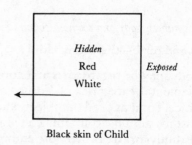

Black skin of Child

FIGURE 5. Healthy child

(ii) The cosmos

This same structure of ideas recurs in another image which will now be explored, that of cosmos. In Yoruba thought the sky is white and the earth is red. Those of us who have English minds like to think that the sky is blue, but both in Britain and even more in West Africa, the sky, sadly, is more frequently white than blue, and the fall of white rain and even the occasional white hailstone completes the identification.[2] It is the brick-coloured sub-soil (*ilèpa*) which Yorubas call red. Above it, except on paths and other spaces open to the elements, is the richer top-soil (*ilèdú*), which is black.[3]

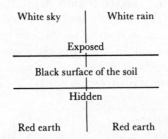

FIGURE 6. The cosmos: fertile land

(iii) Redness revealed

The three diagrams (Figures 4, 5, and 6) illustrate three healthy relationships between the colours red, white, and black in the human body and in the cosmos. In essence they state that whenever red and white, blood and semen, earth and rain, combine in secret beneath a black surface then there is health and fertility, and that any other permutation may in general be regarded as dangerous. Subsequent chapters will consider other unhealthy permutations of colours—where red and white become confused; where black invades red; and where red and white emerge together into the open. Here, however, I shall discuss briefly those regular and only mildly dangerous occasions when redness emerges into the open.

A healthy woman of child-bearing age, according to my informants, will menstruate regularly for five days each month.

During this period she should not have sexual intercourse with her husband. Thus semen will not flow into the vagina of the woman to be hidden in her womb, and the redness, which in copulation and pregnancy should remain hidden, will flow out into the open.

This inversion of intercourse and conception has a parallel in the cosmos. During the dry season, the earth tends to lose its black covering. The vegetation shrivels and the rains do not fall. Just as the flowing menstruation of a woman prevents the occurrence of pregnancy, so too is the growth of vegetation inhibited by the appearance of the red soil on the surface of the earth.

It must be discussed later in more depth how the red earth of the dry season (Chapter 6) and the flow of menstruation (Chapter 5) are each beneficial to humanity despite their immediate opposition to the processes of fertility. For the moment, let us merely define an initial image of the body and of the cosmos as pairs of contrasting states (Figure 7). In one, the

red (and white) hidden	red (and white) revealed
red earth (and water) hidden	red earth (and water) revealed
wet season	dry season
menstrual blood (and semen) hidden	menstrual blood (and semen) revealed
conception (in sexual intercourse)	no conception (during menstrual period)
fertility	infertility
health	illness

FIGURE 7. Image 2

redness of menstruation is hidden within the womb where it may combine with semen to make a child. In the other, redness breaks through its black covering in the form of a menstrual period—a period during which copulation may not take place and during which the woman is temporarily infertile. In the one, the red earth is concealed and rain falls to produce flourishing vegetation. In the other the red earth is revealed, rainfall ceases, and the soil becomes barren.

(c) Eelá *and* ètè

The argument on this topic so far has been analytical and somewhat general, and has indeed taken us far from the recorded remarks of the herbalists. It is possible to see how this framework is implicitly used by the herbalists themselves by looking at the two illnesses known as *èelá* and *ètè*.

(i) *Eelá*

My informants agreed that *èelá* is a dangerous illness affecting small children in which the main symptom is the appearance of 'red', that is light-coloured, blotches in the surface of the skin. The word *ètè* is usually translated as 'leprosy', though as always it is worth mentioning that there may be illnesses which western doctors would not call leprosy known by this name. Like *èelá*, it too is characterized by red patches in the surface of the skin, but it is distinguished by its tendency to 'cut' the fingers and toes of the sufferer. There, briefly, is the area in which all my informants agree; from here their patterns of knowledge diverge.

In addition to the names *èelá* and *ètè*, my informants used a third name, *ara pupa*, which means literally, 'red body'. Awotunde identifies *ara pupa* with the disease *èelá*. Fatoogun on the other hand used the name *ara pupa*, as a synonym for *ètè*. Adebawọ offered yet another more complex categorization; he distinguished three types of *èelá*. 'The first', he said:

ADEBAWỌ. . . . is called *èelá inú* (the *èelá* of the inside) in which the general complexion of the child will become red, but the *èelá* itself (i.e. the distinctive skin rash of light-coloured blotches) will not appear on the body. There is a type of *àgbo* (infusion) which can be used to drive the *èelá* out on the surface of the skin where it can be cured.

There is another type of *èelá* which the Yoruba (i.e. the *Ọyọ*) people call *olóròñtó*. If this affects the child it will pass out watery faeces very frequently. This disease affects the male child more frequently than the female. It is very dangerous because the child's legs will swell up and the skin will start to peel.

Adebawọ explains these two forms of *èelá* as a result of dirt or disease in the womb at the time of conception.

Much more interesting for the purpose of this chapter is his description of a third type of *èelá* which he calls *èelá ara pupa*, and which he also regards as a form of *ẹ̀tẹ̀* or leprosy.

ADEBAWỌ. If a man should have sexual intercourse with a woman while she is menstruating she will give birth to a child with this type of *ẹ̀tẹ̀*. This form of disease does not cut the fingers and toes like the other types but people still run away from the child. There will be black and red patches all over the child.

For Awotunde, on the other hand, all forms of *èelá* are caused when parents conceived the child during or immediately after a menstrual period. He says:

AWOTUNDE. If a man has sexual intercourse with a woman on the same day that the menstruation stops flowing, and if the woman becomes pregnant, the resulting child will be affected by *èelá* when he is three months old. This is because the blood has not finished coming from the womb, it will not mix with the semen and becomes *èelá* on the surface of the child.

These two theories provide a good example of what Kuhn calls 'the articulation of a paradigm'—the definition and solution of a problem using the structure of a widely held belief. Red and white should be joined together hidden in the secrecy of the mother's body (Figure 4) to produce a healthy child (Figure 5) in which the red and white are again combined in the confines of the concealing black skin. But if the white semen and the red blood combine in the open, outside the woman's body, the child will not be healthy. The redness of the menstruation is already moving into the open ('the blood has not finished coming from the womb') when it forms part of the child (Figure 8). But the redness which was still coming from the womb will not remain

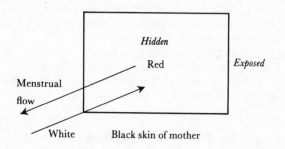

FIGURE 8. Conception of child during menstruation

hidden; it will mix with the semen and become *èelá* on the surface of the skin of the child.

Here, then, is a distortion of an ideal pattern in which the order of the human body is disturbed. This confusion is itself given definition by the paradigm. In effect, a logical transformation has taken place. The infertile menstrual period and the copulation are both healthy female states in which redness is respectively revealed and hidden. When copulation takes place with a menstruating woman the categories of hidden and revealed are, in relation to redness, confounded, and thereby in part inverted. This inversion persists in the new born infant (see Figures 9 and 10).

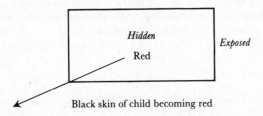

FIGURE 9. Black skin of child becoming red

	Redness hidden	Redness revealed	
Normal copulation	+	−	Health
Healthy child	+	−	
Copulation with menstruating women	−	+	Illness
Child with *èelá*	−	+	

FIGURE 10. Restatement of figures 2, 3, 7, and 8

(ii) *Ẹtẹ̀*

There has been a certain disagreement about the nature of the illness *èelá*. When the illness *ẹtẹ̀* is considered the disagreements become more pronounced. Let me start once more with the area of agreement. All three informants agreed that if a person should live in the same house with a leper, or wear his clothes,

he would soon be afflicted with the illness. similarly, everyone
agreed that it was possible to induce the illness in an enemy by
using bad medicine. Adebawọ seemed to regard himself as
something of an expert on the subject.

ADEBAWỌ. If we dip a stick into a certain medicine and touch any one with
it, the place that the stick touches will be affected by ẹtẹ̀. In ẹta ẹtè (i.e. the
type of medicine which is 'thrown' at someone to induce the disease), they
will soak ataare (alligator pepper) in medicine and use pincers to pick it up
and administer it. If this medicine touches any part of the body or is
stepped on, that place will become diseased unless you can quickly find the
antidote (ẹrọ̀). Another kind of medicine is called atapa (that which stings
and kills) which can be sent to a person's house. It is usually projected
through the hole in a hoe (where the shaft enters the blade).

They usually use medicine for ẹtẹ̀ against individuals, but if it is used, the
disease will soon spread and become a disease of the whole family. For this
reason they always tell them at the Leper Central Hospital at Ogbomọṣọ
not to have sexual relations for if the wife of a leper should conceive she will
give birth to a leper.

All of my informants indicated a general agreement with these
ideas but there were also large areas where they disagreed. One
of these was a statement by Fatoogun that in addition to ẹtẹ̀
being the result of bad medicine, it could also be caused by
burying a dead man wrapped up in a red cloth. There is an *Ifá*
verse recorded by Bascom which explains why white calico and
not red is used to wrap the bodies of the dead. Bascom explains
that the deceased will be reborn as a leper if he is buried with
red (Bascom 1969b: 238–41). Fatoogun himself also recited to
me a very similar version of the same story. This theory rests on
a belief in reincarnation, a belief which is very widespread
among the Yoruba. When someone dies, a grandchild or
greatgrandchild of the same sex born soon after the death may
be taken to be the reincarnation of the dead person who has
returned to the world. When this is suspected by relatives, *Ifá*
or some other form of divination may be used to ascertain that
reincarnation has indeed taken place. This child is then given
one of a large number of names to indicate what has happened.
Among these are *Iyábọ̀* (mother has come), *Yẹ́wáńdé* (mother
has come back), *Babátúndé* (father has returned), *Akíntúndé* (the
brave man has returned) and there are many others.

The belief is both common and deeply rooted, for these

names are to be found among the children of those who have rejected traditional religion in favour of Islam or Christianity, but who, though they no longer believe in reincarnation, are quite aware that the belief exists and are willing to perpetuate its outward forms.

Faced as I was by Fatoogun, who was a supremely intellectual man of the people, I could not forbear from confronting him with what I considered to be a manifest intellectual absurdity in this widespread belief. My reading had indicated to me that not only did the Yoruba believe in reincarnation, they also worshipped their dead ancestors (Schwab 1955, 358, and see also Ojo and Olajubu 1977). How, I wondered, could a man who was dead, and who was worshipped for that very reason, nevertheless be alive and inhabiting the family compound at one and the same time? I therefore asked Fatoogun the following.

BUCKLEY. How is it that a man worships his ancestors while at the same time his ancestor is reborn? Does he worship the little child?

FATOOGUN. (After a moment's thought)[4] When a man dies his heart (ọkọn) goes to heaven and it is this that men worship. It is the man's head that is reborn as a little child. When this child grows old and dies, his own heart goes to heaven. There are always only a certain number of people in the world. When the head (orí) of a man is reborn it becomes the heart of the child, and it is the heart of the dead man that is now worshipped, because it is in heaven and is now the head of the little child. We worship the head because it is in heaven and can go to God (Olódùmarè) and beg for us. Sometimes the head is born into the heart of a small child before the person who is still alive wants to return to heaven and he will soon die.

The head of a man resides in heaven; his heart is in his body in the world. At the death and subsequent rebirth, the head and heart change places. Thus a man can worship his ancestor (his own head) who is in heaven and at the same time know that he is the reincarnation of (the head of) the very same ancestor.

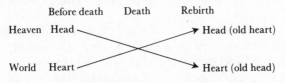

FIGURE 11. The head and heart in reincarnation

Clearly, there may be further ramifications of this idea in the practical life of families and indeed in politics too but I was not able to find time to explore these. One might speculate, for example, about the report (Abraham 1958, *àà̀fìn* (4) C.) that upon the installation of the *Alá.fìn* of Ọyọ, the new king symbolically (perhaps really) eats the heart and afterwards worships the head of his predecessor. On the basis of Fatoogun's remarks, it would seem, that instead of the heart of the dead king going to heaven where it may be worshipped as a head by his successor, it is taken into the body of the new king. Similarly, the head of the dead king is not reborn as the heart of a little child; it remains to be worshipped by the new king, just as it was by the old. The new king, it would appear, becomes identical with the king who has just died (Figure 12).[5]

	Before Death	Death	After Death
Heaven	Head of old king	——————→	Head of new king
World	Heart of old king	——————→	Heart of new king

FIGURE 12. The reincarnation of a king?

Such an interpretation is, of course, merely speculative, but it does indicate a possible fruitful line of investigation, which might reveal, by their very contrast, important structural features, both of royal and non-royal lineages. In any case, I have nowhere discovered a man other than Fatoogun capable of fitting together these complex ideas into a coherent whole. While what he says is entirely compatible with the categories of other Yoruba thinkers, it could possibly be that Fatoogun's brilliant synthesis is idiosyncratic and of limited relevance to the thought and activities of other people in Yorubaland. But however idiosyncratic his opinions, his ideas are always worth serious consideration, both because they are no more idiosyncratic than those of other people, and because he is an exceptionally gifted man.

Part of his theory is that it is only the head of a person that is reborn. Because, in general, it is only the elderly who are reborn, the head of the deceased will already be white with old age. It is possible therefore, that wrapping of the body in white cloth signifies the integration of the whole physical body with the existing whiteness of the head. Whether or not this speculation is correct, it is not at all fanciful to compare the burial ceremony with the sexual act, where the white semen is enclosed in the blackness of the woman's body to mix with the red menstrual blood. In the burial, the white body enters the grave, where it is hidden from view by the black topsoil (*ilẹ̀dú*) so that it may blend with the *redness* of the subsoil (*ilẹ̀pa*). In both cases the results are the same; red and white combine hidden by blackness to produce a child (Figure 13).

I said that not everyone accepted Fatoogun's theory. Adebawọ disagreed with it forcefully. Every family, he said, had different ways of burying their dead which were usually kept secret, but red was not generally prohibited as a burial cloth.

	Redness hidden	Redness revealed	
Normal Burial	+	−	Health
Healthy child	+	−	
Body in Red Cloth	−	+	Illness
ẹ̀tẹ̀	−	+	

FIGURE 13. Burial practices and leprosy

ADEBAWỌ. In the olden days, our forefathers used the red cloth called *alá.árì* (presumably the same as *àlàárì* or *kẹ̀lẹ̀*) to bury their dead. Why did not *they* become lepers? If this belief is correct, why is it that Muslims and Christians, who generally bury their dead in white cloth, are not reborn as white people? The followers of *Ṣòngó* (the god) usually bury their dead with red cloth. Why does not the family of *Ṣòngó* worshippers have *ẹ̀tẹ̀*?

Undoubtedly some of Adebawọ's objections could be explained away by Yoruba detractors. His reference to the practices of Christians and Muslims are irrelevant since they do not in any case break the prohibition which is necessarily concerned with red cloth. Similarly his reference to the worshippers of *Ṣòngó* could undoubtedly be discounted with closer knowledge of the *Ṣòngó* cult and its rituals. *Ṣòngó*, like *Ṣònpònnó* to be discussed below in Chapter 6, is a dangerous god whose emblematic colours are red and white. Perhaps the flouting of normal burial practice is an attempt to avoid offending *Ṣòngó* in much the same way that *Ṣònpònnó* is appeased by disrupting certain corporate activities. At all events, my suspicion is that here is an exception to normal practice which may well prove the rule.

More fundamentally, however, the force of Adebawọ's argument should be respected. In essence, his dismissal of Fatoogun's theory is on empirical grounds: if you look at the facts, he is arguing, you will see that it is just not true. Not that Adebawọ has thrown out the baby of Yoruba paradigms with the bathwater of a specific theory. We have seen even in this chapter that he himself has derived his own explanation of a type of ẹ̀tẹ̀—what he calls èelá ara pupa—from the very same paradigm. Here, as elsewhere, the paradigm has not furnished complete solutions; it was merely a starting-point. From it two different people may arrive at two entirely different and incompatible conclusions.

(d) Health, illness, and Images 1 and 2

Beginning to emerge from this discussion is a picture of what constitutes health and illness. Health would seem to be understood as an ordered structure of the body. Illness is simply the negation or distortion of this ideal structure.

In both èelá and ẹ̀tẹ̀, the illnesses are defined by the appearance of redness on the normally black surface of the skin. It is clear from the informants' remarks that they think that this redness should have remained hidden in the body. The illnesses are caused either by having sexual intercourse with a woman whose menstruation is flowing, or by wrapping a corpse, later to be reincarnated, in red cloth outside the grave. This may be expressed by combining Figures 10 and 13 in Figure 1.

All that has happened in both of these illnesses and in their causes is that the redness which should have been hidden has been revealed and that the conceptually defined ideal structure of the body has therefore been destroyed. In both cases, it has also been an excess of redness which has called forth the unwanted revelation of redness in the sick child.

This understanding of èelá and ẹ̀tẹ̀ has been derived from an image of the human body as a structure of colours (Image 2). Let us now attempt to integrate this second image with the earlier Image 1.

	Redness hidden	Redness revealed
Normal coitus	+	−
Normal burial	+	−
Healthy child	+	−
coitus with menstruating		
woman	−	+
burial with red cloth	−	+
child with *èelá*	−	+
child with *ètè̩*	−	+

FIGURE 14. Health, *èelá* and *ètè̩*

Image 1	diseases hidden in their bag	diseases overflowing their bag
	diseases hidden in the earth	diseases emerging from the earth
	disease beneficial to the body	disease harmful to the body
	moderation in disease	excessive disease
	moderation in habits	excess in habits
	moderation in sex	excess in sex
	bitter, sour, peppery medicine	excess in sweet food and alcohol

Image 2	red (and white) hidden	red (and white) revealed
	red earth (and water) hidden	red earth (and water) revealed
	wet season	dry season
	blood (and semen) hidden	blood (and semen) revealed
	conception	no conception
	fertility	infertility
	health	illness

FIGURE 15. Images 1 and 2

This understanding of the illnesses *èelá* and *ètè̩* has been expressed in terms of Image 2—the image of the human body and cosmos as a structure of colour. Nevertheless, it may be shown that there is a certain similarity between these two illnesses and the illnesses which were considered by means of Image 1. In Figure 14 in which these two models are considered together it will be seen that there is, in both, an emphasis upon the correspondence between health and that which is hidden (whether it be a disease or red earth or menstrual blood). A similar correspondence exists between sickness and that which is revealed.

In Image 1, although the distinction between hidden and revealed is present, it is submerged in the informants' accounts by a greater concern with the dichotomy between moderation and excess. In Image 2, the greater emphasis lies with the opposition of the hidden and revealed. Here too however is a concern with moderation and excess. To have sexual intercourse with a menstruating woman may be regarded not only as an unwise breach of a rule of health, but as a form of sexual excess. Presumably, since one can have sexual intercourse for three weeks out of four, to indulge one's appetite for the fourth week is simply to be greedy, and greed, whether for food, wine, or sex, is, as has been seen, a cause of illness.

More than this, however, sexual intercourse may itself be regarded, like menstruation, as a dangerous form of revelation. I shall return to this subject again, but it is possible to begin to explore this idea here. Sexual intercourse requires at least partial nudity and the ejaculation of semen—i.e. the revelation of that which is normally hidden. To combine sexual intercourse with menstruation is therefore a particularly excessive form of revelation. But the danger in this practice is not of a general nature. It is very specific. It is that a child who is born as a result of the union will have the dangerous illness called èelá.

It may be seen that the illness èelá, while best explained in terms of Image 2, may be readily explained also in terms of Image 1. The two Images are indeed similar in structure and may be combined in a single simplified structure (Figure 15). The illnesses èelá and ètè provide an example of how the body, considered as an idealized structure of coloured elements, may be subject to disruption. In the next two chapters it will be seen that this same ideal structure may be disrupted in other ways. It will then be more clearly seen how the paradigm through

black	red (and white)
red (and white) hidden	red (and white) revealed
health	illness
diseases hidden	diseases revealed
moderation	excess
medicine	food
unpleasant flavours	pleasant flavours
fertility	infertility

FIGURE 16. Simplified paradigm

which Yoruba herbalists understand health are the means by which they also understand illness.

Endnotes

[1] Much of this chapter has been included in my article, 'The Secret, an idea in Yoruba medicinal thought'. In (ed.) J. B. Loudon, *Social Anthropology and Medicine*. Academic Press, London, New York, 1976. It is presented here by permission of the Association of Social Anthropologists.

[2] It is difficult to ask people the question 'What colour is the sky?', without appearing a complete fool. Believing it to be of some importance I asked a number of people, but found them to be as embarrassed as me. Reluctant to expose themselves to ridicule by answering '*funfun*', they often replied with the English 'blue'. A brief discussion usually sorted out the difficulty.

[3] The names *ilèpa* and *ilèdú* are respectively derived from *pupa* and *dúdú*, according to Abraham 1958.

[4] This reply was very loosely paraphrased in my article (Buckley 1976) to allow me to compress much information into a small space.

[5] Bradbury refers to similar beliefs in Benin (Bradbury 1973).

4

Colour and the human body: red and white confounded

There are red and white substances which, when combined together, must be shrouded in secrecy. This is the message of the last chapter. When they are not so concealed, the colours red and white are therefore appropriate as symbols for revelation. Black, the colour which hides red and white, is equally appropriate as a symbol of secrecy. These colours are used to paint the images of gods, but it will later be seen just how complex a symbol a god may be. For the moment let it merely be accepted that red and white must normally be combined behind the blackness of secrecy. From here it is possible to study the relationship between red and white. Red and white fluids in the body may become confused or mingled in such a way as to bring about illness. Just as *èelá* and *ètè* were an ordered confusion, a logical progression away from the ideal of good health, so too are the illnesses in which there is a mingling of red and white.

This chapter will be in two sections. The first will consider a syndrome of distinct but related illnesses of which *èdà* and *sọmúròrò* are the most important. The second will study Fatoogun's understanding of the common illness *ibà* (fever) in its most virulent form, *ibà pọ́njúpọ́njú*.

(a) Ẹdà *and* sọmúròrò

(i) *Ẹdà*

Ẹdà is an illness which affects women. It is characterized by semen (*àtọ̀*) flowing from the vagina of a woman following sexual intercourse. As the informants' descriptions of this illness are recounted, it will first of all be found that it is understood in terms of Image 1, that of simple illnesses. Only later, as *èdà* is examined in relation to illnesses to which it is said to be related will it be seen how *èdà* may be regarded as a logical development of Image 2, the structure of colours in the human body.

ADEBAWǪ. *Ẹdà* is when the semen of the man flows down out of the vagina after sexual intercourse. *Ẹdà* is a single illness but it can affect a woman in three ways. There is a type called *èdà ibúlè* (that which flows when lying down). This is when the semen flows out immediately following intercourse. The second is called *èdà òòró* (that which flows when you stand up) when the semen flows out three or four days after intercourse. The last one is called *èdà òrosùn* (that which flows at menstruation) which occurs five days before menstruation. . . . It is true that a certain white stuff comes from the vagina of a woman but this is different from *èdà*. This is an illness which may affect a woman if she is not properly cared for after she has delivered a child. There will be dirt (*idòtí*) in the womb and the pipe (*okùn ǫmǫ*)[1] will become straight so that after intercourse the semen will come rushing out. Anyone affected by any of the forms of *èdà* cannot become pregnant. It is like pouring water into a broken pot.

Fatoogun explains the illness in this manner.

FATOOGUN. It comes from the semen of men; a virgin cannot complain that *èdà* is worrying her. There are some women who by their nature do not like frequent intercourse. If a man has sexual intercourse three or four times a day with a woman who does not like frequent sexual intercourse, the disease (*àruǹ*), that is to say germs (*kòkòrò*) inside the body of the woman will not allow the semen to stay in and the semen will flow out. It is called *èdà* which means 'that which flows'. There are other women who, even if one has sexual intercourse with them many times, will not have the semen flowing from their womb. It will either develop into a child or she will use the semen to become fat.

Should there be any indication that a woman is becoming affected by *èdà* one should not have intercourse with her too often. An interval of between three and five days should be given between each time. This condition prevents conception. As time goes on, the passage to the womb will become so open that the semen will come out immediately after intercourse. The germs will become accustomed to passing through the route to the womb and germs which eat the semen will cause the semen to flow down. These germs live around the place where the semen is stored (in the woman's belly). Whenever there is any fresh semen in this part of the woman the germs will rush to get at it. The passage of these germs through the route to the womb to eat the semen allows the semen to flow out.

Another informant described the passage of the worm through the semen as like 'putting a hot iron in palm-oil. The semen will

melt (yọ́) and come out.' Adebawọ also associates this illness
with too much sexual intercourse but he sees it as the result of
'corruption'.

ADEBAWỌ. We were told by our grandfathers 'one penis one illness, four
penises five illnesses'.

He is experienced enough however to have seen that ẹ̀dà, which
Abraham (1958 ẹ̀dà, A) identifies as leucorrhoea, can affect
virgins. He explains:

ADEBAWỌ. If we enquire we will find that ẹ̀dà affected her parents before she
was born and ẹ̀dà must therefore affect her also.

Adebawọ does not seem unduly worried that this parenthetical
remark invalidates the whole notion of ẹ̀dà as the flowing of
semen from the vagina. But at first sight this illness is yet
another that has the structure which has been described as
Image 1. It is caused by a disease, in this case a germ (kòkòrò),
which proliferates when a woman is sexually promiscuous or
when, simply, she has too much sex. Also like other diseases of
the genital area, it can be transmitted from one person to
another in the course of the sexual act.

But while undoubtedly ẹ̀dà does participate in the structure
which is here called Image 1, it may also be seen, in the manner
of the last chapter, as an unwholesome development, a disruption of the healthy relationships which normally exist between
the coloured elements of the body.

The paradigm, in the form of Image 2, postulated two
healthy alternatives: one, where red blood combined with
white semen to be hidden in the female body; the other where
the red blood was revealed in menstruation. It was shown that
at a time when the menstrual blood was supposed to remain
hidden—in sexual intercourse—the flow of blood from the
womb would be the cause of a similar flow of redness on to the
skin of any resulting child. The illness èelá (and also, using a
similar logic, ẹ̀tẹ̀) was therefore a distortion of the ideal pattern
of the body's structure but was nevertheless a logical development of tendencies which the paradigm had already defined as
inherent.

With ẹ̀dà there is a similar distortion, for here again there is a
fluid—in this case semen—which should remain hidden, flow-

ing instead out of the womb. But there is an additional factor to consider. In the normal course of events, the fluid which flows from the woman's vagina is red—the normal menstrual flow. In *èdà*, the flow from the vagina is white.

(ii) *Aṣẹ́ lílámi* and *èyọ́* (Water menstruation, watery semen)

It is not yet being argued that the white flow of *èdà* replaces the normal red menstrual flow. *Ẹdà* merely exhibits a formal structure which is, in a way, the opposite of menstruation. There is another illness, called *àṣẹ lílámi* (watery menstruation), in which the menstruation itself becomes white. This is an illness which is distinct from *èdà*, though it is significant that two informants drew a causal relationship between them.

These two men regarded watery menstruation as only one of the illnesses associated with *èdà*, and indeed it does seem proper to regard it as a part of the *èdà* syndrome. Here are two accounts:

BUCKLEY. What causes *èdà*?

AWOTUNDE. If a man whose semen is watery (*olómi*) has sexual intercourse with a woman this will result in *èdà*; that is to say the man has *èdà* and it will also affect the woman he has intercourse with. If they have intercourse about six times the menstruation of the woman will become watery. In the second month her breasts will grow as though she is pregnant. When there are only four or eight days to go before she will see her menstruation, the semen will rush out of her and after that the menstruation will flow and the breast will come to its normal state.

ADEBAWỌ. It is *èdà* that brings about *latọnlatọn* (pains in the legs) *ṣọmúròrò* (swollen breasts) and *ẹ̀hìn dídùn* (backache). At the start of this illness (*èdà*) if the woman has intercourse with a man, the semen will rush down immediately. This will bring about *latọn-latọn*. This will be when it is just about five days before menstruation. By this time the small amount of the semen that has been able to accumulate in the womb will flow out and if someone sees the vulva of the woman it will be as if we have rubbed fresh *ògì*[2] on it. This is followed by *itọn lílá* (*latọnlatọn*) and also *ẹ̀hìn dídùn*.

Then if the woman notices her breast we will see that it is heavier than before and it will be bigger. By this time a woman cannot conceive unless she uses medicine. If the disease remains long in the body of the woman the menstruation will be watery.

These two accounts share several features. Both agree that the breasts of the woman will become heavy; this phenomenon will be discussed shortly. Adebawọ states that the illness is accompanied by *latọnlatọn* and *ẹ̀hìn dídùn*—pain in the legs and pain in the back—and with this Awotunde concurs. Finally both men agree that *ẹ̀dà* is a cause of watery menstruation.

BUCKLEY. Does *àṣẹ́ lílámi* have anything to do with *ẹ̀dà*?

FATOOGUN. *Aṣẹ́ lílámi* is quite different from *ẹ̀dà*. *Aṣẹ́ lílami* is when the menstruation becomes watery and this cannot let the semen become a child. Before menstruation can become pregnancy, it must be clean, good, and fairly thick—but not too thick. If it is not black and is clean, the woman will be able to conceive (below Chapter 5). If the menstruation is watery (*olómi*) the cloth that is used for it will only be red in patches and the blood will not be as red as it normally is. By this we shall know that the menstruation is watery. Medicine should be prepared so that it will not be watery any more. Heat (*ooru*) in the belly (*inú*) is what causes the menstruation to become watery. Medicine should be prepared to make the belly become cool.

These descriptions of watery menstruation and of watery semen allow the completion of the discussion of the *ẹ̀dà* syndrome as it affects the genital region. *Eyọ́* (watery semen) is an illness characterized by a change in the viscosity of the fluid. From being relatively thick, the semen has become thin. A similar transformation takes place in the illness *àṣẹ́ lílámi* (watery menstruation). This is indeed the main sense in which the term '*olómi*' (watery) is used. '*Olómi*' literally means 'that which has water', and the term is used when a thick or viscous substance has become thin like water. When a red substance like blood becomes watery, an additional change is involved. It remains red, but is infused with its opposite, the colour white.

Watery menstruation is thus analogous to the illness *ẹ̀dà* because it involves a similar transformation of a red substance into a white one:

menstruation   →   *ẹ̀dà*
menstruation   →   *àṣẹ́ lílámi*
red   →   white

But watery menstruation is also analogous to watery semen (*èyọ́*) because it involves a transformation from a thick to a thin liquid:

menstruation	→	àṣẹ́ lílámi
semen	→	èyọ́
thick	→	thin

Finally watery semen may be shown to be related to ẹ̀dà itself, for like ẹ̀dà it involves an involuntary flow of white liquid from the genitals:

semen	→	èyọ́
semen	→	ẹ̀dà
whiteness hidden	→	whiteness revealed

Thus it is that these illnesses, closely related in the minds of our informants, are understood according to the same conceptual model.

(iii) Ṣọ̀múròrò

The most significant of all the illnesses which are related to ẹ̀dà is the affliction of the breasts called ṣọmúròrò, ṣọmúrèrè, or àṣẹ́ ọróyọ̀n. In this illness the breast is considered to be somehow infected or infused with redness. Fatoogun shows this by discussing its various names.[3]

FATOOGUN. It gets its name ṣọmúròrò because, when there remain about five days before menstruation, the front of the breast will be shining as if she has rubbed something on it. People will think she is pregnant. It is also called àṣẹ́ ọróyọ̀n because it affects the woman at the time the woman is expecting her menstruation; hence the name àṣẹ́ ọrọ́nyọ̀n.

This association with menstruation came up in various conversations time after time. I asked Awotunde about ṣọmúrèrè.

AWOTUNDE. There are two types of this illness: one is ṣọmúrèrè; the other is àṣẹ́ ọróyọ̀n. Aṣẹ́ ọróyọ̀n causes the breast to become solid and the breast will become red and shiny (ó pọ́n dọ́n). In ṣọmúrèrè the breast will become fat like that of a woman who has been pregnant for two months. It also affects the womb of the woman so that she may not be able to conceive. This type of disease will press the womb and make the menstruation flow. After that the breast will return to normal.

Even more interesting was a comment by a more casual informant.

INFORMANT. When a woman has just given birth her breasts will become big. So also a woman affected by ṣọmúròrò.

BUCKLEY. Is there anything in the breasts of a woman so affected?

INFORMANT. The germs of *ọmúròrò* will change the milk (*omi oyún*). The milk will become red and the child will not be able to suck the breasts. These germs will also block the holes in the nipples so that the milk will not be able to flow very well. The breast will become heavy. The milk will also be red.

I asked Adebawọ the same question and his reply was similar.

ADEBAWỌ. It is a disease that is in the breast and makes it swell up. If a woman has just delivered the breast will become big and the milk will be flowing. This will make the breast lighter. If a woman is not pregnant and she has not delivered; if *her* breast swells up then there is disease inside. The woman will be scratching it. If you press the breast it will be like a bag of *gàrí* (cassava flour). Some of them will be hard and *àgbo* must be prepared to soften it. . . . There is a type of *ọmúròrò* in which the milk will be flowing from the breast when the pregnancy is three months old. This flow must be stopped or else, when the child is born, he will not have good milk to suck. The milk of this type of breast will be mottled red (*omi ọmún a pón ràkọ̀ ràkọ̀*), and if the child should suck it the milk will be thick. If a child sucks this for a month, his complexion will change and he will look like a person affected by *ibà pọ́njú-pọ́njú* (fever with red eyes, i.e. jaundice) (see the second part of this chapter).

Our informants have identified two symptoms of *ọmúròrò*. In the first of these, the breasts will swell up like those of a pregnant woman but with a distinctive solidity or hardness. In the second, the breast becomes infected by redness. This may actually turn her milk red and when it flows the milk will be thick in texture.

This illness clearly forms a similar transformation to that which has already been observed in our discussion of other illnesses in this syndrome but to lend precision to the discussion consideration should first be given to the relationship which obtains between the breasts and genitals of a normal healthy woman. In a healthy woman, the flow from the breasts is of a thin white fluid, while that from the vagina is red and thick. The flow from the breasts and from the vagina cease when the woman becomes pregnant, for there is a rule that no one should suckle a child during pregnancy (Bird 1958, 130; Dow 1977; Matthews 1956; Caldwell and Caldwell 1977; Orubuloye 1979). As in health, so in sickness, the genitals and breasts of the woman are the inverse of each other (Figure 17). As the blood from the vagina becomes thin and white (àṣẹ́ lílámi), so the milk in the breasts becomes thick and red (ṣọmúròrò).

	genitals		breasts		
	hidden	revealed	hidden	revealed	
menstruation		thick red blood		thin white milk	lactation
pregnancy	thick red blood		thin white milk		pregnancy
àṣẹ́ lílámi		thin white blood		thick red milk	ṣọmúròrò

FIGURE 17. Health and illness in genitals and breasts

Fatoogun's description of ṣọmúròrò is somewhat eccentric. Unlike the other two informants he does not believe that ṣọmúròrò can affect a pregnant woman.

FATOOGUN. Any disease in a pregnant woman cannot affect her. If this disease (i.e. ṣọmúròrò) is very powerful she will not be able to conceive, and if she does conceive, the disease cannot develop. All these diseases will mix with the water, blood, and fat for the child. Ṣọmúròró cannot affect any pregnant woman, but if there are too many (germs) in the body of the woman, the only thing it can turn to is ọmú dídùn (pain in the breasts) and it can turn the milk red or prevent it flowing. This can be cured with medicine but it is different from ṣọmúròrò.

We might note that in passing, Fatoogun here provides an additional twist to Image 1. Not only are diseases beneficial to the body they also combine inside a woman's body to help her create a child. He is not alone in thinking this. An old lady herbalist in Ibadan offered a similar opinion.

MRS AJAYI. Women have many different types of diseases. There are forty-one types of disease in woman and without any one of them she cannot give birth to children.

This idea leads Fatoogun to a curious conclusion. When a woman is pregnant, the germs which might cause *ǫmúròrò* do not in fact do so but contribute to the health of the child. Only if there are too many in her body do they cause a separate but similar illness. All he is doing, however, is to distinguish this second illness *ǫmú dídùn* in a pregnant woman from *ǫmúròrò* in one who is not pregnant. The other informants simply regard them as identical.

In his description of *ǫmúròrò* itself, however, Fatoogun gives an interesting variation on the existing theme.

FATOOGUN. It is the germs that cause *ǫmúròrò* that usually make the breasts become big. They will also block the way that enables menstruation to become pregnancy. All this menstruation will go to the breast together with the semen. The breast will become big. The top of the breast will become black as though she were pregnant. Unless the germs are cured, the woman will not become pregnant. If they are cured and the woman becomes pregnant it is then that good milk can be restored to the breast.

It has already been shown that *ǫmúròrò* may be regarded as a mixing of red and white in the breasts. Fatoogun however has denied that there is any milk in the breasts of the woman affected by *ǫmúròrò*. To achieve what is the same formal structure Fatoogun asserts that the menstruation goes to the breasts 'together with the semen'. The genitals have become barren because of *èdà*, but it looks as though the germs that cause *ǫmúròrò* have caused the breasts to become pregnant.

(b) Ibà *(fever)*

In the second section of this chapter, I wish to concentrate entirely upon Fatoogun's description of the illness *ibà*. For him, as for all the Yoruba with whom I discussed this, the illness *ibà* can be distinguished as two separate illnesses. One of these is the basic illness *ibà* (malaria or fever), the second is the more dangerous *ibà pǫnjúpǫnjú* (yellow fever or jaundice).[4] Fatoogun regards *ibà* as merely a milder form of *ibà pǫnjúpǫnjú* and I shall approach it through his discussion of the more extreme form of illness.

FATOOGUN. *Ibà pǫnjúpǫnjú* is caused by, for example, if the eyes of a man affected by the disease are yellow, just like the pool of water containing

fallen leaves.[5] This sort of disease usually affects the water in the body.
When the water in the body is coloured it tends to affect the eyes also, for we
know that eyes contain water. There will be pains all over the body. This
disease (àrùn) will make the water and the blood work against each other.
What usually causes the fever is too much heat (ooru). When excessive heat
enters the body it causes ibà pọ́njúpọ́njú. When this type of heat enters the
blood, the blood is weakened, hence the disease will fill the whole of the
body. It is not only caused by heat, however, and not only through living in
a hot room, but also by eating hot things. Among the edible things (oǹjíjẹ)
which result in ibà pọ́njúpọ́njú is hot ẹ̀bà.[6] If you eat cold ẹ̀bà and then do
something that warms the body this may also cause ibà pọ́njúpọ́njú or ibà
pọ́njúpọ́ntọ̀.[7] Ẹ̀kọ gbígbónọ́ (hot cornstarch gruel) has the opposite effect and
prevents the blood being spoiled. It will expel the excessive water by
perspiration and by the passing of urine.

   People who sit in a hot room may get ibà pọ́njúpọ́njú because the blood
does not like anything too hot. This heat may change the blood to water.
Thus the person will feel affected by pọ́njúpọ́njú.

That it is heat which makes the blood turn to water is an idea to
which Adebawọ refers elsewhere (p. 201), Fatoogun suggests
here that the water in the eyes and the urine are turned red as
the blood becomes watery and merges with it. This becomes
clearer as Fatoogun's remarks continue.

FATOOGUN. Ibà is cured by bitter things. This is because the bitter things are
   able to draw together both the excess of water in the body and the disease
   (àrùn) to expel it. Blood likes things which are bitter because diseases
   cannot live with anything that is bitter. This medicine will be able to
   separate the water from the blood and the person will perspire and expel
   the disease so that the person will get better. A man who has the illness will
   feel cold even though he sits in a warm place. The perspiration indicates
   that the blood is taking its own route and that they (i.e. blood and water)
   will not obstruct each other. Omi yóò máa bá tìrẹ̀ lọ; ẹjẹ̀ yóò si máa bá ọ̀nọ̀ tìrẹ̀ lọ.
   (Water will travel its own way; blood will travel its own way.) Then the
   person may be well.
      This is why it is said: If ibà pọ́njúpọ́njú affects a person he will be told not to
   eat hot yam, for this will give him ibà pọ́njúpọ́njú in his blood. The type of
   medicine used is both bitter and able to make the person perspire. With
   many of them the medicine itself is taken hot and the person must cover
   himself with a wrapper, so that the heat of the medicine may fight against
   the heat in the body.

This account speaks for itself. Ibà is a disease encouraged to
develop by certain types of heat. The illness takes the form of

the mingling of blood and water in the body. However, in the last few sentences Fatoogun has quietly dropped a bombshell.

FATOOGUN. The kind of heat that cures this *ibà* is like the heat of medicinal leaves which we cook. We should know that food which does not suit the body, or heat from an iron sheet underneath the dwelling house, or sun that burns (*pa*—lit kills) us too much is what brings this *ibà*. If it is not this bad heat that brings this *ibà*, why is it that the heat of the leaf that we cook conquers *ibà apọ́njú*? We should know that it is heat of a different kind that brings *ibà apọ́njú*?

Fatoogun seems to be arguing by these rhetorical questions that his conclusion is a logical necessity as well as having a mere basis in fact. In addition he is also giving a motley list of types of heat which are said to cause *ibà pọ́njúpọ́njú*.

My first question was to ask why hot *ẹ̀bà* (cassava flour porridge) caused *ibà pọ́njúpọ́njú* and why hot *ẹ̀kọ* (cornstarch porridge) was able to cure it. His reply added very little to the discussion.

FATOOGUN. When taking hot *ẹ̀bà*, one is in danger of contracting *pọ́njúpọ́njú* or *pọ́njúpọ́ntọ̀*. Hot *ẹ̀ko* has the effect of correcting the excess of water in the body. If there is any swollen part of the body—this is usually the result of bad blood—hot *ẹ̀kọ* will heal the place so that the blood will be able to move about. The excess of water will come out through perspiration and through freely urinating. That is why hot *ẹ̀kọ* cannot cause any disease of the blood.

This is all very well as an *ad hoc* reason why hot *ẹ̀kọ* can be used to cure the disease. It is in fact a common enough ingredient in many medicines as will be seen from the appendices. What this account does not explain is the central idea that one sort of heat (*ooru*) can fight and defeat another sort. To understand this notion I asked another question of Fatoogun:

BUCKLEY. When we were discussing *ibà* you suggested that it was heat which cured it. How is it that the heat of *àgbo* (medicinal infusion) can cure a disease which is itself caused by heat?

FATOOGUN. There are many kinds of warmth in the body. The one that results in *ibà* is the one that heats the blood when they get into contact. This type of heat, that which comes from the sun (*oòrùn*), also that which comes from the earth (*ilẹ̀*) can result in *ibà*. Heat also comes from hot yam (*iṣu*). If a person is feeling cold to the extent that he is shaking, and he should get into contact with this type of heat, he will get *ibà*. Other heat like this comes from food made from cassava. If this type of food is taken when it is hot, it can result in *ibà*. This is why people should not allow themselves to sit in the sun for too long. If the person is sitting in the sun, he will perspire, but there will come a time when the person no longer sweats. This results in *ibà pónjúpónjú*. On the other hand there are other forms of heat which cannot result in *pónjúpónjú* (fever). When a person has been working in the sun and leaves the sun, the heat that has already been in his body will heat the blood in order to get out of the body. This heat will spoil the blood and turn it into *ibà*. If you want to know whether *ibà* is caused by the heat of the sun (all you need to do is to) sit in the sun for two hours. The heat of hot *àgbo*, the power of the leaves collected in the pot together with the heat will work in the body and will fight the heat that has resulted in *ibà* and drive it out. This can be seen by the perspiration. The heat of the leaves together with their power are the main thing that drives *ibà* from the body.

It would be easy perhaps to dismiss these apparently confused statements as an attempt by Fatoogun to rationalize contradictions in his own point of view. Heat causes disease; heat cures it; hence there must be two kinds of heat. Certainly it is true that no other informant gave me Fatoogun's highly developed interpretation of this illness.

On the other hand the contradiction, if not Fatoogun's solution, is present in the thought of other people. *Agbo* is frequently administered hot. *Agúnmu* and *ètù* are often taken with *èkọ* (cornstarch porridge) diluted with hot water (*èkọ gbígbónó*) and the appendices contain many medicines in which ingredients are used against disease because of their 'heat'.

Fatoogun has provided lists of the two types of heat and these I have set out in Figure 18. One tends to confound the distinct red and white identities of blood and water in the body; the other separates the blood and water and also drives out the disease. By confining the discussion initially to the consumable items on this list in the top half of the diagram, two alternative ways of distinguishing them, seem to emerge. First they can be contrasted along the lines which were set out in the discussion of the *èdà ṣọmúròrò* collection of diseases. *Ẹbà* and the other forms of cassava and yam are viscous and thick in texture (*wón kí*) while both *èkọ gbígbónó* and *àgbo* are watery (*olómi*). A second possibility is the one that Fatoogun himself uses. He says that one has the heat of medicine; the other, presumably, has the heat of food.

Heat which causes *pọ́njúpọ́njú*			heat which cures *pọ́njúpọ́njú*
Consumable	yam	⎫ when	hot *èkọ*
	all types of	⎬ served	bitter and pungent herbs
	cassava	⎭ hot	hot *àgbo*
			medicines

Non-consumable	sitting in a hot room	heat of a wrapper
	heat of iron under the house floor	
	hot earth	
	heat caused by working in the hot sun	

FIGURE 18. Heat and *ibà pọ́njúpọ́njú*

The first of these possibilities creates more problems than it solves. Why should Fatoogun believe that taking something because it is liquid has 'the effect of correcting the excess of water in the body'? For such reasoning to be possible one would require some evidence that Yoruba medicines were constructed on the homeopathic hair-of-the-dog principle, and no such evidence is forthcoming. Fatoogun himself regards the two types of heat as antagonistic not identical. We must rely therefore on Fatoogun's own interpretation.

Fatoogun's assertion that the heat of the medicine cures *ibà* because it is the heat of a medicine is not simply a tautology. Most medicines, but especially those for *ibà* and *ibà* and *ibà pọ́njúpọ́njú*, are exceedingly bitter. If the two types of heat are distinguishable on the basis of food/medicine then they are also distinguishable on the basis of sweet/bitter.

Nevertheless it is insufficient simply to reduce this distinction of health-bringing heat and illness-bringing heat to one of bitterness and sweetness, for this would only take account of the top half of Figure 18. None of the items in the bottom half is either bitter or sweet. If it were merely a question of bitterness and sweetness there would have to be four rather than two types of heat and in any case Fatoogun would have been able to say so since it is a familiar enough idea.

Consider now the possible grounds for distinguishing between the two types of heat in the bottom half of Figure 18. At first sight there seems to be little, for example, to distinguish the heat which comes from being enclosed in a wrapper from that which comes from being in a hot room. On closer examination, however, a single distinguishing feature emerges.

When Fatoogun states that *ibà* is caused by sitting in a hot room, those people who live in a cold climate will immediately conjure up the image of an enclosed stuffy space with closed doors and windows. In cooler climes the outside is a source of cold and people seek protection by 'wrapping up warm' in thick clothing or by sealing the doors and windows and lighting a fire inside the house.

In Nigeria, the situation is precisely the opposite. A hot room in Nigeria is not one in which the doors and shutters have been shut; it is a room where they have been foolishly left open. Heat in the form of sunlight is then allowed to enter the house making the temperature unbearable. Metal roofs, too, no matter what their advantages over thatch in the rainy season, also have the undesirable effect of transmitting heat into the house. To these Fatoogun adds the less likely possibility that heat may be transmitted from the earth by means of a metal sheet underneath the floor of the house.

The heat which makes a room hot and which causes *ibà* may thus be described as the 'heat of the outside'. Clothing and the doors and windows of the house are used by Yoruba people to protect them from this type of heat which induces illness. In contrast Fatoogun also says that there is a heat which arises from being enclosed in a wrapper and which is curative. This may be described as the 'heat of the inside'.

Fatoogun regards the heat of food as being precisely similar to that which comes from being exposed to the heat of the sky and earth. Conversely, the heat of medicine is seen to be similar to the heat caused by the wrapper. This may be expressed by a formula:

heat of the inside : heat of the outside :: heat of medicine : heat of food

or more succinctly:

inside : outside :: medicine : food

It is possible now tentatively to interpret Fatoogun's remarks about *ibà pọ́njúpọ́njú*. The heat which comes from outside, from the sun and from the earth and the heat from food grown in the earth (cassava and yam are tubers) can cause disease to develop so that the ideal order in the body becomes confused. Red and white fluids mingle in the body, and a man whose body is hot will shiver with cold. But the heat which comes from being enclosed and the heat of medicine (*ẹkọ* is made from maize which is, of course, not a root crop) can drive away disease and rearrange these red and white fluids so that they may travel in their respective correct paths.

It will be noted that the 'outside' is not here absolutely synonymous with the category 'revealed' which has been expressed as the opposite of 'hidden'. Indeed, the earth, which in relation to the world is 'outside', is a place wherein objects may be hidden. Not only the dead, but also gods and diseases are hidden in the earth. On a horizontal plane it will later be seen that outside of a town—the forest—can similarly be used as a hiding-place.

The problem is that the heat from outside, whether that of forest, earth, or sky which is normally because it is outside, has for various reasons come into the open. What is here being expressed is the idea that not only the body of a person, but also his clothing and house protect him from the heat of the outside. When this heat becomes excessive the diseases within the body develop and become manifest.

In subsequent chapters the idea of heat will be examined further, and it will be shown that the concept of the heat of the outside as a causal factor in illness is quite compatible with the image which has already been discussed. When this has been done it will be clear that although Fatoogun's description of *ibà pọ́njúpọ́njú* is not one which is commonly agreed by Yoruba herbalists, it is nevertheless one which is derived from structures of thought more generally shared by Yoruba people.

Endnotes

[1] Adebawọ uses the phrase *okùn ọmọ* in a different way from Fatoogun for whom it is a rope tying the semen to the menstruation.

[2] *ògì* is pounded maize soaked in water before it is used to make *ẹkọ* (cornstarch porridge).

³ *Ṣọmúròrò se+ọmú+ròrò* lit. make breast red.
  Ṣọmúrèrè se+ọmú+rèrè lit. make breast shine.
  Aṣẹ́ ọróyọ̀n Aṣẹ́+orí+yọ̀n lit. menstruation on the head of the breast.

⁴ *Ibà pọ́njúpọ́njú* (lit. fever with red eyes) *ibà pọ́njúpọ́ntọ̀* (lit. fever with red eyes, red urine) *ibà kójúpọ́n*.

⁵ The first sentences were somewhat confused and are here only loosely translated. The account improves as he gets into his stride.

⁶ A thick porridge made from cassava which has been dried and pounded to make a flour.

⁷ The distinction here drawn is between cases of the illness where the eyes (*ojú*) go yellow (*pọ́n*) and where the yellowness affects both the eyes (*ojú*) and the urine (*ìtọ̀*).

5

Colour and the human body: black blood

There are at least three distinct illnesses which my Yoruba herbalists associated with black blood: black menstruation (*àṣẹ dúdú*); pains in the body and limbs (*àwọ́ká* or *làkúègbé*); and pellagra (*inọ́.run*).[1] The concept 'black blood' or 'dark blood' is not one which is clearly and obviously to be located in empirical fact. No doubt if one looks hard enough one can indeed perceive, for example, that menstrual blood is darker at some times than at others. European doctors with whom I discussed this insisted that while anaemia might affect the colour of the blood making it paler, and while arterial blood was a brighter red than that of the veins, there was no common pathological condition which would turn the blood significantly more dark.

It may well be that European doctors do not see black blood because they do not look for it. Perhaps dark-coloured menstruation is a feature of certain illnesses that has been overlooked by western medicine. Whatever the truth of this, it is clear that one has to look for black blood with some care before it may be seen in empirical reality. My task, therefore, is to inquire why black blood is looked for, and why, when it is perceived, it is regarded as a significant symptom by Yoruba herbalists. I shall proceed as before to give an exposition of the informants' statements and then to show how these statements represent a development of the original paradigmatic structure.

(a) Aṣẹ dúdú *(black menstruation)*

Here is a simple statement of the illness, *àṣẹ dúdú*.

MRS AJAYI. This illness is caused by a certain type of worm. This worm is not too long and it is red in colour. It usually causes the ache in the thighs which begins five days before the flowing of the menstruation. The menstruation will be black when it flows and the eyes of the woman will not be clear.

Adebawǫ attributes black menstruation to causes which are by now familiar.

BUCKLEY. I heard that if a woman eats sweet things this can affect menstruation.

ADEBAWǪ. If a woman eats sweet things this cannot cause *àṣẹ́ dúdú* (directly). The diseases that this can bring are *jẹ̀díjẹ̀dí* and *tápà*, and if these are not cured in good time they can result in black menstruation.

But he has another explanation:

ADEBAWǪ. If a woman delivers a child and is not well cared for this can result in black menstruation. There are several names for each type of (illness involving) menstruation: *àṣẹ́ dúdú*, *àṣẹ́ lílámi*, *àṣẹ́ ológbò*. If a woman menstruates for five days, the disease is not as great as it is for a woman who menstruates for only two days. If a woman has a miscarriage and she does not see her menstruation before having sexual intercourse, pure blood will not come out, and by the time she sees her menstruation it will have turned black. This is because the womb is not clear before she has sexual intercourse.

The symptoms of the condition are quite straightforward: the woman's menstruation is dark in colour (*dúdú*) and it continues for less than the normal 'five days'. All my informants would agree with the next statement:

ADEBAWǪ. There is no woman affected by *àṣẹ́ dúdú* who can become pregnant.

(b) Làkúègbé *(rheumatism)*

Fatoogun understands black menstruation to be part of a wider collection of diseases involving black blood. One of these, strange as it may seem at first, is *làkúègbé*, generally translated as 'rheumatism' (cf. Abraham 1958, *làkúrègbê*).

FATOOGUN. There is a disease called *làkúègbé* which causes *àṣẹ́ dúdú*. *Làkúègbé* is of two types. There is one that swells in different places in the body. If it affects the thighs it may swell up and hurt the person until it is treated with *àgbo* or with an embrocation. If it is a man, it may affect the scrotum causing it to swell. This is different from *ìpá*. Swelling in the scrotum that is not *ìpá* can always be diagnosed as *làkúègbé*. If you cut the place where *làkúègbé* affects the person, black blood will come out. If it affects a woman it may therefore cause *àṣẹ́ dúdú* because blood from this area can easily be carried to the womb.

Fatoogun is not alone in this belief.

BUCKLEY. What causes *làkúègbé*?

INFORMANT. Black blood causes *làkúègbé*, when it becomes thick in a spot on the body, it gives pain to the person affected.

BUCKLEY. What causes *làkúègbé*, and what is it?

AWOTUNDE. If the blood is dirty and there are holes in the bones of a person, or if someone is working too much and does not take good medicine, the blood will flow into the bones and mix with the contents of the bones. This will become *làkúègbé*, and the bones will hurt the person. Thus they say '*làkúègbé a ṛmọ² nínú eegun*' (*làkúègbé* that hurts a person inside the bones).

Adebawọ does not agree with this but this is because he distinguishes a number of illnesses which for Fatoogun and other informants fall under one single category of *làkúègbé*.

BUCKLEY. Does *làkúègbé* have anything to do with black blood?

ADEBAWỌ. No, there is no blood in the place where *làkúègbe* affects the person, i.e. inside the joints of the bones. Black blood is what causes *àwọ́ká* and *lóbùútù*.

In distinguishing *àwọ́ká* from *làkúègbé*, Adebawọ differs from Fatoogun who told me in reply to my question:

BUCKLEY. What is *àwọ́ká*?

FATOOGUN. It is *làkúègbé* which is called *àwọ́ká*. They call it *àwọ́ká* because the disease can affect one part of the body, and the next day can affect somewhere else.[3]

Adebawọ frankly admits he does not know the cause of *làkúègbé*.

BUCKLEY. What causes *làkúègbé*?

ADEBAWỌ. *Làkúègbé* is a dangerous disease. If it affects someone the person will not be able to walk. We have tried to find out what causes it. Some people say that it is a certain fluid (*omi*) in the joints of the body. If it dries, this can result in *làkúègbé*; but this is not the cause. *Agúnmu* and *àgbo* are used to cure it. This disease does not affect any place but the knees.

There are three types. The Ijẹṣa people call it *ẹlẹ́bùútù*. The Ijẹbu (people call it) *lóbùútù*. The third one (name) is called *àrúnmọléegun*. This last one affects all the bones of the body. He will not be able to stand up. The person will also become thin unless we prepare a good (medicinal) soap and *àgbo* for him. This does not swell up in the body because it affects the bones and not the flesh. The one called *lóbùútù* can swell up in any part of the body. There is another one called *àwọ́ká*. This one can swell up in any part of the body. Each of these diseases can only be cured with a different type of medicine. That is to say, we cannot use the same medicine for *àwọ́ká* and for *àrúnmọléegun*.

To conclude this brief exposition of the ideas of these two men concerning these illnesses we need only look at Fatoogun's ideas about the disease called *lóbùútù* (this is also called *olóbùútù*, *lófùútù* or *elébùútù*).

BUCKLEY. What is *lófùútù*?

FATOOGUN. This is a type of disease that turns the blood into water, and any part of the body that is affected will swell up. It is very painful and it can give out pus (*èétú*). The witches use this disease against people.

In short, Adebawọ does not know the causes of *làkúègbé*, the severe version of which he calls *àrúnmọléegun*. He is however sure that this is a disease of the bone and is not caused by the blood. For him *àwọ́ká* or *lóbùútù* is a disease of the flesh caused by black blood. In contrast Fatoogun regards *làkúègbé* and *àwọ́ká* as the same illness caused by black blood and he contrasts this with *lófùútù* which is caused by watery blood (Figure 19).

Fatoogun		Adebawọ	
Caused by black blood	Caused by watery blood	Caused by black blood	Not caused by the blood
làkúègbé	*lófùútù*	*làkúègbé*	*lóbùútù*
àwọ́kà		*àrúnmọléegun*	*àwọ́kà*

FIGURE 19. Divergences in the names and causes of some illnesses

For Adebawọ, it seems unbelievable that illnesses of the bones and joints should be caused by black blood; so he reserves this explanation for illnesses in this group which cause swellings in the flesh. Fatoogun, on the other hand, chooses not to draw a rigid distinction between *àwọ́ká* and *làkúègbé*. Instead he contrasts two types of swelling *àwọ́ká* and *lófùútù* saying that one is caused by black blood the other by watery blood.

(c) Inọ.run *(pellagra)*

In the last chapter were discussed illnesses in which the blood
became watery, i.e. light-coloured and thin. This chapter
considers illnesses in which the blood turns thick and dark.
Prince discusses these two alternative unhealthy types of blood
in a most interesting article (1966). He admirably records the
words of some half-dozen informants as they were asked to
discuss a concept '*aiperi*'. Prince's own intention is to compare
the statements of Yoruba herbalists with his own medical
knowledge in order to translate indigenous terms into those of
medical science. Here are the statements of his informants:

FIRST INFORMANT. *Aiperi* is a disease from Heaven. Anyone will suffer it if
he does not take the right precautions, and eat the right foods. Children
may also have it. There are two kinds, the white and the black. The two are
usually in equal parts; if black is more than white it causes a disease called
inarun; if white is more than black it causes weakness of the body and the
person has *ela* and *ipa orere*. In the white, the water is excessive in the blood,
the blood is thin and circulation is weak (p. 877).

SECOND INFORMANT. *Aiperi* is a blood disease. It is caused by carelessness. It
is caused by eating foods that are not agreeable; too much cassava may
cause it or too much she-goat or beef. There is the black kind, called *inarun*
where the blood turns black, and the white kind where the blood turns to
water (p. 877).

THIRD INFORMANT. *Aiperi*, the name itself means 'the thing that can't be
named'. Some say it cannot be named because it is so bad that to name it
would bring it on; others say it is because the disease has so many forms. It
is composed of different diseases, yet without it a person cannot be born.
Animals and fowls also have it. Anything that has blood has it. There is
black *aiperi* called *inarun*, this gives skin rashes, black blood, dimness of
vision, impotence, and barrenness; it may turn to madness if it is too
intense. There is also white *aiperi* in which the blood changes to water, the
patient will look pale, there is swelling of the body, skin rashes (*ela*), the
stomach swells up and the hands and feet swell also. The strongest *aiperi* is
giri and *warapa* (words for convulsive seizures). These latter are neither
black nor white (p. 887).

These three firm statements would induce most people to agree
with the definitive pronouncement, 'Yoruba herbalists think
that there are at least two types of "*aiperi*", one black, and the

other white', and indeed Prince assumes that this is the case. To this must be added a cautionary note. Not one of my own informants, and here I include many casual contacts as well as my main informants, had ever heard of black or white *àìperí* and did not relate the term *àìperí* to any illness other than convulsions (*gìrì*).

Prince's informants, unlike my own, were willing to characterize black and watery blood as the harmful result of an imbalance between two contrasting forms of the disease '*àìperí*', but even though my informants refused to recognize the word '*àìperí*' in this context, it is clear both from the previous chapter, and from their remarks here, that they do in fact draw some distinction. Healthy blood is red and fairly thick; unhealthy blood can be either thin and watery, or too thick and black.

The disease called *inọ́.run* is, both in Prince's account and for my own informants, at the heart of the problem of black blood. Fatoogun describes it here:

FATOOGUN. *Inọ́.run* has a different effect upon different people. If *inọ́.run* is too much in a person's body, it will turn the person's blood black. As the blood moves around the body it will carry with it the black colour which *inọ́.run* usually turns the blood into. This blackness appears with menstruation. When the *inọ́.run* appears in one part of the body, it will be just like itches or *ifọn*. If it is cured in one place in some way, it will crop up elsewhere. This sort of disease will not eat deep into the flesh. Any blood which passes through this place will be completely changed into black blood. If it does not appear on the skin, it can nevertheless sink deep into the flesh, changing the blood into black and causing pain, both in the flesh and in the bone.

Adebawọ's description is less precise but more flamboyant.

ADEBAWỌ. *Inọ́.run* is a very bad disease; it usually affects the skin. I think it is because of its power that our grandfathers called it *inọ́.run* (fire of heaven). Even this name is not enough for it. If this disease affects someone, a small knife or a penny will not be very far away from him (i.e. to use for scratching himself). And if the person is scratching his body he will not be able to notice what people are saying to him (so engrossed in the scratching will he be).

FATOOGUN. *Inọ́.run* usually causes *àṣẹ́ dúdú*. It is the cause of the black blood which therefore appears at menstruation. There are cases of *inọ́.run* in women in which the *inọ́.run* appears on the surface of the skin but does not cause *àṣẹ́ dúdú*. This is a sign that the *inọ́.run* has not penetrated deep into the flesh.

If a woman has *inǫ.run* and if her husband also has it and she gives birth
to a female child, it is very likely that the girl will never bear a child unless
medicine is given to her right from birth. This is because the child has
inherited black blood from her parents. If the menstruation of the girl is not
pure—that is to say if it is black—she cannot become pregnant.

One of the most interesting features of Prince's account is what
he speculates to be the nature of '*aiperi*'—a kind of 'philosophical life-force that everyone possesses, indeed cannot do
without, yet which in excess can produce disease. This force is
ultimately related to blood.' He confesses himself unable to
understand 'how an excess of life force could give rise to a
symptom of depletion; that an excess should cause a convulsion
seems more reasonable'. And he complains that his informants
were unhelpful in this matter, since 'none of them had a
philosophical bent; all seemed to be lost when they strayed
from the concrete example' (Prince 1966, p. 878).

No doubt Prince's difficulties were due to his over-
enthusiastic and premature attempt to interpret his informants' statements. What they actually say on the subject is this:
'It (*aiperi*) is composed of different diseases, yet without it a
person cannot be born. . . . Anything that has blood has it', and
'*Aiperi* is a disease from Heaven', a phrase which he rightly
understands to mean that people are born with it.

There is in his informants' descriptions given above, no
'philosophical life-force', but rather a repetition of the structure
which became familiar in Chapter Two as Image 1. For his
informants, the different forms of '*aiperi*' are 'diseases', which in
proper quantities and in proper proportions, produce good
health and are indeed necessary to birth and life itself. When
these 'diseases' become too abundant in the body they can
cause specific kinds of ill-health. Prince's error has been to
regard the '*aiperi*' of his account as a unique concept, where as
in fact it is merely a disease or set of diseases with properties
exactly similar to many other diseases in Yoruba medicinal
thought.

Some of my informants share Prince's informants' opinion of
inǫ.run.

MRS AJAYI. *Inǫ.run* is caused by a worm. *Inǫ.run* and the worms live very close
to each other. When the worms peck at the bag of *inǫ.run* the disease will go

all over the body. It can cause bad eyesight. This can be cured by *agúnmu*
and soap.

BUCKLEY. What are the symptoms of *inọ́.run*?

MRS AJAYI. It usually swells in patches on the legs. Everybody has it in the
body. Without it the penis cannot stand erect; if a woman does not have it
the menstruation will not flow.

BUCKLEY. What good does *inọ́.run* do in the body?

FATOOGUN. God has created it in the body of every human being. If there is
none in the body of a woman the blood cannot flow and turn into
pregnancy. So also in men, the absence of *inọ́.run* in the body of men
prevents the semen becoming pregnancy. If it is too much in the body it can
cause other illnesses such as *làkúègbé* and bad eyesight.

Adebawọ, typically, was suspicious of the idea that diseases
could benefit the health of a person.

ADEBAWỌ. I don't believe that *inọ́.run* is born together with a person. If we
should look into it we will find that it is negligence of the body or failure to
eat good food—that these are the causes of *inọ́.run*.

A little later Fatoogun elaborated on the role of *inọ́.run* in the
body:

FATOOGUN. *Inọ́.run* is created by God in the blood of every person. If there is
no *inọ́.run* in the blood of the person, the blood cannot move around. It
affects someone when there is too much in the blood. *Inọ́.run* also gives
power to other diseases. *Inọ́.run* permits heat (*ooru*) to be in the blood and
without heat the blood will not move around the body but it is the main
function of the blood to pass heat round the body. There is no disease in the
body that is not the work of *inọ́.run*. For example, although there is no blood
to be found in the intestines (*ifun*), one should notice that the belly is always
warm. The warmth in the belly helps to transform the food. The warmth in
the blood stops the body from decaying. If the body gets too warm it can
result in (the illness) *inọ́.run*. Or the heat from the *inọ́.run* may assist the
progress of another disease which affects the body. There are some women
whose stomachs rumble. This is due to *jẹ̀díjẹ̀dí*, and it is the warmth that
makes these worms happy.

When worms (he is no longer referring to *jẹ̀díjẹ̀dí* specifically) reach the
womb they will try to suck the blood and this may delay menstruation. The
lateness of the period will cause the blood to become black—the warmth—
too much heat will already have made it black. Medicine for *àṣẹ́ dúdú* (black
menstruation) can kill the worms and enable menstruation to come
regularly and be red.

This final account allows the discussion to be tied together.

First of all, Fatoogun identifies two causes of black menstruation. Like Adebawǫ he regards it as the result of a delay or inhibition of the menstrual flow through the action of worms. The worms themselves may be encouraged by the action of *inǫ.run*, but *inǫ.run* alone may independently cause black menstruation simply by turning the blood black. The identification of blackness with the hiding of menstruation through the activity of worms, substantiates our paradigmatic structure, but it also contributes to a better understanding of the disease *inǫ.run*. Fatoogun says that *inǫ.run* provides the blood with warmth, and it has already been established that in his view there are at least two kinds of heat. If the hypothesis of the last chapter is true, these two kinds of heat may be characterized as 'of the outside' and 'of the inside'. The former, which includes the heat of the sun, of the earth, and of food, is what causes diseases to flourish. The latter destroys and hides them.

Inǫ.run, as Fatoogun has characterized it, is paradoxical in nature. On the one hand, it is a form of heat which causes diseases to flourish. This places it firmly in the category of 'heat of the outside'. But on the other hand *inǫ.run*, at root is merely another disease which was present inside the body at birth and which therefore is emphatically on the inside of the body and therefore enclosed.

The solution to this dilemma lies in the name of the disease. All my informants agreed that the name '*inǫ.run*' meant the 'fire of Heaven'. The significance of this name was not explained to me except to the extent that it referred to the importance of the disease as the 'first created by God', or the 'most important of all the diseases in the body'. Even Prince who has no particular interest in such matters lays special emphasis on the relationship between '*inarun*' and the sun adding 'that *inarun* itself means according to some informants "heavenly fire"' (Prince 1966, 878).

If there is a special affinity between *inǫ.run* and the 'heat of the outside', there is a danger of drawing false conclusions. Let us compare *inǫ.run* with other illnesses. When the blood has become watery, when semen flows from a vagina or when breasts become heavy with thick red fluid, there is a series of pathological rearrangements of fluids within the confines of the body. Black blood is, on the contrary, an invasion of the blood by a colour which normally remains on the outside of the body; on the surface of the skin. Because this colour is the colour of secrecy, one effect of the *inọ́.run* may be not only to darken the blood of menstruation, but to delay and conceal it. In addition, one of Prince's informants and one of my own said that the black blood caused bad eyesight. *Inọ́.run* also causes a skin rash, but this rash contrasts sharply with that of *èelá* and *ẹ̀tẹ̀*, described in Chapter 3. *Eelá* and *ẹ̀tẹ̀* are illnesses in which the redness from within affects the black skin outside. *Inọ́.run* is the precise opposite, for here it is the blackness outside which affects the red blood within. The skin of a healthy person is already black; the effect of the *inọ́.run* is to make the skin even blacker than before.

Although the colour black is to be found on the outside of the body, it would be a mistake to associate its development in the illness *inọ́.run* with the fact that the heat which causes it also comes from outside. My informants have already made it clear that they regard heat as the cause of several illnesses which, as has just been indicated, have the opposite characteristics to *inọ́.run*, namely *ẹ̀dà* and *ibà pọ́njúpọ́njú*.

It would seem that excessive heat applied to the body from outside is merely one more means whereby diseases (and particularly diseases of the blood) can be induced to overflow their bag and cause mischief.

(d) Colour and the human body: some concluding remarks

In the course of three chapters a number of illnesses have been examined in which an important feature has been the colour of bodily substances. Each of these illnesses seems to confirm much of what Douglas (1966) has to say, namely that evil or pollution is best understood as a denial of the categories which the human psyche imposes upon and demands from the social and natural world.

To this however must be added a caveat. As Sperber (1975, 1976) makes clear, it is impossible for a semantic knowledge to contain anomalies. Anomalies exist only in relation to ideal structures existing in the form of encyclopaedic knowledge. The categories which are denied by illness or pollution are not semantic categories, but categories of understanding.

The illnesses which have been described in these three chapters are all deviations from the pattern established as normal in the human body (Image 2). As the blood became black, as redness disfigured the black skin, as the menstruation became white and the milk red, the clear cut order of the body was denied. The possible permutations of these categories were not exhausted by my own informants, and no doubt other people would have different ideas. Prince (1966), for example, seems to indicate that some Yoruba men consciously regard healthy red blood as standing between two extremes of blackness (and thickness) and whiteness (and thinness).

The important point is that health in Yoruba thought seems always to occupy a middle position between the extremes which constitute illness. Illness, or more precisely the diseases which cause illness, may not therefore be regarded as wholly evil. Diseases are, rather, components in the general picture of health.

It was noted earlier, in the context of Image 1, that herbalists occasionally stated that diseases were beneficial, but it was also observed that such statements were seldom elaborated and were often brief. Moreover informants did not take into account the benefits of disease when they constructed their medicines. The central balance to be maintained is that between the hidden and the revealed. By being moderate in his habits, and by taking precautions against the dangerous heat, a person may allow the diseases in his body to stay hidden. Thus is illness prevented. But when sweet food is eaten to excess, or when a woman over-indulges her sexual appetites, then the worms and germs overflow their bags and cause mischief. Although both the hidden and the revealed are necessary to good health, it is important to note that the balance of advantage is usually to be gained from the hiding of the elements which make up the body within the black covering of the skin. In principle, diseases must be present in the body. (Adebawọ usually adopted what must be regarded as an eccentric position on this issue.) But the endeavours of the herbalists are directed to keeping them few in number and hidden.

The same balance of advantage is to be found in the image of the female body in good health (Image 2). Here again, the most satisfactory situation is when the red and white fluids are hidden in pregnancy. When the husband's semen is contained within her body, she not only fulfils her own and her husband's dearest wish, which is to have children, she also becomes less susceptible to illness. The opposite condition, that of menstruation, and also the diseases which can disrupt this harmonious pattern are necessary, but dangerous.

Much of the ethnography of medicine has been impressed with the recurrent idea that the healthy body is somehow in harmony. This is particularly true of studies of medicinal systems in the New World, but is the case elsewhere, including Africa (Bisilliat 1976; Colson 1976; Cosminsky 1977; Foster 1979; Harwood 1971; Logan 1973; Madsen 1955; Mazes 1968; Nash 1967; Ngubane 1976, 1977; Rubel 1960). In the ideas of my Yoruba informants, it seems that there is a similar preoccupation. Indeed, the oppositions of hot/cool, wet/dry and so on are strongly reminiscent of medicinal systems throughout the world.

Yoruba herbalists, however, seem to have made a nice synthesis between the basic principles of humoral medicine and those of germ theory. For them, illness is the result both of the actions of germs and worms, and of the excessive development of necessary bodily substances. Beneath a concealing framework, red and white bodily fluids, and also a plethora of germs and worms perform appropriate, if not always well defined, functions to produce a healthy body. It may sometimes be that concealment is tempered with revelation. The menstruation must flow, the skin must not be too black, the diseases must not be confined. But in general, the darkness of secrecy provides a safe haven within which, protected from the heat without, the elements of the body may constitute the tranquillity of good health.

Endnotes

[1] Prince (1966) identified *inǫ.run* with pellagra by a careful comparison of the Yoruba and European concepts. For his informants '*inarun*' = '*aiperi dudu*'.

[2] The word '*Ǫmǫ*' in the contraction '*ǫmǫ*' here should be taken as '*ǫmǫ ènìǫ̀n*', roughly—'son of man'.

[3] *Awǫ́ká* can mean 'perambulation' (Abraham 1958 *wǫ́* A 2(c)vii).

6

Ifá, Ṣ̀ọnpọ̀nnọ́, and the palm-tree

In general, Yoruba medicine is distinct from Yoruba religion. The Yoruba have a large pantheon of gods (*òrìṣà*) and spirits (*ẹbọra*) presided over by God (*Olodumarè* or *Qlọ́.run*) and by the Earth (*Ilẹ̀*). There are occasions when medicines are used as part of cult activity, but the practice of medicine as such is not in general dependent upon religion. Nor, as has been shown, is the occurrence of illness generally related to the activities of spiritual beings.

There are two important exceptions to this general rule. The first is the god *Ṣ̀ọnpọ̀nnọ́*, who is the god who brings the illness which I shall call 'smallpox', and he also causes a type of madness (*wèrè Ṣ̀ọnpọ̀nnọ́*). The second is the god *Ifá*, the god of divination. The priests of *Ifá*, the *babaláwo*, are the custodians of 256 groups of verses which in principle embrace the whole of Yoruba knowledge about the cosmos. These verses include the incantations (*ọfọ̀*) which, as will be seen in the next chapter, are of vital importance in Yoruba medicine.

Although there have been a number of descriptive accounts of both *Ifá* and *Ṣ̀ọnpọ̀nnọ́*, there has not been any serious attempt to penetrate to the essence of the symbolism expressed in the two cults. This is no doubt because the ideas contained therein sometimes appear to be bizarre, disconnected, and complex. Only Idowu's account of *Ṣ̀ọnpọ̀nnọ́* (1962, 96–101) discusses this symbolism at all, but since his is a general work on Yoruba religion, he does not exhaust the subject completely. Barber's fascinating discussion (1981) is more a commentary upon *òrìṣà* cults as a whole than it is upon *Ṣ̀ọnpọ̀nnọ́* in particular, even though he provides an important focus for her article. Barber's paper, and also the account of *Ṣ̀ọnpọ̀nnọ́* by Simpson (1980), serves as a reminder that in any discussion of Yoruba thought we are confronted, not by a monolithic system of belief, but rather a set of often mutually inconsistent opinions. Barber says that in the town of Okuku there are several quite distinct cults of Ṣọ̀npọ̀nnọ́ each of which see Ṣọ̀npọ̀nnọ́ in a significantly different manner. In the Ibadan of Simpson's description, however, there is but one cult, albeit embracing considerable complexity, in which no doubt is also to be found a wide variation of opinion between the god's different followers. The literature on Ifá, on the other hand, is massive (e.g. Abimbọla 1964, 1965a, 1965b, 1968, 1973b, 1976; Bascom 1941, 1943, 1961, 1966, 1969b; Boston, 1974; Clarke 1939; McClelland 1966; Ojo 1968; Park 1963; Prince 1964b; Sowande n.d.) and it is surveyed in a masterly way by Bascom (1969b, 13 ff.) whose account of divination techniques and of the beliefs and practices of the cult is the finest to date. Some of the most valuable work on the Ifá cult has been the simple recording, transcription, and translation of the verses of the cult, amongst which the work of Abimbọla stands out as especially scrupulous.

My own approach to the pattern of ideas and practices concerned with Ifá and Ṣọ̀npọ̀nnọ́ will be to select from the almost unmanageable complexity some of the more prevalent themes and to compare them. The first task will be to explore some of the ideas relating to Ṣọ̀npọ̀nnọ́ alone, and to explain them as far as possible within the framework established by the previous discussion. This exposition, however, breaks down as we come to look upon the special symbolic relationship which exists between Ṣọ̀npọ̀nnọ́ and the palm-tree. To elucidate this requires discussion of the palm-tree as it affects the cult of Ifá. Finally, returning to Ṣọ̀npọ̀nnọ́ there will be an examination of the relationship which is posed between him and Ifá, in a mythical story of a battle between the two gods. Not only will this comparison give a better understanding of the symbolism of Ifá and Ṣọ̀npọ̀nnọ́, it will allow the further development of the structure of the paradigm.

(a) Ṣọ̀npọ̀nnọ́

(i) Hot earth and the wind

The illness which I call 'smallpox', but which seems to include less serious ailments such as chicken-pox, has a connection with the wind, and also with the hot earth. Smallpox is usually referred to simply by the ordinary name (*orúkọ*) of the god Ṣọ̀npọ̀nnọ́, but it may also be called 'Hot Earth' (*Ilẹ̀ẹ́gbónọ́*), sometimes shortened to *Egbóṇọ́*. People are however sometimes reluctant to use these names to refer either to the god or the illness. Instead they may be called *Ọba* (the king), *Ọbalùayé* (king of the world), *Olùwayé* (lord of the world), or *Oló.de* (owner of the outside).[1] The phrase 'Hot Earth' can also be euphemistically transformed to 'Cold Earth' (*Ilẹ̀ Tútù*) but, as Adebawọ explained, this is not due to any ambiguity in the personality of the god.

BUCKLEY. Why do they call *Ṣọ̀npọ̀nnọ́ Ilẹ̀égbónọ́* and *Ilẹ̀ Tútù*?

ADEBAWỌ. It was called *Egbónọ́* in the olden days, but when they found that the illness spread more and more when they called it by its name *Egbónọ́*, they stopped calling it *Egbónọ́* and changed it from *Ilẹ̀égbónọ́* (Hot Earth) to *Ilẹ̀ Tútù* (Cold Earth), so that the god might no longer be annoyed. They must not weep in the house where *Egbónọ́* affects a person. There are three towns where they can curse with *Ṣọ̀npọ̀nnọ́* (i.e. use his name in mock cursing) and it will not affect them. These are Ekiti, Ileṣa, and Ẹgba. This is because there they know the medicine to prevent it. In other towns they must not play or curse with *Ṣọ̀npọ̀nnọ́*. Hence the proverb: '*Ẹni tí Ṣọngó bá tojúurẹ̀ wọlẹ̀ láí kò ní bú Ọba kò so*' (he in whose sight *Ṣọngó* enters the earth, he will never abuse the king who did not hang).[2]

Hot earth then is called 'cold earth' but this contradictory usage does not indicate ambiguity. There are Yoruba gods—the most famous is *Eṣù*—whose personalities are quite emphatically ambiguous, but this is not the case with *Ṣọ̀npọ̀nnọ́*.

The connection between hot earth and *Ṣọ̀npọ̀nnọ́* was indirectly explained to me by Fatoogun who gave me a general description of the god's activities:

FATOOGUN. Whenever *Ṣọ̀npọ̀nnọ́* comes into the world, he is accompanied by *eburú* (spirits) otherwise known as *wọ̀rọ̀kọ̀*. These are the things that cause the bad wind (*atẹ́gun búburú*). When this bad wind blows on to anyone this will become *Egbónọ́* (smallpox), the person will become hot and *Ṣọ̀npọ̀nnọ́* will be coming out of this body. *Ṣọ̀npọ̀nnọ́* uses a type of arrow known as *ọfà Ṣọ̀npọ̀nnọ́*. Wherever he shoots his arrow (*ọfà*) into the air, smallpox will affect the person, or tree, or animal, wherever the wind from the arrow touches. *Wọ̀rọ̀kọ̀* comes out of the arrow in the form of wind. This is why old men pray that 'evil wind may not beat us' (*afẹ́fẹ́ búburú kò ní fẹ́ lù wá o*).

Another way *Ṣọ̀npọ̀nnọ́* affects someone is through the witches (*ìyáàmi àjẹ́*). Witches borrow the wind from *Ṣọ̀npọ̀nnọ́* and fight anyone they want to fight with it. It is as if a man goes to borrow a cutlass (*àdá*) from another man that the witches borrow the wind from *Ṣọ̀npọ̀nnọ́*. This is why, if

Ṣǫnpǫnnǫ́ affects anyone and they consult *Ifá* about it, *Ifá* may tell them that
it is witches who are fighting the person.

Another way *Ṣǫnpǫnnǫ́* affects someone is that there are some men who
know about medicine, who can prepare a medicine which they can put in
the house of a person they want to fight, so that *Ṣǫnpǫnnǫ́* can affect the
person.

Ṣǫnpǫnnǫ́ always visits the world during the months of the dry season.
Then he will visit the world (*ayé*) and also the heaven (*ǫrun*) and he will
affect both plants and human beings, so that the plants will shrivel up (*ro*).
This is why it is said 'dry season is killing people; dry season is coming; the
coward feels anxious; the chest of lazy people is jumping with convulsions'
(*'Ẹ̀ẹ̀r.ún pá; ǫgbẹ̀lẹ́ ńbǫ ominú ńkǫ ojo; ayá ńfǫ̀ òle gìrì!'*). This type of coward is
the sort who already knows that *Ṣǫnpǫnnǫ́* visits the world at this time of
year. Lazy people will be praying that they might survive the dry season; it
is all because of *Ṣǫnpǫnnǫ́*.

Fatoogun has clearly associated *Ṣǫnpǫnnǫ́* with the hot, dry
season (*èèrùn*) and with the hottest time of day (*ǫsǫ́n*).

The dry season, as Fatoogun points out, is a time of 'bad
winds'. At the height of this season, the dry harmattan winds
sweep southward from the Sahara, shrivelling the vegetation.
Where the forest covers the soil, it is only the trees and plants
themselves which are affected, but where vegetation is more
sparse the earth itself is transformed.

It will be remembered that the earth is perceived by the
Yoruba as having two layers. One is brick-red laterite (*ilẹ̀pa*)
and this is usually covered by a thin, but important black top-
soil (*ilẹ̀dú*) which gives the earth its fertility. Under the impact
of the dry wind of the harmattan, and particularly during the
middle of the day, when the temperature rises to its peak, the
black soil is eroded, leaving exposed only the barren red soil of
the *ilẹ̀pa*. For the Yoruba, hot earth has always a real tendency
to become red earth.

The relationship between the appearance of red on the
surface of the earth and smallpox on the surface of the skin is
thus strikingly similar to the illnesses *èelá* and *ẹ̀tẹ̀* which were
discussed in Chapter 3. Smallpox is, however, different from
both *èelá* and *ẹ̀tẹ̀*, for it should not be understood merely as
dangerously open redness. I discussed smallpox informally
with a wide range of informants, and a number of different
themes emerged. Among them four came specially to my

notice. The first was that the body always became exceedingly
hot; second, that the surface of the skin became rough 'as
though there were small stones just beneath the surface'; third,
that red and white blotches appeared on the skin; fourth, that
the patient would become wild and say foolish things.

Leaving aside for the moment the delirium or madness (*wèrè*)
associated with smallpox, it is plain to see that these ideas have
almost completed the association between hot earth and smallpox. As redness appears on the skin, the skin is both hot and
stony, like the hot red earth.

But the skin does not become merely red. In contrast to *èelá*
and *ètè*, the spots of *Ṣònpònnó* are described as being both red
and white. Red and white is in fact, the typical symbolic
colouring of the god *Ṣònpònnó*. I purchased a ferocious-looking
statue of the dangerous god brightly coloured in red, white, and
black spots (in British English they would be described as red,
white, and blue), but in all my discussions both with my prime
informants and with many more casual acquaintances, I was
told that the black spots were unnecessary and that the red and
white spots were the sign of the god *Ṣònpònnó*, and also that they
depicted the illness for which he was responsible.

The use of both red and white in *Ṣònpònnó* symbolism may be
explained by an observation made by Idowu (1962, 95).
According to him, when water is thrown out on to the earth, it is
customary to apologize to *Ṣònpònnó* in a brief prayer. The hot
red earth it seems, is dangerous, but there is particular danger
when red earth, and white water mingle together in the open.
The mingling of red and white is acceptable when it takes place
in the secrecy of earth or body, but not when it is visible on the
surface (Figure 20).

(ii) *Ṣònpònnó*, dancing and drumming

It is common Yoruba knowledge that *Ṣònpònnó* dislikes festivities of any kind, or at any rate that festivities which occur when
he is around are dangerous. During smallpox epidemics card
games, ludo, and draughts are forbidden, as are such activities
as dancing and drumming (MacLean 1964, 20). The burial
ceremony given to a smallpox victim is also said to be markedly
different. Normally a man is buried in his own compound.
Indeed until comparatively recently, and perhaps to this day

Health

Black Earth		Black Skin	
Red	White	Red	White
Earth	Water	Blood	Semen/Water
Hidden		Hidden	

Smallpox

Black Earth Eroded		Black Skin Eroded	
Red	White	Red	White
Earth	Water	Spots	Spots
Revealed		Revealed	

FIGURE 20. Health and Smallpox

away from the larger towns, he might be buried immediately below the mud bed on which he slept during his lifetime. In contrast, the burial of a *Ṣọ̀npọ̀nnọ́* victim is said to be performed in the forest and secretly by the priests of *Ṣọ̀npọ̀nnọ́* (Idowu 1962, 95–101). If the family should wish to mark the death with drumming and dancing, they will usually postpone the festivities until a time when *Ṣọ̀npọ̀nnọ́*'s immediate threat has receded.

Here is Awotunde's account of the practice:

AWOTUNDE. When *Ṣọ̀npọ̀nnọ́* kills a person, no one should rejoice. For if there are any (funeral) celebrations he will be annoyed that despite the evil he has done to these people, they are still happy. He will then affect many other people. God has given *Ṣọ̀npọ̀nnọ́* such a power that if he kills in anyone's family they must not be angry but must instead be thanking *Ṣọ̀npọ̀nnọ́* or else he will be angry that people are not aware of the evil that he has done. This is why people usually call *Ṣọ̀npọ̀nnọ́ 'Alá.padúpẹ́'* ('the owner of kill and thank'). Anyone that *Ṣọ̀npọ̀nnọ́* kills, we should not say that he died, but rather '*ó yọ̀ lọ*' ('he rejoiced and went'), because if it is said that the person died, (*ó kú*) *Ṣọ̀npọ̀nnọ́* will be annoyed that people are calling him a murderer (*àpàìọ̀*).

MacLean (1964 21) suggests that there may perhaps be an empirical justification for these practices. Knowledge of the tendency of smallpox to spread to those who come into contact with it undoubtedly exists and brings with it a reluctance to meet those closely associated with a smallpox victim. I once accompanied Adebawọ to the house where a small child had just died of a skin illness attributed to *Ṣọ̀npọ̀nnọ́*. After handling the dead child he was very careful to wash his hands thoroughly, to avoid contracting the disease himself. Despite this I do not feel inclined to reduce the complex beliefs of the *Ṣọ̀npọ̀nnọ́* cult to a rather vague belief in infection.

More apposite here is the suggestion of Needham that drumming is associated with communication with the gods (1967). Among the Yoruba, as elsewhere in West Africa, percussive instruments are undoubtedly associated with communication, both musical and verbal. Drumming often imitates verbal communication and drums are used to speak to the gods as well as to men. It is true also that percussion of a less rhythmic kind is used when the diviner taps his board to summon spirits in *Ifá* divination.

Certainly it is the case that *Ṣọ̀npọ̀nnọ́* is thought to be attracted into the town by the sound of drumming. It is reasonable to suppose that in the dry season, or when *Ṣọ̀npọ̀nnọ́* is abroad, people would abstain from activities which might attract him or his spirits into the town. In the following story, *Ṣọ̀npọ̀nnọ́* is portrayed as a person who dearly wishes to participate in the dancing and drumming of town life. Unfortunately, his presence is deemed unacceptable to his fellows and he is rejected. The myth suggests that it is because he is unable to participate in the activities of urban life that he seeks to infect people with smallpox.

Shan-kpanna is old and lame, and is depicted as limping along with the aid of a stick. According to a myth he has a withered leg. One day, when the gods were all assembled at the palace of *Obatala*, and were dancing and making merry, *Shan-kpanna* endeavoured to join in the dance, but, owing to his deformity, stumbled, and fell. All the gods and goddesses thereupon burst out laughing, and *Shan-kpanna*, in revenge, strove to infect them with smallpox, but *Obatala* came to the rescue and seizing his spear, drove *Shan-kpanna* away. From that day *Shan-kpanna* was forbidden to associate with the other gods, and he became an outcast who has since lived in desolate and uninhabited tracts of country' (Ellis 1898, 73).

This story may conveniently be approached in the manner which Lévi-Strauss developed in his early articles on the study of myth (1955). The most obvious contrast to emerge in the story is that between the gods *Ọbàtálá* and *Ṣọnpọ̀nnọ́* themselves. The first of these is healthy and he dances together with the other gods. *Ṣọnpọ̀nnọ́*, however, is lame and cannot dance.

There are two attempts to mediate this contrast between the gods. First of all *Ṣọnpọ̀nnọ́* seeks to be like the others by trying to dance. He fails to do this, and is laughed at for his pains. *Ṣọnpọ̀nnọ́* secondly strives to make the other gods like himself by infecting them with smallpox. In this too he is unsuccessful, and *Ọbàtálá* drives him back into the forest.

With this second failure to resolve the opposition between the two gods, between health and sickness and between dancing and lameness, the picture is complete. *Ọbàtálá* and the healthy gods are able to enjoy themselves in the safety of the palace; *Ṣọnpọ̀nnọ́* is hidden in the forest where he may do no more harm.

The story may then be expressed diagrammatically as a structure of opposites:

Culture	Anti-Culture	Failed Attempts at Mediation
Ọbàtálá	*Ṣọnpọ̀nnọ́*	
Dancing	Lameness	*Ṣọnpọ̀nnọ́* tries to dance
Health	Sickness	*Ṣọnpọ̀nnọ́* tries to make others ill
(*Ṣọnpọ̀nnọ́* in desolate, isolated places)	(*Ṣọnpọ̀nnọ́* in town with other people)	

FIGURE 21. *Ṣọnpọ̀nnọ́* and *Ọbàtálá*

For the sake of completeness, I have added to Figure 21 a further pair of opposed concepts—those of culture and anti-culture. It was suggested in previous chapters that my informants regard many aspects of good health as poised midway between the extremes of excessive revelation and excessive secrecy. The Yoruba town seems also to be thought healthy when balanced between these same extremes. Yoruba people typically live in towns, in villages, or in the forest dwellings at the farm. Each of these types of habitation consists of clearings in the forest—open patches of land created, at least originally, by removing the vegetation. Many of the myths and rituals which recount the origin of particular towns celebrate this primordial clearing of the forest. I have already shown that Ṣọ̀npọ̀nnọ́ is thought to be at his most dangerous where there is hot earth, and that the hot earth of the dry season is likely to be the red laterite (ilẹ̀pa). This hot, dry, red earth is most obviously encountered not in the forests, but in the towns, villages and farms. Indeed, even away from the centres of urban life, such is the tendency of deforested farmland exposed to the elements quickly to become barren, that farmers (when they can afford it) allow their farms to become overgrown with forest so as to restore the land to a fertile condition covered by the richer, black earth. However, Yoruba culture does not exist primarily in the open spaces of the town where the earth is apparent. Rather, it may be found in the shrines, the Ogbóni lodges, the palace and the family compounds, which are cool and shady. It is here that the secrets of the town are kept.

The Yoruba farmer is typically torn between on the one hand the forest and farm, and on the other his house and the town. In the forest, knowledge is in danger of being too much hidden; in the town, it is in danger of becoming too visible. A number of examples could be offered here to illustrate this dichotomy between town and forest. Here I shall give only one, an extract from a verse quoted from Bascom (1969b, 252).

Aro of the house and Aro of the farm were two friends. The diviner said that they should make a sacrifice lest they both meet death at the same time. Aro of the house refused to sacrifice, Aro of the farm also failed to please Eshu. Aro of the house, died in the house, and Aro of the farm, died in the farm. They said that Aro of the farm should be carried to the house. When they carried Aro of the farm to the house, they said that his children should come and begin the entertainment for the dead for their father. But they said that they had been so long at the farm that they no longer knew how the drums should be beaten. Because of this the people of Ifa say that 'Aro stayed at the farm so long that he no longer knew how the drums should be beaten.'

This extract draws an explicit relationship between the forest (or farm) and ignorance of vital ritual, and the house (or town) and knowledge. Specifically, the knowledge which is so vital is associated with dancing and drumming. Dancing and drumming are singularly associated with the town and with the activity of corporate groups within the town. It usually occurs in the festivals associated with cult groups, but it also plays an important role in lineage celebrations. The drummer is able, not only to play music appropriate to the occasion, but also to speak through his music, using tonal variation to convey messages which praise the town, lineage, or cult groups and their leaders and antecedents as these are appropriate. These praise songs are themselves an important part of Yoruba urban culture, and are owned either by specific corporate groups within the town, or by the town itself.

Dancing is inseparable from drumming. Like music, dancing is at one level merely fun, but it is ultimately regarded as an expression belonging to a specific corporate group. As such, it is ultimately the means whereby knowledge about the corporate group is displayed to the outside world.

As Bascom's verse suggests, nowhere is the association of dancing and drumming with corporate life more apparent than in funeral ritual, to which *Ṣọnpọ̀nnọ́* takes particular exception. The funeral combines in its different stages both mourning and elaborate festivities, neither of which is tolerated by the god. Each lineage has its own peculiar rituals which are kept secret from outsiders and from which outsiders are in part excluded.

I have already shown that *Ṣọnpọ̀nnọ́*'s tendency is always to carry the revelation of that which is hidden to unacceptable extremes. Family compounds which are also the burial places of the dead, are places where the lineage keeps its secrets hidden. *Ṣọnpọ̀nnọ́* lives in the forest, but, like other forest-dwellers, he is attracted to the town by the lure of dancing and drumming and by the enjoyable celebrations which attend the expressions of urban corporate life. The burial ceremony is one in which there is a delicate balance between the need to involve others and the need also to keep aspects of the ritual secret. *Ṣọnpọ̀nnọ́* however is a 'hot' god who reveals the red earth and presumably also that which is concealed within it. On occasions which already involve dangerous revelation, his presence is therefore unwelcome. To protect individuals and groups from his dangerous heat, it is therefore considered wise to refrain from dancing and drumming, and to bury his victims in isolated parts of the forest where they and their illness may remain hidden.

Ṣọ̀npọ̀nnọ́'s dislike of traditional celebrations and his insistence that victims of smallpox be buried in the forest is a denial of corporate urban life. More generally, his objection to all forms of dancing and drumming is an objection to the corporate life of the whole town and of its constituent institutions. Ṣọ̀npọ̀nnọ́, the embodiment of the dangerous heat of the outside, is antagonized by manifestations of the closed corporate institutions from which as an outsider he too is excluded.

(iii) Ṣọ̀npọ̀nnọ́ and the palm-tree

Ṣọ̀npọ̀nnọ́ is closely related in Yoruba thought to the palm-tree, and, while this relationship may not be fully explained in the context of Ṣọ̀npọ̀nnọ́ alone, it may be initially defined. The associations may be quickly listed:

1. Palm wine (ẹmu) is used to keep Ṣọ̀npọ̀nnọ́ away.
2. The broom normally used to sweep the floor, which is made from the stripped mid-ribs (ọwá) of the palm-fronds, is sometimes used to symbolize Ṣọ̀npọ̀nnọ́, and, during a small-pox epidemic, it is forbidden to use it to sweep the floor.
3. Palm-oil (epo) is used as an antidote (èrọ̀) to smallpox.
4. Palm-kernel oil (àdín) is offered to Ṣọ̀npọ̀nnọ́ only in a deliberate attempt to antagonize him (cf. Idowu 1962).

This section will consider only the first two of these points.

The first concerns palm wine. During a smallpox epidemic it is common for men to drink palm wine to keep the god and his disease away. Palm wine is sometimes splashed around the verandah and courtyards of houses for a similar purpose, and I was told that it could be also smeared on the face. The last practice was once explained to me as a gesture of friendship towards the god. Ṣọ̀npọ̀nnọ́ does not afflict those who already bear his markings, and the frothy dregs of palm wine smeared on the face are similar to the symptoms of the disease.

The odd thing about Ṣọ̀npọ̀nnọ́'s attitude to palm wine is that it seems to contradict all that we have learned about his dislike of festivities. While he strongly disapproves of those who dance, drum, and otherwise enjoy themselves, Ṣọnpọnnọ seems to approve of those who drink palm wine.

It has already been suggested that Ṣọnpọnnọ's principal objection to dancing and drumming lies in the fact that dancing and drumming gives affirmation to the internal culture of corporate groups in the town from which Ṣọnpọnnọ is excluded. If this is correct, it would seem to indicate that palm wine has the opposite significance, that in some sense it represents the openness and outward orientation associated with Ṣọnpọnnọ himself.

This association was reinforced by a brief restatement of the myth of Ṣọnpọnnọ and Ọbàtálá.

BUCKLEY. Is it true that Ọbàtálá fought with Ṣọnpọnnọ?

INFORMANT. It is true, this is because Ọbàtálá does not like palm wine (ẹmu) whereas Ṣọnpọnnọ likes it. Ọbàtála likes only the wine from the raffia palm (ọtí ògùrọ̀) but Ṣọnpọnnọ likes palm wine. That was what caused their quarrel. Ọbàtálá drove Ṣọnpọnnọ from the house because he is more powerful than Ṣọnpọnnọ.

This vague reference is scarcely an adequate foundation for a complete theory about the place of palm wine in Yoruba thought, but it may be tentatively used to reinforce our position. Around the common motif of a quarrel between Ọbàtálá and Ṣọnpọnnọ in which the latter is driven out of the house (or palace), are found a new set of circumstances. The central antagonism has ceased to be an opposition of lameness and health, and of dancing and not dancing (Figure 22(A)). Instead it has become a quarrel over drinking habits (Figure 22(B)): Ọbàtálá who does not drink palm wine, is contrasted with Ṣọnpọnnọ who does.

A		B	
Ọbàtálá	*Ṣọnpọnnọ*	*Ọbàtálá*	*Ṣọnpọnnọ*
culture	anti-culture	culture	anti-culture
palace	forest	house	outside
dancing	lameness	raffia wine	palm wine
health	illness		

FIGURE 22. Two pictures of the opposition between *Ọbàtála* and Ṣọnpọnnọ

To pursue this line of inquiry to the end, it would be necessary
fully to investigate not merely the cults of *Ifá* and *Ṣọ̀npọ̀nnọ́*, but
that of *Ọbàtálá* as well, and this would lead too far from the
subject. But what is published about the relationship between
Ọbàtálá and palm wine (cf. Idowu 1962) also seems to reinforce
the argument that palm wine is associated with revelation. As a
'white' *òrìṣà*, *Ọbàtálá* declines to eat anything which is red. He
takes neither palm-oil, blood, nor red cola-nut, and insists on
being offered the bloodless snail with its white fluid (*omi ìgbín*),
the white cola (*obì ifin*), and white shea butter (*òrí*) (Idowu
1962; Awolalu 1979, 22). For such a god, the whiteness of palm
wine would seem to make it an obvious choice for a gift, but he
rejects it in favour of the similar but milder raffia wine. But
Ọbàtálá is not merely white; he is a god who gives order to the
inside. He has already been portrayed as a king in a palace
defending his subjects against *Ṣọ̀npọ̀nnọ́*. He is also the god who
forms the features of children inside the womb (Idowu 1962,
91). Similarly, he is the god who, on the command of *Olódùmarè*
(God,) came from heaven into the world in order to create it
(Idowu 1962, 19).

The whiteness of palm wine might seem to make it a suitable
drink for *Ọbàtálá*, but if my hypothesis is correct its association
with revelation makes it unsuitable for a god devoted to the
work of creation on the inside of the world, of the town and of
the womb. A variant of the creation story, (Idowu 1962, 22)
shows us that when coming to the world in order to create it
Ọbàtálá stopped to drink palm wine. He thus failed to complete
his task and the work was performed by another.

It appears, therefore, that, at least as a working hypothesis,
it is the association of palm wine with revelation and hence
with the destruction of internal order that makes it both unsuitable as an offering to *Ọbàtálá* and appropriate as a gift to
Ṣọ̀npọ̀nnọ́.

The second major connection between *Ṣọ̀npọ̀nnọ́* and the
palm-tree which I wish to consider here is that which he has
with the broom (*ìgbálẹ̀*) made from the mid-rib (*ọwá*) of the
palm fronds. Abraham asserts that: 'The image of this god is
represented by a broom made from palm-branches smeared
with *osùn* (camwood) and during a smallpox epidemic, people
sweep a room where a sick person lies with the leaves of *ọ̀ṣẹ́pòtu*

which symbolise his emblem, the broom (*ọ̀wọ̀*)' (Abraham
1958, *ṣọ̀npọ̀n:nọ́n* (2) (f)).

There is certainly some connection between the broom made
from palm-fronds, that made from *ọ̀ṣẹ́pòtu*, and *Ṣọ̀npọ̀nnọ́*, but it
is unlikely to be as simple as Abraham thinks.

Awotunde describes the relationship thus:

AWOTUNDE. The servants of *Ṣọ̀npọ̀nnọ́* roam about the world during the dry
season, and always take with them their brooms which they use to touch
people. The name of these servants is *èbùrú*. If the servants of *Ṣọ̀npọ̀nnọ́* touch
the person with the broom, all the places that the broom touch will swell
up. (It was later demonstrated to me that the pressure on the skin from the
handle-end of the palm-broom, where the twigs have been bound tightly
together, produces a patch of marks similar to pock marks.) This is why
they tell people not to use brooms in the season. This is why they tell people
who live with the affected person, not to sweep the room, because if they
sweep with the broom, *Ṣọ̀npọ̀nnọ́* will affect everybody in the house. *Ọ̀ṣẹ́pòtu*
is just like an intimate friend (*ọ̀rẹ́ tímọ́ tímọ́*) to *Ṣọ̀npọ̀nnọ́* whenever the *èbùrú*
find *ọ̀ṣẹ́pòtu* they will not fight against the person.

A roughly similar opinion was advanced by a casual
acquaintance:

BUCKLEY. Why do they not use a broom to sweep the floor when a person is
affected by *Ṣọ̀npọ̀nnọ́*?

INFORMANT. If a broom is used to sweep the floor *Ṣọ̀npọ̀nnọ́* will kill the person
affected by it. The broom can only be used when the person affected has
been cured. *Ṣọ̀npọ̀nnọ́* does not like the broom.

BUCKLEY. Why do they use *ọ̀ṣẹ́pòtu*?

INFORMANT. They use *ọ̀ṣẹ́pòtu* instead of the broom to prevent *Ṣọ̀npọ̀nnọ́* from
spreading to the other people in the house. If *ọ̀ṣẹ́pòtu* is used to sweep the
ground, the person affected by *Ṣọ̀npọ̀nnọ́* will be easily cured.

And this indeed seems to be the general opinion. *Ọ̀ṣẹ́pòtu* is used
to sweep the floor not because, as Abraham suggests, it sym-
bolizes the ordinary broom, but because in some way it
contrasts with it. Awotunde thinks that it is because of the
marks on the skin which are inflicted by the broom in the hands
of *Ṣọ̀npọ̀nnọ́*'s servants, but there are other explanations. I asked
another informant why they use the *ọ̀ṣẹ́pòtu* and he suggested:

INFORMANT. This is because it does not sound like the ordinary broom.

The grass-leaves called *ọ̀ṣẹ́pòtu* are quite stiff, so they can be tied
into a bundle suitable for use as a broom, but they are much

softer than the mid-rib of the palm-frond which is more commonly used for this purpose. Whereas the palm-broom makes a whistling swishing sound, the broom from ọ̀sẹ́pòtu is almost silent in use.

Here then my informant is associating the sound of the palm broom with the onset of smallpox and, in the context of some earlier observations, it would seem to be a reasonable association. The wind is what afflicts people with smallpox, and sounds such as whistling and whispering, which remind men of the wind, are believed to be dangerous when Ṣọ̀npọ̀nnọ́ is abroad.

These explanations may be regarded as sufficiently cogent in themselves. The marks made on the skin by the base of the broom can be demonstrated to be similar to those of smallpox, and the sound of the broom is indeed like that of the wind which causes the illness. But since the palm-tree and its products are so widely used in religious symbolism, and since the leaves themselves from which the palm-broom is constructed have a clear ritual function, we should re-examine the significance of the broom in the more general context of the palm-tree as a whole.

(b) Ifá

Any adequate discussion of Yoruba traditional culture must lead to the subject of *Ifá* whence perhaps it must go on to that of *Ogbóni*. Together, these two cults must be regarded as the embodiment of the most significant truths of Yoruba culture. Certainly they are so regarded by those who participate in them.

Ifá is the main Yoruba oracle. Its priests (*babaláwo*) have to learn a vast number of verses by heart, a feat that would put a Freemason to shame. Divination consists in the selection of a single group of verses from this large body by means of a mechanical process. It takes place when an individual is at some life-crisis, when some important decisions have to be taken, at birth, marriage or death, or when misfortune threatens. *Ifá* is consulted by individuals on their own behalf or on behalf of social groups. Lineage heads, chiefs and kings must all consult *Ifá* at regular intervals and at times of uncertainty.

(i) *Ifá* and the palm-tree

Central to the cult of *Ifá* are the sixteen palm-nuts (*ikin Ifá*) presented to each *babaláwo* (priest of *Ifá*) when he completes his training. By gaining an understanding of the *ikin Ifá*, it will be possible to gain an understanding of the palm-tree. Thence the discussion may return to the subject of *Ṣọnpọnnọ* for whom the palm-tree also has significance. This process will however touch upon some of the most esoteric aspects of Yoruba life.

The sixteen black palm-nuts (*ikin*) at the heart of *Ifá* ritual are kept carefully by their owner in a closed container. Sacrifices may be made to the palm-nuts by the *babaláwo* as an offering to *Ifá*. The nuts are the means whereby the diviner is able to communicate with *Ifá* and therefore instruct his client by the chanting of an appropriate group of verses. Sometimes a metal chain symbolic of the nuts is used.

The palm-nuts of *Ifá* (*èkùrọ́ Ifá* or *ikin Ifá*) used in this form of divination are quite different from the ordinary palm-nuts (*èkùrọ́*) cultivated by Yoruba farmers, though they are sufficiently similar for one to be mistaken for the other. The ordinary palm-nuts (*èkùrọ́*) come from the oil-palm (*ọ̀pẹ*) *Elaeis Guineensis* which has many uses, both secular and sacred and is to be seen almost everywhere in Western Nigeria. The palm-nuts of *Ifá* (*ikin Ifá* or simply *ikin*) come from a similar but distinct species of tree called *ọ̀pẹ Ifá* (or *ọ̀pẹfá* or *ọ̀pẹ lífá*) *Elaeis Idolatrica*, which is seldom used except in connection with *Ifá* ritual. Because of the similarity between the two trees, discussion of the palm-tree and palm-nuts of *Ifá* usually implied a comparison with the ordinary oil-palm.

The palm-tree of *Ifá* has three distinctive features to which my informants alluded. It is branched; the nuts have more than three 'eyes'; and the oil from the palm-fruit, when it is cooked, overflows the pot. This is much feared and is treated with the greatest respect by many Yoruba people. Such a tree grew in the driveway of the school compound where my wife taught in Ibadan (St Anne's), and occasional damage to it was widely believed by the schoolgirls to be responsible for serious misfortunes afflicting the girls and their families. It was, as individuals often told me in English, 'a strange tree'.

The palm-tree of *Ifá* that I knew had two branches or heads (*orí* = head), but they are reputed to have as many as sixteen heads—a number which has great significance in *Ifá*. It is said too that the *ikin* (nut) has four or more 'eyes' (*ojú*). The first set of *ikin ifá* which I saw were perfectly formed with four 'eyes' or small holes symmetrically and clearly spaced around the top of the nut. My first reaction upon seeing them was to think that the holes had been carefully bored with a small drill. The nuts were shining black and, considering how common palm-nuts are in Nigeria, they had the startling effect of inducing in me a great aesthetic, or even numinous pleasure, having about them a quality of magnificent simplicity.

Adebawọ, whose *ikin* they were, insisted:

ADEBAWỌ. Each of the nuts has four eyes each. This is the strange thing about these nuts.

And when I commented upon their strikingly black appearance, he said:

ADEBAWỌ. The thing has a kernel (*ọmọ*) inside, just like the ordinary *èkùró*. It is because of the blackness that they call it *èdú ọpẹ Ifẹ* (the black one of the palm tree of *Ifẹ*).

I wish that I could claim that my awe-inspired reaction when perceiving these perfect little nuts could be related to the logical structure of beliefs surrounding them. Aesthetic perfection is, after all, closely related to logical perfection. Unfortunately such perfection seems not always to be required by the *babaláwo* in their palm-nuts and it is even doubtful whether the presence of four eyes in the palm-nuts is even universally considered necessary.

Bascom (1969b, 27) says that in Ifẹ, the town most closely associated with *Ifá*, only the nuts with four eyes are used and that those with three are unacceptable, but that there is an account in Dennett (1906, 246) that *Ifá* is represented by palm-nuts with four to ten or more 'eyelets', and he gives a number of instances of variation. While it does seem that most *babaláwo* do in fact use nuts with only four eyes, there do seem to be other possibilities.

Fatoogun gave me a long account of the nature of *ikin Ifá*, which I shall quote almost in full, adding glosses and comments.

FATOOGUN. The thing that is central to the meaning of *Ifá* (*nǹkọn tí ó wà nínú itú.mọ̀ Ifá*) is that it is sixteen *ikin* that we cast in *Ifá*. *Ikin* is its name. The reason why it is *ikin* is that if you want to look into the *Ifá* that they cast (i.e.at the nuts), you will find that it is four, six, or five eyes that *Ifá* bears.

It is at the foot of the *ọ̀pẹ ifá* only that we can find this type of nut (*èkùrọ́*). These will not be the kind with three eyes, but only those with four, five, six, or eight. The last number (i.e. the maximum) of eyes is sixteen. Where the one has sixteen eyes, birds will die there if they pass the place. If animals pass through the place, they will die there. It is only the person who brings the thing of atonement (*ohun ètùtù*) in his hand (i.e. something to sacrifice) who is able to reach the foot of the palm-tree.

Have you seen this type of palm-tree? It grows very suddenly. And a message will be sent home that they should tell the diviner (*awo*), for example the head of the diviners (*olórí awo*), or the king of the town, that *Ifá* came down here. When they give him the message, and when they reach the place it is there that they will meet it.

This palm-tree can grow two heads (branches) or three, sixteen heads or four. The reason it is different from other palm-trees is that it is three eyes (*ojú mẹ́ta mẹ́ta mẹ́ta*) that all the *èkùrọ́ ọ̀pẹ* have in the world. It is the one of *Ifá* that is different.

What emerges from this account is first the contrast between the two kinds of palm-nut. One sort has three eyes, the other has any number between four and sixteen. Second, there is a contrast between the ordinary palm (*igi ọ̀pẹ*) which has only one head, and *ọ̀pẹfá* which can have any number of heads (branches) from two to sixteen.

The contrast is particularly strongly drawn by Fatoogun around the number sixteen, but there is also an indication from Adebawọ's own *ikin ifá* and in the account given by Bascom (1969, 27) that four is also significant in this configuration of numbers.

	palm-tree *ọ̀pẹ*	palm-tree of *Ifá* *ọ̀pẹ ifá*
number of branches (*orí*)	1	any number
number of 'eyes' on nuts	3	but especially 4 and 16

FIGURE 23. The palm-tree and the palm-tree *Ifá*

These numbers, one, three, four, and sixteen, are very important to Yoruba thought. They are closely related to the structure which has been established and also to the symbolism of the left and right hands. Before, however, we plunge into the delights of Yoruba number symbolism and the meaning of the left and the right hands, let us consider the next statements in Fatoogun's account.

FATOOGUN. When it (*igi ọpẹ Ifá*) grows and they do not recognize it, if they cut the bunch (of fruit) of this palm-tree together with the (ordinary) palm-fruit (*èkùrọ́ ẹyìn*), when they put them on the fire, the oil will overflow completely whatever type of fire they use to cook it (i.e. a hot or a slow fire). So they will not be able to see any of the oil from the *ọpẹ lífá* together with ordinary palm-oil, and it will also overflow the other oil.

Now this last remark may be merely a statement of simple empirical fact, and no more, but I was interested to find that Adebawọ makes precisely the same observation.

ADEBAWỌ. They use it (*ikin Ifá*) because it has four eyes. If those who are making oil (*epo*) mistakenly cut a bunch (of palm-fruit) from *ọpẹ Ifá* and cook it together with other palm-nuts, those who use the oil, for example the sellers of *àkàrà*,[3] they will be unable to use it because when it is cooking the oil will overflow into the fire.

Bascom too, who is one of the few writers on the subject even to mention, let alone go into detail about, the peculiarities of *ọpẹ Ifá*, also draws attention to the fact that, when heated, the oil from this palm-tree overflows the cooking-pot (Bascom 1969b, 27). I have already shown that the image of overflowing is significant in Yoruba medicine.

(ii) Left, right, and Yoruba numerology

We are approaching one of the most difficult and basic ideas of Yoruba thought. It is particularly difficult because of the secrecy which envelops it.

The number three is closely associated with the secret cult of *Ogbóni*, which though its old judicial role has largely become defunct, still thrives as the Reformed *Ogbóni* Fraternity. Adebawọ was a member of this fraternity but, even at a late period in our association, when he would tell me virtually anything else I needed to know, he refused to tell me about number three. Similarly when I asked about number four:

ADEBAWO. I cannot tell you about four, because if I tell you about four I am
at the same time telling you about three.

Morton Williams, whose interpretative studies of Yoruba ideas
are the most thoughtful to date, has made an excellent study of
Ogbóni in Oyọ (1960b) and he relates the number symbolism
which is so much part of the cult with the distinction between
the left and right hands (see also Beck 1978a; Beidelman 1973;
Bril 1979; Chelhod 1964; Fox 1973; Hertz 1909; Kruyt 1941; La
Flesche 1916; Littlejohn 1967; G. Lloyd 1962; Needham 1960,
1967b; Nicolas 1968; Rigby 1966; Weischoff 1938; for studies of
the left and right hands). Morton Williams draws attention to
the use of the number three in contrast to the 'emphasis on
dualism, in for example the pairing of the gods—and stress on
the number four and its square sixteen' (1960b, 373). His
suggestion is that just as the left hand, also used by *Ogbóni*, is
unclean and not used for such purposes as writing and eating,
so the number three is similarly offensive; one would not offer
three objects to a god or to a guest (1960b, 373). 'The
preeminence they give to the left hand suggests that they
perceive that they cannot reject one side of themselves but must
accept the unclean—that which is hidden and knowledge that
is forbidden—one can see in the image of three, set against what
we know to be the significance of four for the Yoruba, a sign of
incompleteness and therefore a concern with process and time'
(1960b, 373).

Ogbóni, he suggests, with its preoccupation with three and
the left hand, in contrast with four and the right, is able to
transcend the particular truths of the lesser cults (among which
he includes even *Ifá*). 'The rituals of the *òrìṣà* cease to captivate
the more thoughtful of them and to be reduced to a technique
for gaining magical power from the *òrìṣà*; through their
experience, age, and closeness to death, they have transcended
the ordinary *òrìṣà* "truths"—the conception expressed through
the cults—leaving only Earth as the absolute certainty in the
future' (1960b, 373).

I do not wish to disagree very forcefully with Morton
Williams here, but I feel that this interpretation of three and of
the left hand raises certain difficulties which can be overthrown
by developing his ideas a little further. First of all however I

heartily concur that the left hand is associated with the number three. Members of *Ogbóni* indicate to each other that they are members of the cult by shaking with the left hand, or by knocking sharply three times upon the door. It is said that it is even possible to send a letter through the post without a postage stamp, by simply marking the envelope with three spots as a sign to *Ogbóni* members in the Post Office.

A similar connection between three and the left hand, exists in medicine and food. Medicines are usually eaten with the left hand (*àsèjẹ* is, as far as I can gather, an exception to this) and, when they are accompanied by incantation, the verse, or significant parts of it, are chanted three times. Food, however, is never eaten with the left hand, and it is particularly noticeable that, before a meal, only the right hand is washed. Similarly food is never offered to anyone in units of three, and, should this rule be broken, the recipient may take serious offence. This restriction does not apply to medicine. The left hand is also prohibited for writing. I met no Yoruba who was 'left-handed'. My wife, who always writes with her left hand, found that this was always remarked upon, and that reactions to it varied from surprise to anger. Morton Williams interprets the left hand and the number three as 'unclean', and there is some truth in this. The left hand is used to clean the anus after defecation and this would seem to support his interpretation. Unfortunately this does not account for the significance of three or the left hand in medicine. What is more, he claims that since four is associated with completeness, three is related to incompleteness. This would seem to contradict what he goes on to say about the *Ogbóni* cult, that it transcends the particularity of the truths of the other cults. It would seem that if this were true, three and the left hand would imply, not incompleteness, but indeed its contrary.

One of my most interesting interviews took place with a member of *Ogbóni* with whom I was very friendly. He knew that I was interested in the significance of these numbers, but was usually very reticent in imparting information. One day, with a show of great confidentiality, he took me to a room where we could be alone (I had no tape recorder with me) and he explained the importance of three for *Ogbóni*. This is the proverb he gave me: '*Aàrò mẹ́ta kìí dọbẹ̀ẹnu*' (The three stones of the hearth will not spill the soup). This, he said, showed that it was the earth (*ilẹ̀*) which supported the world (*ayé*). I tried to discuss this further with him, but he refused and the conversation was concluded. On the face of it, this proverb states no more than the obvious. Morton Williams has shown us (1964) that the Yoruba universe has three layers *ilẹ̀* (earth), *ayé* (world), and *ọ̀run* (sky). The earth therefore supports the world. The analogy with the cooking-pot seemed initially to have mild interest. But as I speculated further I found that it became more and more intriguing.

It is not surprising to find the cooking-pot used as an analogy for the womb. Some medicines (e.g. pp. 214–18) point explicitly to this comparison. In the literature also, there are a number of references which indicate that the cooking-pot (*ìkòkò*) or the calabash (*igbá*) are used as metaphors or symbols for the world bounded by the sky and earth. Ellis (1894, 41–2) portrays the world as a calabash containing the male god '*Obatala*' (the top half of the calabash) with '*Odudua*', the female god, as the bottom half. Dennett (1910, 153–5) tells a story of how the 'calabash of Ife' was broken; gods and famous men came to try and mend it but in vain; the rains failed, hunger came and not until the calabash was mended was harmony and tranquillity restored.

The metaphor in fact implies two numbers. The first is three, the three stones, or pillars of earth, the second is one, the cooking-pot itself. Morton Williams, quite correctly in my view, has identified the twos, fours, and sixteens with the plenitude, the completeness of the Yoruba world. But if the metaphor of the cooking-pot and hearth is applied to his description of *Ogbóni*, a somewhat different interpretation may be found for the number three.

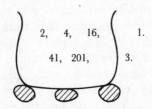

FIGURE 24. The cooking-pot and numbers

Two, four, and sixteen are, we have already seen, representative numbers for the plethora which *is not* three or one. Moreover, from within the cooking-pot, the three stones of the hearth (*ààrò*) are what is hidden. There are here several developments of the same theme (Figure 25). But can this image of the world and the human body as a cooking-pot be reconciled with Image 2, the world comprehended through the colours of the body itself?

Ogbóni member	Three hearth-stones one cooking-pot	containing *ọbẹ̀* (soup)
Morton Williams (1960a)	One earth	transcending multiplicity of cults (201 *òrìṣà*)
Adebawọ on *èdà* pp. 214–18	One calabash-like womb	holds blood and semen
Mrs Ajayi and Fatoogun	One female body	holds blood and semen and (41) diseases
Dennett (1910) Ellis (1894)	calabash	holds the world or two *òrìṣà*

FIGURE 25. Containers

In its simplest form, the Image 2 took the form of red and white mingling, at conception, behind the blackness of secrecy. One informant suggested that the diseases in the woman's body which contributed to the creation of the child numbered forty-one. We have here then two, forty-one, and two-hundred-and-one, mixed together as though in a cooking-pot. It may be significant that until the introduction of enamelled dishes, and indeed for many cooking purposes today, cooking-pots are traditionally black.

The red and white fluids of our model were, of course, the female menstrual blood and the male semen. Male and female are in fact related to the numerology of the Yoruba. It seems to be generally believed that women have two fewer ribs than men. Men have nine ribs; women have but seven. This seems to

be a wholly indigenous belief, independent of the similar one
found in the first pages of the Bible. It is believed, but it seems
to have little consequence beyond the fact that, very occasionally in certain medicines, ingredients are specified to be
included in quantities of seven for women and nine for men. It
happens sometimes too that when incisions are made for the
purpose of rubbing in medicine, seven cuts are made for women
and nine for men.[4]

Bril (1979) argues that in West Africa the distinction
between the numbers nine and seven is commonly associated
with that between male and female and he argues that the sum
of such numbers—in this case sixteen—indicates the unity of
creation. He complains however that he cannot find much
evidence of the number sixteen in the literature. This is,
perhaps, rather surprising. At any rate, the union of red and
white has in Yoruba symbolism a numerological counterpart in
the union of seven and nine, sixteen. Hence we find the pattern
of Figure 26.

Three	Seven-and-nine (16)
Black	Red and white
left	right
hidden	revealed
unity	diversity

FIGURE 26. Numerology and other themes

It appears, then, that the left hand is the hand that hides, and
the right hand is the hand of revelation. We may further suggest
a rationale for this association. The left and right halves of the
average human body are, unless one engages in surgical
research, completely symmetrical, save in one respect. The
heart is to be found only on the left of the body. For most
Yoruba the heart (ọkọ̀n) is the place where knowledge (òye) is
stored, and all significant knowledge is secret (awo) (cf. Chapter 7).

The use of the left hand to cleanse the anus after defecation
suggests that defecation is itself a form of hiding—an idea
which is happily consonant with earlier conclusions (Image 1).
What is not immediately apparent, and must therefore be

discussed later, is why the left hand should be prohibited for writing and for the consumption of food, while it is used when one wishes to eat medicine. If my hypothesis is correct, it will have to be shown that medicine and food are respectively associated with secrecy and revelation.

The image of the cooking-pot therefore not only gives us a means to see the significance of the various numbers used by the Yoruba, but also it shows why Morton Williams is precisely correct when he says that *Ogbóni* transcends the particular truths of the ordinary *òrìṣà* cults. As a container, the earth, associated with the number three and the left hand, embraces the whole world. The right hand and the other representative numbers, four, sixteen, forty-one, and two-hundred-and-one, signify, as Morton Williams asserts, the completeness of the world. Three and the left hand give to this disordered completeness its hidden unity. This hidden unity is the earth.

(iii) The palm-tree as a container

Returning to the discussion of the two types of palm-tree, it may be seen how this symbolic structure is relevant. The two trees stand contrasted with one another on the basis of the same two opposed sets of numbers. Strange as it may at first appear, these two palm-trees have opposed characteristics in that one is identified as a container, while the other is identified with the contents (Figure 27).

Qpẹ	*Qpẹ Ifá*
1-headed tree	2-16-headed tree
3-eye nut	4-16-eye nut
container	contents

FIGURE 27. The palm-tree as container

It is not to be inferred from this, of course, that the one palm-tree contains the other as a pot contains soup. But, since the ordinary palm-tree is apparently regarded as a container analogous to the womb, it may be asked what it is that the palm-tree does in fact contain.

The ordinary palm-tree contains two natural fluids: one is white; the other is red. The white palm wine is the sap of the palm-tree which may easily be revealed by knocking a small hole in the inflorescence at the top of the tree. The red palm-oil is not so easily obtained. It is found in the bunches of palm-fruit (*ẹyìn*) also found at the top of the tree, and may only be released by a long process of cooking. Once it is extracted it may be cooked over a fire in complete safety, for it does not overflow the pot.

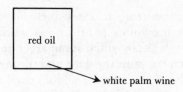

FIGURE 28. The palm-tree (*ọ̀pẹ*)

The palm-tree of *Ifá* is similar to the ordinary oil-palm, but it differs in crucial respects. Its palm-nuts, despite their blackness, have as many as sixteen 'eyes' which can kill animals, birds, and human beings. Its oil, while similar in appearance to ordinary palm-oil, has the (literally) dangerous property that, when cooked, it quickly overflows the pot into the fire until the pot is empty. Just as outflowing menstruation is dangerous when, at conception, the womb becomes a container for a child (Chapter Three), so the outflowing palm-oil from the palm-tree of *Ifá* is dangerous in the cooking-pot.

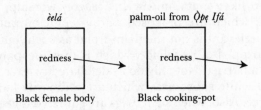

FIGURE 29. The body and the cooking-pot

This characterization of the ordinary palm-tree as a container provides an understanding of its role in relation to *Ṣǫ̀npǫ̀nnǫ́*. It would seem that just as the palm-tree contains red

and white fluids, so the remainder of the palm-tree and especially those parts found near to the oil and wine, would provide
satisfactory fabric for containing other things.

In Appendix C, it will indeed be shown that the hair (*lẹ̀wù*)
found upon the male inflorescence (*àrọ̀n ọ̀pe*) and upon the stem
of the palm-tree is used to stem the flow of harmful liquids in a
medicine for *ẹdà*, but it is in the leaves that this hiding facility is
more obvious.

The palm-frond (*imọ̀*) is extensively used in ritual. Most
commonly it is the young palm-fronds (*mọ̀rìwò ọ̀pẹ*) which are
employed, for it is these which stand erect and encircle the top
of the tree which contains the wine and the oil. The older fronds
which droop down the tree are seldom used. The main use for
palm fronds is to provide a barrier. Sometimes this barrier is of
the most practical sort, for the palm-fronds are extensively used
as material for thatching. Nowadays, thatching occurs only on
the smaller farm houses and shacks, but within living memory
the palm-frond was the main means of protecting the occupants
of a household from sun and rain outside and dangers. Often
the barrier created by the palm-fronds is merely symbolic.
Where there is a sacred grove or some other form of sacred
place, the road may be sealed by a small partition made of
palm-fronds. Anyone who sees such a barrier, will know that,
by passing it, he is entering a realm where a god or spirit is
present.

The palm-frond has an important function in *Ṣọ̀npọ̀nnọ́*
worship, but its use here is not as a barrier, for *Ṣọ̀npọ̀nnọ́* is not a
god who likes containment. In *Ṣọ̀npọ̀nnọ́* worship, and in the
customs which are practised during epidemics of smallpox,
what is relevant is not the palm-frond as such, but rather the
frond stripped of its foliage, which is thus incapable of being
used as a barrier. Not only do its defoliated twigs 'reveal' those
red and white substances which are ordinarily hidden in the
palm-tree. Also, when such twigs are gathered together to form
a broom they are a singularly efficient means of removing
whatever covers the earth. Not only does the broom remove
rubbish, but, especially in a town, it may brush away the black
soil to reveal the red earth beneath. When it is stripped of
foliage, the mid rib of the palm-frond used as a broom is thus
doubly appropriate as a symbol of *Ṣọ̀npọ̀nnọ́*.

(iv) Palm-nuts, *Ifá* and *Ṣọnpọ̀nnọ́*

Both the palm-nuts of *Ifá* and the ordinary palm-nuts may be regarded as microcosms of their parents. The nuts of the ordinary palm-tree are obtained only from the tree which has not been tapped for palm wine. Like a human child, they are the product of a union of red and white fluids enclosed within a concealing framework. When they emerge from the tree, they are black outside and are surmounted by three eyes, the three of secrecy. This peculiarly concealed structure of palm-nuts explains *Ṣọnpọ̀nnọ́*'s special hostility to the oil which is extracted from them (*àdín*). Idowu writes (1962, 95–101) that it is possible to direct the anger of *Ṣọnpọ̀nnọ́* towards an enemy by offering him palm-kernel oil (*àdín*), taking care to mention to him that this oil was sent to him by the enemy. The general hostility which *Ṣọnpọ̀nnọ́* demonstrates to all manifestations of secrecy makes it likely that this procedure would be effective.

The palm-nuts of *Ifá*, however, are obtainable only from a tree which, though similar to the concealing presence of the ordinary palm-tree, at the same time embodies an opposite principle. The palm-tree of *Ifá* contains wine and oil, and these are concealed as with the ordinary palm-tree by palm-fronds and by the hair on the inflorescence. Similarly when the nuts are born they embody in their very blackness a symbolic secrecy. Yet, unlike the oil from the ordinary palm-tree, that which is obtained from this 'strange tree' is volatile, and spills easily from the pot. The nuts themselves, the *ikin Ifá*, which provide the focus of so much Yoruba thought, are also found to embody the openness associated with the numbers four and sixteen. In *Ifá* and its symbols are to be found both secrecy and revelation.

(v) Revelation and secrecy in *Ifá*

We have now given an explanation of every detail of Fatoogun's exposition, so far as the palm-tree of *Ifá* is concerned, with one single exception. We have not explained why those *Ifá* palm-nuts which have sixteen eyes can cause birds and animals to die, and why men must bring a sacrifice when approaching the tree. But his exposition has not yet been fully quoted and it should be pursued to the end to demonstrate the usefulness of this interpretation of the two kinds of palm-tree.

FATOOGUN. In this (the foregoing) is the contract that God has given to *Ifá* from heaven, that they should use (the palm-nuts) to divine. So that everyone can obtain it anywhere, that is why he used this palm-tree as a covenant (*májèmú*) to use in divining (*àyèwó*), because if it is a thing which is more expensive than this, how can many people have it, and use it to divine. That is why it is in the body of the palm-tree that *Ifá* put the sign of the covenant.

There is in this statement, which I have heard repeated by others, a sense of wonder that God should choose such a humble thing as a palm-nut (if not the common variety) to pass his messages to man. It contains the paradox found in many religions including Christianity, of transcendence and immanence, of the 'wholly other', the *mysterium* and *tremendum* (Otto 1917 *passim*), a sense of the distance yet closeness of the divine. Through *Ifá* and through his palm-nuts, God's truth is both hidden and revealed.

Fatoogun now turns to the technicalities of manipulating the palm-nuts in divination.

FATOOGUN. When he (the diviner) takes the sixteen *ikin Ifá* they will be the size of the hands, eight in the right hand and eight in the left hand. He will put them together and will say, 'right is together, left is together' (*ọ̀tún jọ, òsì í jọ*). He will begin to cast *Ifá*. When he takes *Ifá* ('*Ifá*' here means the palm-nuts) he will hold them in the left hand and will put the right hand on top of them (the motion is of the two hands being slapped together). He will use the right hand to take all the nuts from the left hand, and if one remains, he will use two fingers to mark the earth (*wọ́n ó bá fi ìka wéjì tẹ̀lẹ̀*). If he tries to take the nuts, there may remain two alone (in the left hand). He will use the one finger to mark the earth. . . . If three remain in the hand, he will know that *odù* has not grown, he will recast it. If there are none left in the hand, he will know that *odù* has not grown (*odù ò tíì hù*) and he will say '*òfìfo ilẹ̀ kò máa ńta isu o! a fi ka kọbẹ̀ si*') ('Empty ground does not sell yams oh! unless we dig heaps upon it'). This is the proverb they say to *Ifá*, they will cast it again until it grows one or it grows two. Then they will continue to mark it in different ways until the *odù* will grow.

From this account, which is parallel in all respects to those of Bascom (1969b) and others, we can suggest the way in which the symbolic structures are explored and developed in the ritual of *Ifá* divination.

First, to clarify what Fatoogun is saying, the process involves a number of stages:

a. The nuts are divided equally between the two hands.

b. They are beaten together.

c. All but one or two nuts are taken from the left hand.

d. If one nut remains two marks (*ojú*) are made in the dust (*iyẹròsùn*) in the divining tray (*ọpón Ifá*) with the right hand.

e. If two nuts remain one mark is made in the dust.

f. It is repeated until the *odù* has grown, i.e. until there are eight sets of marks on the round tray.

g. The diviner is then able to chant the verses of the *odù*.

h. Sacrifice is made.

It will be noticed that in the ritual of divination two contrasting numbers are used. The first of these is obviously sixteen, but the other, which is less obvious, is the number three. The sixteen palm-nuts in both hands are beaten together and snatched, so that in the left hand (the hand of secrecy), one or two nuts remain. With the right hand (the hand of revelation) the number is made up to three by marking in the dust on the divining tray, one or two marks (*ojú*) as determined by the number of nuts in the left hand.

The dust of the divining board itself is singularly appropriate for the revelation of hidden truths. This dust (*ìyẹròsùn*) is collected from the foot of the camwood tree. The wood of the tree is deep red in colour, and the dust emerges from within the tree through the action of insects. The dust therefore itself is red wood hidden in the tree which has been revealed outside the tree.

But what is revealed by the marks in the dust is not the whole truth of the *Ifá* corpus of verses. The whole secret truth is in the number three, and with each separate manipulation of the palm-nuts, only a portion of three is revealed in the right hand. If one mark is revealed by the right hand in the dust, two nuts remain hidden in the left hand. If two marks are revealed, one nut remains hidden.

As divination proceeds, a figure grows on the divining board. But this figure also reveals only a small part of the truth. Each completed figure represents an *odù*, but as there are 256 possible permutations within the system, the revelation of one *odù* implies that 255 remain hidden.

Ifá reveals the truth, but at any one time, he reveals only a small proportion of it, keeping the remainder hidden. Yet even in this minute revelation of *Ifá*'s truth there is danger. As the verses connected with the *odù* are chanted, the client will learn that he must make a sacrifice. Each verse in the *Ifá* corpus prescribes a sacrifice and directly or by implication, each verse suggests that, should the sacrifice not be made, the client will himself suffer misfortune or death.

If the revelation of hidden truths brings danger or death, then *Ifá* provides the most satisfactory context for its revelation. In divination there is a delicate balance between the revelation of truth and its concealment. As truth is revealed in a controlled and ritualized way, much of it remains hidden, so that the client may avoid the devastation of the uncontrolled revelation of misfortune and death. Unlike *Ṣọnpọnnọ* who hates concealment and brings the uncontrollable openness of smallpox, *Ifá* is able to control his openness with secrecy.

(c) Ifá *and* Ṣọnpọnnọ

This analysis has come some considerable way towards an understanding of the two gods *Ifá* and *Ṣọnpọnnọ* and also towards an understanding of the two types of palm tree which feature so much in Yoruba symbolism. *Ṣọnpọnnọ* the dangerous god of smallpox is associated with the hot earth, the bad wind, and the open spaces, and is the enemy of all aspects of Yoruba urban, corporate culture. *Ifá*, the god of divination, brings peace and harmony to individuals and corporate groups by means of the balance between revelation and secrecy which constitutes culture. Already it is clear that there is some contrast between the two gods, and because of the discussion of the role of the two types of palm-trees it is possible to make this contrast more explicit.

A first step in this direct comparison will be an analysis of two variants of a myth recounting a battle between the two gods. Through it, it will be possible to consolidate the previous conclusions. The story in effect gives definition to the central ambiguity in *Ifá*'s personality. It poses the problem of how a peace-bringing god such as *Ifá* should paradoxically have many of the qualities of *Ṣọnpọnnọ*, and it also provides a mythical solution. From this definition of the two gods, it will be possible to progress to an understanding of the rather obscure connection between the gods of smallpox and madness.

(i) A myth of *Ifá* and *Ṣọ̀npọ̀nnọ́*

The first version of this myth was elicited when I asked Fatoogun about the colouring upon my statue of *Ṣọ̀npọ̀nnọ́*.

BUCKLEY. Why is my carving painted red, white, and black?

FATOOGUN. When *Ṣọ̀npọ̀nnọ́* was coming from heaven, *Olúdùmarè* (God) gave him many colours, and when *Ṣọ̀npọ̀nnọ́* arrived in the world, he began to fight with all the children of *Olódùmarè*.[5] When *Olódùmarè* saw this, he called *Ọrúnmìlà* (the first diviner of the *Ifá* cult), that he should fight *Ṣọ̀npọ̀nnọ́* and conquer him. *Ọrúnmìlà* left (the town of) Ile Ifẹ to fight *Ṣọ̀npọ̀nnọ́* at Oke Oya. When he got there he could not find *Ṣọ̀npọ̀nnọ́* and he met him on the way home to *Ifẹ*. They began to fight. There were 200 flames (*inọ́*) on the head of *Ṣọ̀npọ̀nnọ́*, and *Ọrúnmìlà* quenched all these flames until only sixteen flames remained. He brought *Ṣọ̀npọ̀nnọ́* to Ifẹ. When they arrived at the gate *Ọrúnmìlà* called for water and he drank all the water in Ifẹ. He called for palm-oil (*epo*) and drank all the oil. He then called for blood, and drank the blood of all the animals, and they had to start killing the people to find enough blood for *Ọrúnmìlà* to drink. *Ọrúnmìlà* thought he was trying to save the lives of the people, but now he was killing them. He told *Ṣọ̀npọ̀nnọ́* that he should not kill the people in the way that he had been doing, but that he should instead use disease. It was on that day that *Ọrúnmìlà* spoke 200 languages, and from that day there have been many different languages in the world. When *Ọrúnmìlà* recovered from his injuries he decorated himself with the colours of *Ṣọ̀npọ̀nnọ́*. He jumped from the palace to his house at Igeti and the day is remembered in Ifẹ to the present time. Anyone established as *Aràbà* (the head priest of *Ifá*) must commemorate this day. *Aràbà* usually paints his body in these colours during the celebrations.

Awotunde gave me this version which differs somewhat in detail but the broad outline is the same.

BUCKLEY. In some towns in the festival of *Ifá*, *babaláwo* (priests of *Ifá*) paint themselves with the same colours as *Ṣọ̀npọ̀nnọ́*. Why is this?

AWOTUNDE. When *Ọrúnmìlà* went to fight *Ṣọ̀npọ̀nnọ́* at Ile Ifẹ, he was first of all overpowered by *Ṣọ̀npọ̀nnọ́*, but he afterwards beat him. When he had overpowered *Ṣọ̀npọ̀nnọ́*, *Ọrúnmìlà* said that they should give him all the water in Ifẹ. They gave him this and he drank it. But this did not defeat the disease. After this, he said that they should give him all the blood to drink. They gave him this, killing many animals, but to no effect. After this, they complained to *Ifá* that he had come to save the people from *Ṣọ̀npọ̀nnọ́* but that in doing so, he had killed all the animals. *Ifá* then went to his house. When they celebrate how *Ifá* came to Ifẹ̀ they usually dress like this (indicating the statue). They do it at Ile Ifẹ̀ calling it *ọdùn Agbọ́nnìrè*.[6] *Aràbà* is the name of the person who dances like this every year. He runs from the palace to the house of *Ọrúnmìlà*.

These two variants of this story provide explanations for the paradox which lies at the heart of *Ifá* ritual and which has been a major theme of this chapter. The myth seems to solve a pair of related problems. The first of these has do do with the personality of the god. *Ọrúnmìlà*'s role, both generally and in this story, is to defeat evil and to bring health, security, prosperity, and life to the town and its inhabitants. Yet the first story says '*Ọrúnmìlà* thought he was trying to save the lives of the people, but now he was killing them.' And the second relates 'They complained to *Ifá* that he had come to save the people from *Ṣọ̀npọ̀nnọ́*, but in doing so, he had killed all the animals.' That is the first problem defined by these accounts. The second, however, is similar. *Ifá* is the archetypal 'secret'. His priests are called 'father the owner of the secret' (*babaláwo*). Yet his symbolic colouring is not black, the colour of secrecy; it is, at least in this context, the red and white of revelation, danger, and death.

In one sense *Ifá* and *Ṣọ̀npọ̀nnọ́* may be regarded as the total opposite of each other. *Ifá* is a god who lives in the town, indeed, whose very presence in the town may be said to constitute it. He is the secret (*awo*) who is privy to the secrets of all the corporate groups in the town and who embodies, in the verses of his many *odù*, all of Yoruba cultural life. His verses also contain the incantations of (*ọfọ̀*) which inform men of the hidden power of medicinal ingredients (see the next chapter), and because of this he affords to individuals the prospect of personal health and prosperity.

Ṣọ̀npọ̀nnọ́, on the contrary, is a god so dangerous that he must be kept in the forest. Of all the Yoruba gods, he is the only one who is hardly ever worshipped in the town. When sacrifice is made to him, it is cast away into the bush. His hostility to the town and to the secrets of the corporate groups therein is manifest in several ways, of which his dislike of dancing and drumming is only the most trivial. Much more serious is the smallpox with which he destroys both individuals and whole communities. Where *Ifá* is the god of secrets and of the inside, *Șònpònnó*, with his red and white spots of smallpox and of revelation, is the owner of the outside. It will be noted that I do not come to this conclusion because of *Șònpònnó*'s epithet *Oló.de* which literally may be translated 'owner of the outside'; my analysis does however show why this epithet is appropriate.

If *Șònpònnó* and *Ifá* are most clearly and obviously seen to be utterly different in character we may readily understand the problem defined by the myths. It is a problem created by the internal inconsistencies of *Ifá*'s personality. The secrecy of *Ifá* is associated with the colour black, yet his colouring is that of revelation—red and white. His numbers are four and sixteen, but also three. He is a god of peace and salvation who brings harmony to the town and health to its members, yet he demands sacrifice, and at times, he wantonly kills both animals and men to assist him in his task.

Herein lies the paradox within the idea of *Ifá* and it is the reconciliation of this paradox which is attempted in the stories.

(ii) *Ifá* and the madness of *Șònpònnó*

So far we have seen *Șònpònnó* only as the bringer of smallpox; he must now be seen in relation to the madness which he inflicts on individuals.

FATOOGUN. *Șònpònnó* can make a person made (*wèrè*). If the wind does not give a man smallpox, it can enter a man's heart (*okòn*) and cause him to speak all kinds of nonsense. For a person will be speaking only to the *eburú* (servants of *Șònpònnó*) and people will not be able to understand what he is saying. (It will be remembered that for Fatoogun the bad wind (*afééfé búburú*) and the children of *Șònpònnó* are identical.) The person affected will think that he is doing the right thing, and all other people will seem to him to be animals. He will think that he is the only wise person; thus he will be mad.

In view of the comparison which has already been made of *Ifá* and *Șònpònnó* it is extremely interesting to find in these remarks about *Șònpònnó* a close parallel with the cult of *Ifá*. Just as *Șònpònnó* has servants who enter the hearts of men and speak to them, so also does *Ifá*.

Central to the ritual of the *Ifá* cult is, as we have seen, the selection of a group of verses which are chanted by the *babaláwo*. Each group of verses is called an *odù* and has a name derived from that of the sixteen primary *odù* which are senior to the other 240. But the *odù Ifá* are more than mere collections of verses. As Bascom tells us (1969b, 47–9) they are generally regarded as intelligent beings who take an active part in divination. The *babaláwo* who chants the verses is not merely exercising his memory; he has fallen under the guidance of one of these *odù* spirits. The *odù*, as Bascom correctly states are neither *ẹbọra* (spirits) nor *òrìṣà* (gods), for they exist as a distinct category of being, but like gods and spirits, they have a measure of independence and the more important ones are offered sacrifice. I have indeed witnessed a sacrifice to the most important *odù*, *Ejì ogbè*, in *Ojà ọba* in Ibadan.

Fatoogun himself certainly regards the two groups of spirits in sharp contrast to each other.

BUCKLEY. Can we say that the children of *Ṣọnpọnnọ́* are in many ways similar to the *odù Ifá*, or are they the opposite?

FATOOGUN. They are not similar. *Eburú* and *wọ̀rọ̀kọ̀* are the children of *Ṣọnpọnnọ́*, and there are more of them than there are people in the world. They have no other work than to be used by *Ṣọnpọnnọ́* as tools for fighting. Some of them he may send against human beings, animals, and trees. They usually ride on the air.

Each of the *odù Ifá* has its own assignment given to it by *Qló.run* (God) and they are still doing their work to this day. They take care of human beings by curing their sickness, giving them children, giving money to them, and protecting them from their enemies. They also prevent wars. If bad spirits (*ẹbọra Burúkú*) are coming from heaven, they can stop them or prevent them from harming human beings. There is one who is in charge of air, to see that the wind is always blowing, one in charge of the rain, one in charge of the sun. There is one who is to open the door for human beings to enter heaven, and also one who opens the door for children coming into the world. There is one on the *àpáta agbarisaala* (rock at the gateway from heaven) whose mission is to ask the people coming into the world their purpose. He will advise those who wish to come to the world to do bad things to change their purpose. The servants of *Ṣọnpọnnọ́* are exactly the opposite.

Fatoogun here draws a proper contrast between the two groups of spirits; one is 'good' the other 'bad', but his own version of the myth of *Ifá* and *Ṣọnpọnnọ́* calls into question the extreme nature of this contrast, for *Ifá* is a god who also brings death to the town.

So also it is when the two groups of spirits whisper into the hearts of men. When the odù Ifá whisper to the babaláwo, they allow him to state the hidden truths necessary to the salvation of the town. The eburú Ṣǫnpǫnnǫ on the other hand whisper to men causing them to speak nonsense and ultimately to see men as animals. On the level of speech, Ifá and his servants induce culture, Ṣǫnpǫnnǫ brings anti-culture in the form of insanity.

Yet this simple contrast too is belied by the myth of Ifá and Ṣǫnpǫnnǫ. In the first version, as a direct result of his contact and infection by Ṣǫnpǫnnǫ, Ifá 'spoke 200 languages and from that day there were many different languages in the world'. As he rampaged round the town, killing animals and men, Ifá's voice, like that of Ṣǫnpǫnnǫ had become a Babel of confusion.[7]

We may now draw together the strands of our argument. Ṣǫnpǫnnǫ is totally self-consistent. He is a god of the outside, hidden from the town when he is distant from it, but who destroys the town, its people and its culture when he is near. Ifá is opposed to him, but only by his lack of self-consistency. He is everything that Ṣǫnpǫnnǫ is not, a quiet, peaceful god, concerned with maintaining the culture, health, and well-being of the town and its inhabitants. Yet at times, he transforms himself into a vicious and vindictive god with properties precisely analagous to those of Ṣǫnpǫnnǫ. The contrast between them may be expressed diagrammatically (see Figure 30).

(iii) Good and evil: secrecy and openness

From Figure 30 we might be inclined to derive a direct and clear relationship between secrecy and revelation on the one hand and good and evil on the other. To a considerable extent the Yoruba do the same. It has been noted that disease is beneficial only when it is hidden, and that menstruation is dangerous when it is revealed. In general the Yoruba are more preoccupied with the danger of revelation, than with that of secrecy. The openness associated with red and white brings smallpox, madness, and death whether it is associated with Ifá or Ṣǫnpǫnnǫ. The word burúkú (evil) occurs so often in the context of Ṣǫnpǫnnǫ, that it is very difficult to avoid this conclusion.

It should, however, be realized that Ṣǫnpǫnnǫ is not merely evil; he also brings benefit to the world.

	Ifá	*Ṣọ̀npọ̀nnọ́*
Hidden in the town	Revelation in the town	Revelation in the town
Words of servants bring order and peace	Words of servants bring confusion	Words of servants bring confusion
Life to nature	Death to nature	Death to nature
Health to individuals	Sickness to individuals	Sickness to individuals
Order to communities	Disorder to communities	Disorder to communities
Associated with black	Associated with red and white	Associated with red and white

FIGURE 30. Ambiguity in *Ifá*; self-consistency in *Ṣọ̀npọ̀nnọ́*

BUCKLEY. Does *Ṣọ̀npọ̀nnọ́* do any good?

FATOOGUN. Yes, *Ṣọ̀npọ̀nnọ́* does good as well as evil. Every *ẹbọra* (spirit) has its own form of help that it can do for people. *Ṣọ̀npọ̀nnọ́* is also the owner of the sun, and we all know that the sun does some good for us. He is the one who is responsible for the movements of the sun in the sky like a canoe. He is also responsible for the dry season, and for all the things that derive benefit from the dry season. The good that *Ṣọ̀npọ̀nnọ́* does seems greater than the harm.

The reason that *Ṣọ̀npọ̀nnọ́* does bad things to some people is because of their bad character, and the ones responsible for these bad things are *eburú* and *wọ̀rọ̀kọ̀*. They can fight with trees and animals as well as human beings. It can be stopped with sacrifice.

Once when there were many diseases affecting human beings, it was *Ṣọ̀npọ̀nnọ́* who brought pepper (*ata*) to the world so that when people ate it, it would eradicate some of the diseases.

Ṣọ̀npọ̀nnọ́ brings the advantages of revelation as well as some of the more lurid disadvantages. Like the diseases in the second chapter, like the menstruation in the third, and the heat of the outside in the fourth and fifth, *Ṣọ̀npọ̀nnọ́* must make his presence felt if the world is to survive.

His evil is precisely similar to that of *Ifá*. Much of *Ifá* practice consists in the revelation of truths and in death. But this revelation, however unpleasant, is completely necessary to the health of the individual and the town. The benefits from both *Ifá* and from *Ṣọnpọnnọ* are due to the fact that both gods are normally hidden.

Ṣọnpọnnọ, with his defoliated palm-fronds, his red and white symbolic colouring, his hot earth, his smallpox and his madness, is so unambiguously revealing that he must be excluded from the town. *Ifá*'s ambiguity, balancing black with red and white, three with sixteen, left with right, means that his occasional revelations are controlled by a generalized blanket of secrecy. For *Ifá* and *Ṣọnpọnnọ*, as for menstruation and the disease, concealment is important, but the good health and prosperity of individuals and social groups does not reside entirely in secrecy. In most situations concealment of hidden truths and hidden bodily substances is imperative, but it is only by maintaining a correct balance between revelation and secrecy that good can be achieved.

(d) The paradigm

This chapter has brought together a number of images which need to be restated and integrated in the overall pattern of the paradigm. The first pattern which is here of interest concerns the myth of *Ọbàtálá* and *Ṣọnpọnnọ* (see above pp. 104 ff.). This, together with a variant, was expressed diagrammatically in Figure 22 which with slight alterations may be reproduced as Figure 31.

Ọbàtálá	*Ṣọnpọnnọ*
culture	anti-culture
safe in town	dangerous in town
sheltered places, shrines, palaces, towns	open places
dancing	lameness
health	illness

FIGURE 31. *Ṣọnpọnnọ* and *Ọbàtálá*

Next to be discussed were the images of the two palm-trees, the familiar oil-palm and the rather mysterious palm-tree of *Ifá*, and also the use of palm-nuts in divination. The results of these discussions may be expressed in Figures 32 and 33.

Oil-palm	Palm-tree of *Ifá*
1 'head'	2–16 'heads'
3 'eyed' nut	4–16 'eyed' nut
container	contents

FIGURE 32. The two palm-trees

three	seven and nine (16)
black	red and white
left	right
hidden	revealed
unity	diversity

FIGURE 33. Right, left, and numbers

Ifá was further considered in contrast to *Ṣọnpọnnọ*. It was found that *Ṣọnpọnnọ* was distressingly unambiguous in his dangerous habits, while *Ifá* contained a central ambiguity. Since *Ṣọnpọnnọ*'s attributes may be regarded as merely a facet of *Ifá*'s ambiguous nature, it will suffice here merely to express the ambiguity in *Ifá*.

black	red and white
secrecy	revelation
life	death
health	illness
order	disorder

FIGURE 34. Ambiguity in *Ifá*

By placing these different structures together it becomes quite clear that they may indeed be regarded as different aspects of the same unified paradigm. Their essential features may readily be integrated into Images 1 and 2 in the manner of Figure 35.

The chapter may be concluded by returning to the image of the cooking-pot and the hearth, which was given to me in the

life	death
fertility	infertility
health	illness
order and peace	disorder
medicine	food
unpleasant flavours	pleasant flavours
moderation in sexual behavior	excess in sexual behaviour
moderation in eating	overindulgence in eating
1, 3	4, 16, 41, 201, etc.
unity	diversity
hidden	revealed
container	contents
containment	overflowing
cultivated	uncultivated
palm-tree	palm-tree of *Ifá*
sheltered places, shrines, palace, houses	open spaces
dancing	inability to dance
culture	anti-culture
heat of inside	heat of outside
cool	hot
black	red and white

FIGURE 35. Statement of paradigm

form of the proverb: *àdrò mẹ́ta kìí dọbẹ̀ẹnu* (the three stones of the hearth do not spill the soup). When I was told this proverb it was in an atmosphere of the utmost secrecy as though I was being told the deepest truth of Yoruba esoteric knowledge. I now believe that this was indeed the case.

Standing on its three stones, the cooking-pot containing soup is an image of totality. All of its elements are necessary, the pot itself, the three stones, the contents of the pot and the fire outside. But each of these elements must be present in moderation. If the heat from outside, for example, becomes too excessive, the soup will overflow. In this, the image of the hearth reflects that of the human body.

Diseases, if subjected to too much heat from outside, will overflow their bags and will cause illness. Similarly, when the earth is subjected to too much heat or, which amounts to the same thing, when the 'hot' god *Ṣònpònnó* emerges from the forest, the redness beneath the surface of the earth or the skin will also overflow the black covering, where it will mingle with whiteness on the surface.

If the pot is given too much food, it will overflow. So also will the bags of disease if they are given too much food. Semen, it seems, is similar to food, for the diseases feed upon semen. Dirt may be allowed to settle at the bottom of a pot of water by means of the use of the bitter mineral alum. In the same way, bitter medicine will drive the diseases in the body downwards so that they cease to cause injury, and so that they may be removed and thrown into the forest.

The three stones of the hearth together with the black cooking-pot are the secret, the container which permits birth, health, order, and peace to exist in the world in the corporate groups of the town and in the body of the individual.

In cooking, in the body, and in social relations, the first imperative is concealment. But in no area of life is it sufficient merely to seal the pot closed. A pot that has no opening will not serve as a pot, and this is as true in cooking as in other aspects of human life. Despite all the dangers it is necessary to reveal that which is hidden. Menstruation must overflow; diseases must do their work; the dry season must come; there must even be death.

In the simple image of a cooking-pot supported by three stones, we have a symbol for a whole (and very complex) world. It is an image of the world in microcosm. Its articulation may be seen in all of the complicated discussion of illness and medicine which has preceded this chapter, and in all the spectacular diversity which characterizes Yoruba culture. When I was told this proverb, my informant said that this was the secret I was looking for. He said no less than the truth.

This chapter has examined a wide range of images with a brief look at three religious cults, Ṣọ̀npọ̀nnọ́, Ifá, and Ogbóni. Many of the images which have been explored here are 'symbolic' images, in that they are intended to point beyond themselves, evoking other images which are not directly expressed. It will be seen that these symbolic images, the myths of the different gods, the different palm-trees, and the proverb of the cooking-pot participate in a structure which is homologous to structures found in the encyclopaedic knowledge which herbalists have of illness and medicine. Firm conclusions about the relationship between Yoruba symbolism and more general Yoruba encyclopaedic knowledge may not be drawn until another major aspect of Yoruba medicine has been explored. This is the medicinal incantation, and it will be the concern of the next chapter.

Endnotes

[1] Barber (1981, 732) quotes '*Orúkọ mẹ́tadínlógún ni òrìṣà Ṣọnpọnnọ́ pín sí*' (the *òrìṣà Ṣọnpọnnọ́* divides into seventeen names). She further suggests that in the town of Okulin, names refer to different facets of the god's personality. Different devotees find their different needs satisfied by relating to one of these aspects.

[2] *Ṣọ̀ngó*, the god of lightning and thunderbolts, is a dangerous god akin in many respects to *Ṣọ̀npọ̀nnọ́. Ọba kò so*, 'the king (who) did not hang' is a name given to *Ṣọ̀ngó. Ṣọ̀ngó* is not the direct concern of this volume since he has little to do with sickness. Adebawọ merely makes the point that just as anyone with direct experience of *Ṣọ̀ngó* will take care not to annoy him, so also one should treat *Ṣọ̀npọ̀nnọ́* with respect.

[3] *Akàrà* is a rather heavy doughnut made from ground beans and pepper cooked and sold in the market, a great comfort to the hungry anthropologist.

[4] One implication of this might be that the seven tassels on the *làbà Ṣọ̀ngó* (the bag used by priest of *Ṣọ̀ngó* as a resting-place for newly flung thunderbolts) implies that this bag is feminine—an interpretation which fits more closely Morton Williams's and Westcott's general thesis (1962) that the male thunderbolt when removed from the female earth and cooled in palm-oil, should be returned to the female bag for safe keeping. This theory replaces the idea that the seven tassels represent the union of threeness and fourness which they here identify with mystery and completeness. I venture to say, that such a union would be inappropriate in a bag intended to hide a hot thunderbolt, but in the absence of clear statements by informants, which they say (p. 23) were not forthcoming, their guess is, presumably, as good as mine.

[5] These *ọmọ Olódùmarè* may be *òrìṣà* (gods) or simply men. The story suggests the latter, but whichever is intended, the meaning of the whole text is not significantly altered.

[6] *Ọdún* is an annual festival; *Agbọ́nnìrè*, or more commonly *Agbọ́nmìrègún*, is a name given to *Ifá*.

[7] Perhaps as well as Babel, a fruitful comparison is with Pentecost. *Ṣọ̀npọ̀nnọ́* who manifests in the form of a wind is, in Fatoogun's story, crowned with 200 flames. He also causes *Ọrúnmìlà* to speak 200 languages. Unlike the events at Pentecost, which are good, the events of this story are bad. Nevertheless, it will be recalled that St Paul warns the church at Corinth that speaking with tongues should be used sparingly, for it can sound to unbelievers very much like madness (1 Cor. 14: 23). It is an odd coincidence that the liturgical colours used in the Catholic church to commemorate Pentecost should be red and white.

7

Hidden knowledge and rationality: the work of incantation

It has been made clear that a central concern of Yoruba thought is secret knowledge and its revelation. *Ifá* with its countless verses is the embodiment of Yoruba esoteric knowledge as indeed is *Ogbóni* and, in their different ways, the *òrìṣà* cults. In this chapter, the nature of secret knowledge and of revelation will be discussed further in the context of medicinal incantation.

It is important to note that medicines which have an incantation or which contain a ritual do not differ radically from those which do not. The use of incantation does not, for example, carry with it the connotation of non-rationality (as against rationality) that it might carry in the West. Nor is a Yoruba medicinal incantation to be contrasted with herbal medicine in the same manner as faith healing is in Europe contrasted with 'scientific' medicine (Ardener 1973, makes a similar point).

Anyone who practises medicine within the Yoruba tradition is likely to know both medicines with and medicines without incantations. Of both types he will argue that God has given to the ingredients the power to cure an ailment or to assist a client in some other manner. Though the overwhelming majority of medicines to cure illnesses do not contain incantations, there are nevertheless some which do. I have, for example, collected a medicine to cure headache which uses an incantation, even though headaches are caused by germs (below p. 157). And in Appendix C for example there are a number of medicines which include ritual practices used to cure illnesses. Similarly, while incantation may be used in medicines which are directed against 'supernatural' agencies or to counteract sorcery, others have nothing to do with the supernatural.

There is a Yoruba concept, *idón*, which may be translated as 'magic' or 'conjuring'. The magician (*onídón*) may indeed use medicines (*oògùn*) in the performance of his tricks. Magicians are able to render themselves impervious to shotgun pellets or to the cuts of knives, and they may even turn themselves into animals. Such feats form a part of certain cults—*Ṣọ̀ngó* worshippers are frequently magicians as also are some members of *Egúngún* cults—but in essence magicians are entertainers and they are most frequently to be seen performing in the market places. Though they sometimes use medicines which have serious application—the medicine supposedly used by magicians to protect themselves against gunshot wounds is used by soldiers and was certainly employed by the Ibadan tax rioters[1] in 1969—it is the role of the magician as entertainer which distinguishes him from the more serious practitioner of medicine. Nevertheless the magician's knowledge of the more obscure and dangerous medicines, combined with the fact that magicians tend to be wild and unruly people, leads them to be feared and mistrusted.

(a) Curses, prayers, and speaking the truth

It is useful to draw a comparison between the medicinal incantation (*ọfọ̀*) and the curse (*èpè*) or prayer (*àpè*), for, like incantations, curses and prayers are the means whereby hidden truth is revealed. By examining the nature of curses, more light will be shed upon the role of revelation in Yoruba practices.

Needham (1972) has warned against misinterpreting the concepts of other cultures, and his warning is of particular relevance when discussing Yoruba concepts of truth (*òótọ́*). The speaking of truth by means of an incantation is not merely the pronouncement of a neutral statement of fact. Particularly when the truth which is spoken concerns the future, the act of speaking is understood to have a positive impact upon the events of the world (Adeniran 1969).

Cursing may be understood to be a special manner of speaking the truth. Certain people, those who are about to die, old men and also, for reasons which I could not fathom, people whose first top teeth had grown before their bottom teeth are believed to have the power to curse. There are also medicines which allow the individuals who use them to influence events simply by stating what is going to happen.

I had been told that the god Ṣọ̀ngó was reputed to prefer the bitter cola-nut (orógbó) to the more common, segmented, cola-nut (obì). But I had also heard that bitter cola was used in cursing. So I asked Fatoogun about the connection. He replied:

FATOOGUN. Bitter cola (orógbó) is eaten as a trustworthy fruit. You cannot split it into two like ordinary cola (obì) for it is in one piece. Its power comes mainly from the root. If you chew the root of bitter cola for three years and then curse somebody, whatever you say will occur. It will affect the person. This is why Ṣọ̀ngó likes bitter cola, he hates dishonesty.

This brief exposition adds another dimension to the discussion in Chapter 6. Obì (cola) is used in simple divination procedures. The split segments (usually, in my experience four) are thrown and the different configurations are interpreted as positive or negative answers to a question. Orógbó (bitter cola) cannot be so used because it cannot be split. Perhaps the meaning of these remarks by Fatoogun is that obì reveals only the partial truth in a controlled manner in divination, whereas orógbó, being unified, reveals the whole truth in an uncontrolled way. I have an uneasy feeling that much more information is required before the full significance of orógbó can be elucidated.

Ṣọ̀ngó may hate liars, and he may therefore like to be offered orógbó, but there are far too many dishonest (indeed lying) practices in the Ṣọ̀ngó cult to allow the matter to rest there. My personal opinion, which is no more than a hunch, is that the secret of the Ṣọ̀ngó cult is that *the truth is a lie*. This hypothesis explains why Ṣọ̀ngó does not like those who lie—for liars are people who reveal his secret. But that is only my guess.

For the moment, it is sufficient that Fatoogun has clearly identified the ability to curse with the ability to state what will happen in the future. And he relates this ability to speak the truth to concepts of honesty and dishonesty. The ability to speak the truth in this manner was regarded by my informants as inherently dangerous. Though it might be used for beneficial purposes, a person who has such a power may use it inadvertently and cause great misfortune.

Adebawọ told me that a dying man was liable to become cantankerous. Because such a man fell into one of the categories of people who are able to speak the truth, it was by no means unknown for physical force to be used to prevent him speaking.

It seems too that in the past, people about to be sacrificed could get their own back on their killers by cursing them. This was found to be a major inconvenience at public ceremonies. Frequently, therefore, when human sacrifice took place, rituals were performed to prevent the victim's curses being efficacious (Awolalu 1973, 88).

Adebawǫ had a medicine for curses which he kept on a shelf in the room where we usually met to hold our conversations. He is an Ijębu and once told me in his mischievous manner, 'everyone knows that the Ijębu are the owners of curses'. In fact Adebawǫ was a very good-natured man who would be very unlikely to use such a medicine for evil purposes, but he was enough of a showman to be happy to cultivate the notion that he had at his disposal a wide range of spectacular powers.. He did not discuss his own medicine for curses with me because, since it was capable of being used for evil, he did not wish to disseminate information on the subject. He began his account of cursing by discussing some masquerade cults.

ADEBAWǪ. In my town, Ode Ogbolu, we have several important masquerades (egúngún), ękùn, masǫn, moji, agęmo. Anyone who does not possess curse (èpè) must not be a member of their societies for they usually curse each other even though it does not affect them because they know how to avoid it. Olúgbohùn (a type of curse) is owned by the òʂùgbo (ògbóni). This olúgbohùn must not be brought inside the house because, when it is there, anything they say in the house will actually occur. There are other kinds of curse (èpè) that resemble olúgbohùn and no wise man will live in the same house with it. I remember two women who quarrelled in the house of a man who owned medicine for curses (oògùn èpè). One who was pregnant accused the other of spoiling her property. The other said that her own property would be spoiled. The pregnant woman miscarried twins. A medicine for curses (èpè) must be kept away from the house because it is like a sword which does not know or respect the person who made it. The type of èpè that is called olúgbohùn is always kept in the sacred grove of òrò (a cult) or in the part of the forest where egúngún (the masquerade) appears or in the ògbóni lodge . . . We do this because the èpè must not hear bad things.

What emerges from these remarks is that the ability to curse is also the ability to tell the truth. It is in this respect a precisely similar activity to the chanting of an *Ifá* verse, or the recitation of any number of other religious formulas attached to the lesser cults. But, and here is to found a parallel with some of the ideas discussed in the context of *Ṣọ̀npọ̀nnọ́*, because cursing is a form of truth-telling which may become uncontrolled, it is inherently dangerous.

In general, *èpè*, cursing, is considered to be 'bad'. Beneficial forms of cursing, using an inherently similar procedure, are usually known as *àpè* which I have translated as 'prayer'. *Apè* is used, I have been told, to stop the flowing of blood after, for example, an accident. It is also used to 'beg' snakes to withdraw their poison after a snake bite.

(b) Medicinal incantation (ọfọ̀)

Medicinal incantations are, in principle, a part of the *Ifá* corpus, and as such they fit into the pattern which was established in the last chapter. They are similar to the curse or the prayer in that they are a means whereby hidden knowledge may be revealed. The hidden knowledge contained in a medicinal incantation is of a particular type for it reveals the power of the ingredients used in a specific medicine. As in the curse, the medicinal incantation is both a statement of facts about the powers of these ingredients and an invocation of these powers. In the medicines for illnesses which have so far been considered, ritual and incantation are absent. The reason for this is simply that in these medicines the powers of the ingredients are obvious. An ordinary Yoruba farmer is able to walk through the forest reading the plants and trees as a student might read a book.[2] Each leaf and plant has immediately perceptible properties which indicate whether it is useful in medicine. By smelling, tasting, or simply looking at a leaf, most Yoruba people can tell that it has a number of powers that do or do not make it a suitable ingredient for certain medicines. Where such properties are perceptible in nature, there is no need to express them in ritual or incantation.

When I say, however, that a leaf or a root reveals its properties naturally, it is only, of course, in the context of Yoruba paradigms of encyclopaedic knowledge that these properties are revealed. To someone who does not share these paradigms, the trees and plants are dumb. If a herbalist tells a fellow herbalist or even a farmer that he uses, let us say, spring onions in his medicine for headache, the listener will understand why the other might think such an ingredient to be appropriate. To someone who does not share the Yoruba paradigm, the reasoning will remain obscure. It is only where the power of an ingredient is not revealed in this manner that incantation becomes necessary.

Incantation belongs to the technology and not to the sociology of medicine. It is not a communication between doctor and patient. Lévi-Strauss in a celebrated article (1949) argues that, among the Cuna Indians of Central America, medicinal incantation is a psychological device for the benefit of the patient. In the case he examines, a pregnant woman is able to overcome the difficulties of her labour by identifying herself with the travail of a folk-hero as his story is recounted. There are occasions when a similar process is at work in Yoruba medicine. Prince tells of cures for madness in which there are extensive ritual actions sometimes involving *rites de passage*. Here a change in the patient's life is effected by his participation in the ritual, joining in the incantations, singing songs etc. (Prince 1964, 98 ff.). And there are in my own collection a number of medicines which may be interpreted in such terms (e.g. pp. 240–1). These cases however are rare and occasional. Tambiah argues (1968, 202) that 'all ritual, whatever the idiom, is addressed to the human participants and uses a technique which attempts to restructure and integrate the minds and emotions of the actors'. With only occasional exceptions, to argue this in the case of Yoruba medicinal incantations is to stretch his point until it breaks. The tendency to see all folk medicine as psychotherapy (e.g. Kennedy 1967) is one that should be resisted.

The typical Yoruba medicinal incantation is not addressed to the patient; it is addressed either to the medicine, or to the dust on the divining board which may then be added to the medicine. There are occasions where the patient must himself make the incantation, perhaps alone at a crossroad, or at a river, but except in cases such as these, which are unusual, the patient need not even be present when the incantation is spoken. I have witnessed several occasions where the patient has been present while an incantation has been spoken. Here, the herbalist holds the bowl or divining board, next to his mouth, and, in a deliberately low voice, he mutters the incan-

tation into it. Whatever psychological benefit the patient
receives from this procedure can be gained only by his having
been impressed by the herbalist's knowledge. He cannot benefit psychologically from the content of the incantation because
it is virtually inaudible.

A distinction was made earlier between medicines considered at the level of the ingredients and medicines considered
as complete wholes. It is here that this distinction becomes
vital. The powers of the ingredients when used in simple
medicines are, in nature, revealed for anyone with eyes, taste
buds and the encyclopaedic knowledge provided by a Yoruba
upbringing, to see. But when they are combined in medicine,
their separate identities are submerged. The methods of
preparation, the pounding of ingredients in *agúnmu*, *àsèjẹ* and
ọṣẹ, their burning to make *ẹtù*, or the extraction of the fluid in
àgbo, all render the ingredients unrecognizable. Even in the
simplest Yoruba medicine, there is, therefore, a transformation: that which is perceptible, naturally, in the separate
ingredients has become hidden in the completed medicine.

When the powers of the ingredients are not apparent in
nature, the herbalist himself must reveal their hidden power.
This he does usually by chanting an incantation. The incantation will list the different ingredients, and explain how they
all, *when combined together*, will do the task required. Herbalists
may sometimes extract a line or two from an incantation to
explain the powers of a particular plant, but the incantation
properly belongs to the complete medicine.

Here again, there is the same combined cleavage between
that which is revealed and that which is hidden. The powers of
the ingredients are revealed in the incantation, but they are
nevertheless concealed. They are hidden in two ways. First, as
in the simple medicines they are hidden in the construction of
the medicine. But second, they are hidden in the incantation
itself. Incantations are part of the *Ifá* corpus, and are therefore
the esoteric knowledge of herbalists and *balaláwo*. Existing on
the level of the completed medicine, the revelation of the
powers of the ingredients by incantation is, paradoxically, a
hidden revelation.

(c) Some implications of the secrecy of medicine

The distinctions between that which is hidden and that which is revealed casts light upon two important aspects of Yoruba medicinal technology.

First of all, it explains why medicines are taken using the left hand, and not, as with food, with the right. The left hand, it has been argued, is the hand of secrecy, and is therefore appropriate for the consumption of the secret medicine. The use of the right hand to eat food once more evokes the contrast drawn between medicine and food.

Medicine	Food	
Inside	Outside	p. 83
Left	Right	
Hidden	Revealed	p. 121

FIGURE 36. Food and medicine

Second, it provides an explanation of the sexual division of labour in medicine. What requires explanation is the fact that though women dominate in the sale of ingredients for medicines, and though they often know a lot about medicines, they do not usually practise medicine in any systematic way until they reach middle age.

In at least three of the Ibadan markets, Dugbẹ, Ọba, and Ibo.de, there are large sections devoted to the sale of medicinal ingredients in which few men take part. Such women are often willing to diagnose illness, and to tell clients how to prepare medicines, but they do not sell completed medicines. Only a very few women, after they reach the menopause, will prepare and sell any but the simplest medicines. The reason given for this is that menstruation can destroy the power of medicines.

Menstruation, it has been shown, is one of the images of a dangerous form of revelation. It corresponds, roughly, to the overflowing of hot palm-oil from the cooking-pot (p. 123). If it is correct to assume that secrecy is of the essence of completed medicines, then it would follow that medicines, in their combined and hidden state, should be shielded from the revelation which the flow of menstruation implies.

Women do in fact practise medicine in a small way while

they are still of childbearing age, but since many medicines take several weeks to prepare, and since it is often necessary for the professional herbalist to store away a considerable number of medicines so that they may be available on demand, it is impractical for young women to become serious herbalists. While they are menstruating, women must stay away from the room where medicines are stored. They may prepare a few medicines for the treatment of their children's minor ailments, but these must be stored away from their own sleeping quarters. Should a young woman wish to make large quantities of medicines, which would be necessary for her to be taken seriously as a herbalist, she would have to greatly inconvenience the male members of her compound, by keeping her medicines in their living quarters.

This does not, however, prevent her from collecting and selling the ingredients for medicine. It has been argued that the powers of ingredients take two forms. Either they are clearly visible in the natural object itself, in which case, they have no secrecy to be endangered by the revelation of menstruation, or they are hidden in nature, in which case they can be revealed only by incantation in the completed medicine. The rule that menstruating women should be kept away from completed medicines was often closely related in conversation to a rule that sexual intercourse should not be performed in a room where medicines are stored. Here too, the sex act would destroy the power of the medicines. In the final chapter it will be confirmed that the sex act too is regarded as a dangerous form of revelation.

(d) The revelation of the hidden powers of medicines by incantation

In order to illustrate the manner in which the powers of ingredients are revealed by means of incantation, some medicines will be examined whose function is to provide the user with 'good luck'. Although there are some quite complicated ideas associated with these medicines (*oògùn àwúre*), these fortunately need not intrude into our discussion here. *Awúre* itself is discussed in Appendix F. The medicines are intended to provide the client with money, popularity, sexual and marital success, and social standing.

The first medicine to be discussed here will apparently contradict the central point of this chapter, that incantation reveals ingredients' hidden powers. These medicines are ones in which the incantation reveals qualities of medicinal ingredients which are in fact visible in nature. This paradox, however, lacks substance for it will be seen that in each recipe, the role of the incantation is to show how the visible or known qualities of ingredients are useful in relation to a specific problem. What is important to note, however, is that in every case, when showing that the properties of the ingredients are indeed relevant, the reasoning employed is tortuous and far-fetched. This is by no means accidental. If the medicinal solution to the client's problem were at all obvious within the paradigms of Yoruba encyclopaedic knowledge, then no exposition of the ingredients' powers through incantation would be necessary. Incantation is here used precisely because the paradigm has failed to provide the answer.

The following medicine, like many medicinal incantations, contains an allusion to the fact that it has an origin in a more substantial story from the *Ifá* corpus. The different ingredients in this medicine are all well known: the *agbe* bird is blue-black, the colour of indigo; the similar *àlùkò* is well known to be red, the colour of camwood; vultures and ground hornbills eat carrion and they therefore frequent places where sacrifices are made. The blacksmith's poker too is in constant contact with other pieces of metal.

What the incantation suggests is that all of these readily perceptible properties on the different ingredients are signs of their success. Presumably, the different ingredients are supposed to have made the prescribed sacrifice of a pigeon. Thus they have been successful in their various enterprises. Thus too will the client be successful when he has made the same sacrifice and licked the powder made from the ingredients.

Oògùn àwúre (ètù)	Adebawọ
orí igún	head of vulture
orí àkàlà	head of ground-hornbill
orí agbe	head of blue turaco
orí àlùkò	head of red-coloured bird
ìwọ̀nó àgbẹ̀dẹ	poker used in forge

Prepare as *ètù* and sacrifice pigeon (*ẹyẹlé*) to it. The *ètù* should be licked.

Incantation

> *Agbe awo abólúpé*
> *Alùkò òsà awo abóròjí*
> *Dá fágbe*
> *O lọ síbi ìdáró*
> *A díá fá.lùkò*
> *O ńlọ sí mùkosùn*
> *Irọn igún ni ńjẹbọ*
> *Irọn àkàlà ni ńjòkú*
> *Iwọnó àgbẹ̀dẹ kìí wá tiẹ̀*
> *Owó olífẹ, e gbàá.mi wá*
> *Ojúmọ́ kìí mọ́ kí tùrú má.fà*
> *Ẹ mówó tèmi wá fún mi ló.ní òo.*

> *Agbe* the diviner of *abólúpé*
> *Alùkò* of the lagoon, the diviner of riches
> He cast *Ifá* for *agbe*
> He (i.e. *agbe*) went to the place where they prepare indigo
> We cast *Ifá* for *àlùkò*
> He was going to where they paint camwood
> It is the generation of vultures, which eats the sacrifice
> It is the generation of *àkàlà* which eats the corpse
> The poker of the forge is not in need of his own
> The money of the owner of Ifẹ, get it for me
> Day will not break when *tùrú tùrú* will not crawl
> Bring my own money for me today

The next two medicines contain incantations which indicate how naturally occurring features of the ingredients indicate their power to bring good luck.

Oògùn àwúre (agúnmu)   Adebawọ
orí mòrìwò ọpẹ – 7   tips from seven young palm-fronds
ẹyẹlé funfun – 2   two white pigeons

Remove all the feathers and pound the feathers with the palm-frond. This (the frond) should be cut about six inches from the end and the rest of the frond should be pounded with soap. Its power is in the incantation.[3]

Incantation

> *Ifá má. jẹ́ kí owó tuntun tón lọ́wọ́ọ̀mi*
> *Mòrìwò tuntun kìí tón lọ́rùn ọpẹ*
> *Apá ọ̀tún apá òsì lẹyẹlé fíí koreé wọlé*

> *Ifá*, do not let new money finish in my hand.
> Young palm-frond does not finish at the neck of the palm tree.

It is the right and left wing that the pigeon uses to carry good things to the house.

The legs and the head of the pigeon will be also pounded with soap. If it is used for a man, nine palm fronds are cut.[4] *Iyèròsùn* (divining dust) is marked before saying the incantation.

Oògùn Awùre (for money) *(àsèjẹ)*   Awotunde
Ewé olójòngbòdú   leaf of *commelina vogelii*

Cook with *ẹja àrò* (mudfish) for the person to eat.

Incantation

> *Kówó ó. má. tọ́n lọ́wọ́ lágbájá.òo*
> *Omi kìí nínú olójòngbòdú*
> *Kówó ó. má. tọ́n lọ́wọ́ lágbájá*
> *Kire gbogbo ó. má. tọ́n lọ́wọ̀ọmi*
> *Omi kìí tọ́n nínú olójòngbòdú.*

> May money not finish in the hand of so-and-so
> Water does not finish inside *olójòngbòdú*.
> May money not finish in my hand
> Water does not finish inside *olójòngbòdú*.

The idiom used in these two verses '*owó tọ́n lọ́wọ̀ọmi*' is difficult to render accurately in English. Roughly they infer that just as the palm-frond can be seen to extend beyond the trunk of the tree, and just as water can be found beyond the limits of the juicy plant *olójòngbòdú*, so money will be found for the person, beyond the limits of what is already in his hand. But the idea is put more succinctly in Yoruba.

In each of these three medicines the incantation indicates why the ingredients have the power to solve a specific human problem—lack of success. The properties revealed in the incantations may be directly perceived in the ingredients themselves, but only when they have been given an unusual definition in the verses.

Although there are many incantations similar to the one given above, in most incantations, the attempt to relate human problems to directly observable features of objects is abandoned altogether. For it is of the essence of medicinal incantation that the power revealed by the verse is one that is hidden from human gaze.

When the power of an ingredient is not known through direct observation, a herbalist may reply to the question 'What is the power of so-and-so, in such and such a medicine?' in a number of ways. One typical answer is '*Lá.tọlọ́.run lágbáraarẹ̀ ti wá*' (Its power has come from God). This conversation-stopping remark I came to recognize as meaning one of two things: either, 'I do not know the answer to your question', or 'You are asking too many questions and I am not prepared to answer you in depth.' Similar in form, but with much greater content, is the answer, '*Agbáraarẹ̀ wá lá.ti orúkọọrẹ̀*' (Its power comes from its name). This type of answer refers to an important feature of Yoruba medicine, that the name of an ingredient can express its medicinal power which would otherwise remain hidden.

Nearly all Yoruba names, whether of people, gods, plants, animals, or towns, are in certain contexts believed to be derived from other Yoruba words, and Yoruba people take frequent delight in making explicit the derivation of the name, so as to discover the hidden essence of the named object. The long debate over the derivation of the term *Olódùmarè* (God) is an academic version of this typically Yoruba indulgence (Awolalu 1979; Bamgboṣe 1972; Idowu 1962, 32; Lucas 1948, 41; Oduyoye 1971, Chapter 4). Most of the names given to people are chosen to reflect some circumstance of their birth. A reincarnated grandfather is called *Babátúndé* (father has returned) or *Akíntúndé* (the brave man has returned) or some similar name to indicate the fact. Those born into the *Ifá* cult tend to have names like *Fálọlá* (*Ifá* has honour) or *Awókòyá* (the *babaláwo* fought bravely). There is a large number of similarly derived names to fit different circumstances.

The names of ingredients in medicine are also derived from other Yoruba words, but here there are considerable difficulties. Even apart from proper names, it is a common practice in ordinary Yoruba speech to link words together to make compounds, in such a way that a part of one or more of the constituent words is omitted or assimilated. In ordinary conversation this assimilation presents few difficulties. The phrase '*ó takùn*' can, in principle, mean 'he sold the rope' (*tà* + *okùn*) or 'he stretched the rope' (*ta* + *okùn*) or 'he sold the leopard' (*ta* + *ẹkùn*), but this ambiguity can usually be overcome by examining the wider context, or, if this does not help, the speaker may avoid the construction altogether. The same is true of the considerable number of homonyms which are to be found. The syllable '*pa*' for example has some half-dozen quite distinct meanings, but it is only occasionally, as with homonyms in the English language, that they are confused.

If in ordinary conversation, the Yoruba language can be as unambiguous and clear as any other, there is in these features a rich seam of ambiguity which can be exploited by ingenious minds. Journalists are said to avoid political censorship and libel suits by a deliberate use of ambiguous phraseology, though their task is further assisted by the omission of tones in their orthography. For example, without tone-marks the phrase '*ọta ni*' can mean, 'he is an enemy' (*ọtá ni*), or 'he is a good marksman' (*ọ̀ta ni*).

In medicinal incantation where the power of an ingredient is generally assumed to be identical with the supposed derivation of the name, there is considerable room for manipulation. In many medicines, folk derivations of the names of ingredients follow normal Yoruba language rules of assimilation. The first of the medicines in this section are like this:

Oògùn Awúre (*ọṣẹ*)	Awotunde
Awọ ẹtà	skin of civet cat
ọṣẹ	soap

Awo ẹtà is used in medicine for a trader so that he can be selling quickly. It will be pounded with soap and the person will be using the soap to wash his head.

Incantation

> *Ki ńtà lé.ní òo*
> *Ẹtà ni ńkọ́ tà kọmọ ẹrọnko ó.tótà*
> *Ẹtà kìí gbégbáarẹ̀ dọ́jà àìmá.tà*
>
> Let me sell today oh!
> It is civet cat that first sells before the children of other animals sell.
> Civet cat does not carry his calabash to the market
> without selling.

Here it is assumed that the name *ẹtà* (civet cat) is derived from the term *tà* (sold) so that it means 'that which sold'. This follows a regular linguistic rule in Yoruba by which a noun is derived from a verb by the addition of a vowel prefix.

Oògun Awúre (*ẹtù*)	Awotunde
orí awó (= *ẹtù*)	head of guinea-fowl

If a person has no cloth, the head of a guinea-fowl will be burned and put into a small gourd (*àdó*). (This type of gourd is approximately two inches long and useful for preserving very small quantities of medicine.) The person will put the gourd into his box and will be able to buy many clothes. If he has no money, it can also be burned for the person to be licking.

Incantation

    Ẹtù ló ní kára ó. tù mi
    Morówó morówó lẹ́tù ńké.

It is the guinea-fowl that says my body should be comforted (lit. the body should comfort me)
'I see money, I see money', is what guinea fowl cries.

Here not only the name of *ẹtù* is shown to be derived from *tù* (comforted) but its cry *morówó, morówó* is implicitly shown to be a contraction of *mo rí owó*—I see money.

Sometimes it is made possible to reveal the hidden powers of ingredients in an incantation by means of synonyms. In the following medicine, for example, the use of a familiar synonym provides an opportunity for word-play in a medicine for money.

Oògùn Awúre (àsèjẹ)   Adebawọ

Eyin adìẹ 6.	six chicken's eggs
ewé ìrọnjé	a leaf
ewé ajé (= *àyọ̀n*)	leaf of African Satinwood
ewé ẹyinbísowó (= *abísowó*)	leaf of *Ampelocissus Salmonea*
Cook in *àsèjẹ*.	

Incantation

    Tí wọ́n bá pìtọn títí wọn áaní ìrọnọ̀nminìrọn ajé
    Ifá wá ṣe mí bí ará ìrọnọ̀mi kí ñlájé lówó
    Ẹyinbísowó kìí fẹ́ towó kù ní.gbà.kọn
    Gbogbo ara ni ṣẹbuṣẹbu fi ńsajé

If they tell a story they will soon say my generation is a generation of money
Ifá, come and help my family so I may have money in my hand
Ẹyinbísowó will not at any time search for money and fail
It is all of its body that *ṣẹbuṣẹbu* uses as money.

The African Satinwood tree is normally known by the term *àyọ̀n*, but it is also called *ajé*, a homonym for a word meaning 'money'. Indeed so obvious is this relationship that it does not even feature in the incantation. *Irọnjé* can be analysed as *ìron* + *ajé*, 'a generation of money', and the last two syllables of *ęyinbísowó* are shown here in a punning relationship with *owó*, 'money'.

The use of synonyms—even of obscure ones—should be distinguished from the use of names which are only to be found in incantation. In the following medicine dog is given the name *wágbà wágbà*—come and get, come and get. This name is by no means in general use. The revelation of its name gives the person who reveals it power over the dog. A similar use of hidden names is sometimes to be found in the medicines for snake-bite.

ADEBAWǪ. We use the head of a dog in a sort of medicine in which we go to those who are dyeing cloth and collect some indigo water.

Oògùn Awúre (ọṣę)		Adebawǫ
Omi aró	water from indigo dye	
tábà	tobacco	
orí ajá	head of dog	

If the tobacco has already been ground up mark it with *odù Ifá* in the doorway of the house. This is to be used as a (medicinal) soap.

Incantation
> *Bá mi pá, bá mi ré kìí tọ́n nílé aláró*
> *Nńsun, nńbe kìí tọ́n nílé aláṣáà*
> *Wágbà wágbà làape ajá*
> *Okùnrin, obìnrin kę́ę máa pèmí*

> Help me to dye, help me to soak does not stop at the dyer's house.
> I am sniffing, I am wanting does not stop at the tobacconist's house.
> It is Come-and-get-come-and-get that we call dog.
> Men and women may you be calling me.

This type of medicine is prepared for those who have no money to start trading. If the person is washing with the soap, someone will come who will sympathize with him and let him have some money to start his work.

The idea behind this medicine is that just as the dye can be obtained from the dyer, and just as the taking of, and desire for, snuff extends beyond the house of those directly concerned with its manufacture, so wealth may spread to the user of the medicine.

It is tempting, when hearing incantations, to draw the conclusion that the folk-derivations which they often contain are always considered to be the actual derivations of the terms.

This is however a temptation which should be resisted. Consider, for example, the following three medicines. Two are for àwúre (ifẹ́, 'love', being simply one form of good fortune in this instance) and the other is for headache. All of them use the herb akọ réré.

Oògùn ifẹ́ (medicine for love—ọṣẹ́)　　　　　　　　　　　Awotunde
akọ réré　　　　　　　　　　　　　Cassia toro
ọṣẹ́　　　　　　　　　　　　　　soap

It is used for a man who finds it difficult to find a woman who will marry him. Pound the ingredients together. Ifá (i.e. an odù mark) will be marked in ìyẹ̀ròsùn (dust in the divining tray).

Incantation

    i.   Akọ réré ló ni kobìnrin ó. ré mọ́ mi
        Iyẹ̀ròsùn má. jáya tèmi ó. sùnnọ̀
        Akọ réré òun ló ní káya rere ó. máa ré mọ́ mi
        Iyẹ̀ròsùn dákun má. mọ́ jẹ́ẹre té.mi ó. sùnnọ̀
    v.   Ejì ogbè wá rèé gbéere aya tèmi fún mi
        Iwọ ẹjì ogbè
        Ejì ẹjì ni mo mọ agbe
        Ifá wá gbéere aya tèmi fún mi
        Akọ réré òun ló ní kíre aya tèmi ó. máa ré mọ́ mi

    i.   It is akọ réré that says that women should jump across to me
        Divining dust, do not let my wife sleep in the road,
        It is akọ réré that says that a good wife should jump across to me,
        Divining dust, do not let my own good things sleep on the road,
    v.   Ejì ogbè (the first and major odù Ifá) go and bring my own wife to me.
        You, ẹjì ogbè
        It is in twos that I know agbe (the blue turaco)[5]
        Ifá come and bring the goodness of my wife to me,
        It is also akọ réré that says that the goodness of my wife will jump to me.

Oògun Awúre　　　　　　　　　　　　　　　　　Awotunde
Ewé réré　　　　　　　　　　　　Cassia toro
Ewé sìnkìnrínmíní　　　　　　　　unknown leaf
oyin ìgọ̀n　　　　　　　　　　　undiluted honey
epo　　　　　　　　　　　　　palm oil

Grind the leaves and put them in a container; add the honey and palm-oil. He will rub this on his body and people will like him.

Incantation

i.   *Réré o, ló.ni*
      Rere o máa ré mọ́ mi
      Ajé máa fà mọ́ mi ní.gbà.yí òo
      Ewé olúsìnkìnrínmínì, a fàì mọ́ni akóni mọ́ra

v.   *Ire gbogbo máa fà mọ́ mi ní.gbà.yí*
      Ifá, olúsìnkìnrínmínì a fàì mọ́ni akọ́ni mọ́ra
      Réré ló ní kíre ó. máa ré mọ́ mi
      Réré ló ni kíre ó máa ré mọ́ mi
      Oyin mi mi ò

x.   *Bọ́mọdé bá róyin ò*
      A sàkàrà nù
      Bí gbogbo ayé bá bá rí mi kí wọn ó. máa lè gbàgbe mi
      Bọ́mdé bá róyin o a sàkàrà nù.

i.   *Réré* oh! today,
      Goodness jump to me,
      Money will crawl to me now
      Leaf of *olúsìnkìnrìnmínì*, that does not know people that gathers people
      to its body

v.   All good things will crawl to me now
      Ifá, olúsìnkìnrínrínmínì, that does not know people that gathers people
      to its body
      It is *réré* that says good things should jump to me.
      It is *réré* that says all good things should jump to me
      I am honey oh!

x.   If a small child sees honey oh!
      He will throw away his bean-cake (*àkàrà*)
      If all the world sees me let them be unable to forget me
      If a small child sees honey, oh!, he will throw away his bean cake.

Oògun orí fífọ́ (medicine for headache)   Adebawọ
akọ réré   Cassia toro leguminosae
alùbọ́sà eléwé   Spring onion

Grind, and rub on the head.

Incantation

      Réré ni kó ré ohun tí ńfọ́ lágbájá ní orí.yí kúrò ńbẹ̀
      Alùbọ́sà kóo sa gbogbo kòkòrò nọ̀ọ̀ kúrò

      It is *réré* that pares off the thing that is breaking so-and-so in the head,
      Onion, may you cause all those insects to go.

In these three medicines, there is a great play made with the
name of the plant *réré*. In the first incantation there is *ré mọ́*

(jump across, lines, i, ii, and ix) *rété* (good, line iii) with its derivative *ire* (good things, lines iv, v, viii and x) and *rèé* (went to it, line v). In the second incantation, *ré mó*, *rété* and *ire* are also used (lines ii, v, viii and ix) but in a totally different context. And in the third, which is a medicine to kill the germs which cause headache, the innocuous leaf of *rété* is included because the incantation reveals that it has the power to 'pare off' (*ré*) the germs in the head.

It is possible that there is some linguistic connection between the names of the plant *rété* and one or more of the similarly sounding words which accompany it in these incantations. What is not possible, however, is that *rété* be related to all of them. My guess would rather be that none of these words, *ré mó*, *ré*, *ire*, *rere*, or *rè*, has any but the remotest connection with the name *rété*. Rather the diverse powers of this herb have been revealed by a series of puns.

This point is of some consequence for the translation and interpretation of Yoruba incantations. Above all, it is a virtual impossibility to translate a pun from one language to another, but as an added complication, many of the relationships between words which we might regard as punning seem to be regarded by Yoruba as the actual meaning of the word. Pierre Verger makes an awkward compromise in his otherwise useful collection of medicinal incantations (1967). He attempts, in the titles he gives to the verses, a direct translation of the names of the ingredients. For example, he gives as a translation of the name *obì* (cola-nut), the English word 'push'. This he derives from the incantation:

> *Má bi mi s'ọrun obì*
> *Bi mi s'aiye obì*
>
> Do not push me to heaven *obì*
> Do not push me to earth *obì* (pp. 54–5)

In this incantation, *obì* certainly seems to have been derived from the word *bì*, which means 'push'. But is Verger justified when he translates *obì ẹdun* (monkey cola) in the heading of his next incantation (p. 56) as 'Monkey Push'? His mistake in doing this is to regard the derivations which emerge from Yoruba incantations as though they were definitive, existing outside the immediate context of the incantation.

Yoruba names can operate at more then one level at a time. At their simplest they are like any other word in any other language, merely signs which refer to specific kinds of object. *Obì* is the name given to the nut which in English is called 'cola'. In most contexts this is the only meaning of the word *obì*. The incantation however takes the name and shows it to be a medium for the transmission of other information. It contains the knowledge that this nut, when used in medicine, has certain specific powers. By exploring the aetiology (whether plausible or spurious) of the names of the ingredients, the incantation is able to bring to light knowledge about the power of ingredients which would otherwise remain hidden. In ordinary conversation the sign has a clearly defined meaning, and the object to which it refers has clearly-defined properties, each accessible to those with adequate encyclopaedic knowledge. But in incantation, the sign is discovered both to conceal and reveal hidden meanings. When these are revealed, the name is shown to embody facts about the properties of natural ingredients which are inaccessible to Yoruba encyclopaedic knowledge.

(e) Some comments on incantation and rationality

The incantation in Yoruba medicine is a statement of the power which specific ingredients possess when they are combined together. First and foremost, each incantation expresses knowledge about a combination of ingredients. This knowledge, however, is of a different kind from that which was discussed in earlier chapters.

The knowledge which has been the main focus of our discussion has been encyclopaedic knowledge, the common sense and specialist knowledge of herbalists, which, though it may be given symbolic expression by means of ritual, proverb, myth etc., may nevertheless be regarded as a series of articulations of a basic paradigm.

It is being suggested here that despite the use of incantation and ritual there is nevertheless an underlying rationality in Yoruba medicine. Indeed, I wish to assert a belief based upon observation that within Yoruba medicinal practice there is a strong element of critical appraisal akin to, although not identical with, the spirit of scientific enquiry to be found in the

West. It should not be thought that because it has been possible to identify homologies between diverse elements in the Yoruba encyclopaedic knowledge discoverable outside medicinal incantations and because symbolism may sometimes be employed to encapsulate and evoke the principles upon which this encyclopaedic knowledge is built, that herbalists are unable to appraise their work with a critical eye. It is true that the existence of incantations raises certain difficulties for this hypothesis, but these difficulties can be overcome. Let us see then the manner in which herbalists are critical of their medicines and how incantation fits into the rationalistic framework which is here being postulated.

Criticism may be usefully differentiated as empirical and rational criticism. Empirical criticism is the process whereby hypothesis and evidence, or theory and practice are compared and contrasted. Rational criticism lies in the contrasting of a specific theory or hypothesis with generally accepted universal principles. My contention is that Yoruba herbalists habitually exercise both kinds of criticism in their work.

Eichinger Ferro-Luzzi (1978) argues that analogical thinking is incompatible with the 'trial and error' of empirical criticism. She claims that it is wrong in principle to regard, for example, food taboos as appropriate responses to 'real' nutritional circumstances. She is not merely making the valid phenomenological point that the so-called 'real' world of science belongs to the experience of people from one culture and that the world of the food taboo belongs to another people whose vision of the world is necessarily different. Her view is more all-embracing and dubious. It is, rather, that food taboos are part of a system of analogical thought and are thus unconnected with the scientifically verifiable world. Her view is understandable, but only because anthropologists tend to regard the statements of exotic peoples which do not accord with their own paradigms of encyclopaedic knowledge as 'symbolism'. Neumann (1978) argues against her, using as an example the widespread belief that hunting big game after having been in close contact with a menstruating woman is dangerous. Apparently, it is scientifically verifiable that this practice is dangerous (Neumann, 1978, 414–15).

There is indeed no reason to suppose that analogical thinking is incompatible with empirical testing, with trial and error. For, as is shown throughout this volume a single paradigm can generate many different versions of the same set of circumstances, and these versions, though analogous, may be incompatible with each other. These different versions of the same circumstances are available for empirical testing.

By insisting on the pragmatic and instrumental nature of even the symbolic forms of Yoruba medicine, it would seem that I am returning to a Frazerian or Tylorian view shorn perhaps of its Edwardian or Victorian self-confidence. For as Downie remarks (1970, 45) *vis-à-vis* some comments of Beattie, 'It would seem that Frazer is wrong in thinking of magic as instrumental and that this error is shared by those who practise magic.' What is upsetting about the contretemps between Eichinger Ferro-Luzzi and Neumann is that anthropologists should be surprised and even a little worried that professional hunters might actually know something about the behaviour of the game they stalk. My own suspicion is that just as certain social circumstances and accepted paradigms may lead hunters to discover the fact that menstrual blood antagonizes game, so also Yoruba herbalists, guided by their paradigms, have made genuine discoveries about the nature of illness and the means of curing it.

My experience of Yoruba herbalists is that they constantly subject their medicinal knowledge to empirical criticism. They may not be as rigorous in their testing of medicines as a western scientist—there are no 'controlled experiments'—but herbalists are constantly aware that not all medicines are equally effective, and they are very free in their condemnation of the medicines of other herbalists, arguing usually that the other man's medicines do not work. Adebawọ, in particular, could pour scorn upon received opinion—whether the European view that malaria was caused by mosquitoes, or the Yoruba one that leprosy is caused by burying the dead with red cloth. And his sceptical attitude was not at all peculiar to him alone.

There is, for example, a commonly held belief, that to touch a chameleon (*agẹmọ*) is to invite the onset of an illness in which the skin peels from the body. I have watched people attempting to catch this animal for use in medicine go to inordinate and sometimes hilarious lengths to avoid touching it. When such a

person was in the market one day attempting to sell a
chameleon to a dealer, the dealer horrified all around her by
placing her hand into the small cage and picking the animal up.
Presumably, because the dealer was familiar with chameleons,
her experience had taught her that they were in fact completely
harmless.

The people who use medicine do so usually for one reason
only—they want the medicine to work. Of course in the field of
medicine there is always a degree of failure. If a medicine were
discarded every time it failed to cure a patient there would be
no medicines in either Africa or Europe. Conversely, an enor-
mous proportion of people recover from illness whether or not
they are treated. This creates difficulties in making valid
empirical judgements about the effectiveness of medicines. But
nevertheless, such judgements are undoubtedly made both by
Yoruba herbalists and by their patients, and I was convinced
by occasional parenthetical remarks that herbalists did discard
medicinal recipes which did not give a satisfactory rate of
success.

This sort of empirical 'testing' of medicines—albeit performed in a rough and ready manner—is as likely to be
employed in relation to medicines which have incantation as to
those without. Where there is no incantation there is no serious
difficulty in abandoning a recipe. Where there is an incantation, the fact that the medicine does not work carries with it
the imputation that the incantation is fraudulent—and
perhaps that the herbalist is incompetent or dishonest. It need
perhaps not be said that the frequent clandestine accusations
made by herbalists against their rivals (my main informants
were remarkably free of such back-biting) are not altogether
disinterested. But they are very common and imply that
medicines are by no means unhesitatingly accepted as valuable
cures.

The other main ground for criticism which may be applied to
encyclopaedic knowledge is reason, and here the fact that a
medicine has an incantation makes a more substantial difference. When a herbalist—or indeed anyone with an interest
in such matters—considers a recipe for a medicine in which
there is no incantation, he will be able to make an intelligent
and wholly a priori judgement about whether it is likely to

work. (This assumes a moderate understanding of the illness or problem and a reasonable knowledge of the ingredients.) But where there is an incantation in the medicine, no individual is able to make this sort of intelligent judgement unless he knows whether the incantation is or is not an authentic medicinal incantation. In other words, rational criticism cannot determine directly whether or not the knowledge contained within the incantation is true. The incantation thus has the effect of insulating the knowledge embodied within it from rational criticism.

Before this is regarded as indicative of the non-rationality of the Yoruba, let it be stated that this phenomenon is equally common in Europe. The idea that 'space is curved', for example, is wholly foreign to my own common sense, and yet I assent to it. The reason I do so is that somewhere, on the radio perhaps, or in a newspaper, I was told that scientists say that 'space is curved'. Since it is part of my own encyclopaedic knowledge that the opinions of reputable scientists should be respected even where they contradict my own common sense, so it is part of the encyclopaedic knowledge of most Yoruba people that the rather odd knowledge enshrined in authentic medicinal incantations is also true. If the form of the incantation, the manner in which it is spoken, but above all, the fact that it *is* an incantation insulates the knowledge contained in it from rational criticism, it also provides the means whereby this knowledge may be incorporated within encyclopaedic knowledge.

In the ordinary, everyday experience of a Yoruba herbalist, there is nothing directly to suggest for example that a combination of the skulls of a monkey, a leopard, a crocodile, and a human being together have the power to bring a person wealth (pp. 247–9). This knowledge exists for him only in an incantation. Once this incantation is recognized to be a valid and authentic incantation, then the knowledge may become part of the herbalist's encyclopaedia. For there is a body of knowledge about the knowledge contained in incantations (meta-knowledge) which is wholly compatible with Yoruba paradigms. If an incantation is an authentic one, then it is in principle part of the *Ifá* corpus, and the information stated within it is therefore true. The word 'true' is here being used in the sense referred to at the beginning of this chapter. It is not merely that the knowledge within the incantation is factually correct, but that it becomes factually correct through having been spoken.

So far, my argument has remained quite close to that of Sperber (1974). However, it is necessary to qualify and expand certain features of Sperber's original statement. Sperber argues that the main function of symbolic statements is to be 'the delimitation of a field' of knowledge hidden in the memory so that it may be awakened and surveyed for relevant material. Symbols, he says, 'provide a second mode of access to the memory: evocation when invocation (as usually provided by conceptual representations) fails' (Sperber 1974, 121). In Chapter 6 a number of symbolic representations have already been discussed which have precisely this evocative function, and the argument will return to these in the final chapter. Sperber's idea that symbols have an evocative function may indeed be regarded as true of most symbols. But it is not universally true, and it is not true of Yoruba medicinal incantation.

First of all the medicinal incantation is not primarily a means of evoking anything, at least not from the memory of the patient or the herbalist. By stretching Sperber's argument a little it might be possible to suggest that the *ingredients* have forgotten what their powers were and that the herbalist hopes to evoke these forgotten powers from the memory of the ingredients. This notion does at least account for much of the data. But the incantation is of little value to the herbalist's memory save as a rather cumbersome mnemonic. For secondly, what is expressed in the incantation does not merely delimit 'a field in which the required information may be found' (Sperber 1974, 121). The incantation does not evoke a wide field of potentially useful knowledge. Rather, the knowledge contained in it, though it is often shrouded in obscure language and allusions, is very specific. It says that a combination of certain ingredients has the power to do a very particular type of pragmatic task.

Identifying an item of knowledge as part of a type of symbolic knowledge (knowledge in quotes) may be regarded as having at least three functions. Two of these are interdependent. First, it insulates the knowledge from the sort of rational criticism to which encyclopaedic knowledge is usually subjected. Second, it simultaneously allows the knowledge to be integrated as an insulated total unit into the rationality of encyclopaedic knowledge at the level of meta-knowledge. The third function is quite distinct from these and may or may not appear when the knowledge is set apart in this manner. This is the function of evocation. Clearly, there are times when knowledge 'in quotes' evokes other knowledge which may have become buried in memory. But equally, there are times when it does not.

The central theme of this chapter has been the nature of hidden knowledge, and especially the nature of that knowledge which is contained in medicinal incantation. It has been shown that the knowledge within the incantation is incompatible with the structure of the Yoruba paradigm and hence with the principles of the common sense, or even of the specialist knowledge of Yoruba herbalists. Nevertheless, herbalists have a knowledge about incantations as such which *is* compatible with the Yoruba paradigm. It is this meta-knowledge which allows rational Yoruba herbalists to believe that the knowledge in the incantation is true.

Nearly the whole of this volume has been devoted to informants' comments upon the technology of Yoruba medicine. In the final chapter, there will be an attempt to draw together some of the loose ends. It will also be suggested that the paradigm which has been shown to be the basic framework for my informants' remarks about medicine may also be relevant to the study of aspects of social life.

Endnotes

[1] The official report stated that the rioters carried 'charms and other dangerous weapons'.
[2] This image is Professor R. G. Armstrong's in a private conversation.
[3] There are two parts to this medicine. *Agúnmu* is made from the tip of the palm-fronds and the feathers, the remainder of the frond is pounded with the head and legs of the pigeons and with soap.
[4] The use of 9 for a man, 7 for a woman is explained above p. 120–1.
[5] This line implies that some part of *agbe*, a feather or the head, could usefully be included in this soap.

8

Food, wine, sex and medicine in social relationships

It has been suggested that beneath the diverse and often complex statements of informants about the nature of illness and medicine, there is a common, and, at root, simple structure of thought which has been called a paradigm. The notion will now be carried further by suggesting that the same paradigm provides the basis for certain social relationships. In the course of this work, a contrast has been drawn between the idea of medicine and that of food related to the contrast between the hidden and the revealed. Medicine tends to hide disease, food tends to reveal it. This correspondence has been shown to provide a satisfactory explanation for much of the technology of medicine, but it has yet to be given a direct and readily comprehensible validity.

When the basic diseases, the 'germs' and 'worms', were considered in Chapter 2, it was shown that food, because it is 'sweet', causes the diseases to flourish, perhaps overflowing their bag so as to cause illness. Medicine has an opposite effect; it kills the diseases or drives them back into their bag or out of the body as excrement whence they may be hidden in the forest. It has also been suggested, that while the natural properties of ingredients both of medicine and food are usually revealed to the observer, the process of preparing a medicine effectively conceals the identity and hence the properties of the individual ingredients. This, combined with the fact that in medicines, certain hidden powers of ingredients may be revealed only by chanting of esoteric verses, enables the herbalist to conceal his recipes from those who might wish to learn them.

In contrast, recipes for food are well known. It is possible to determine with some accuracy the contents of any specific dish of food that is offered to one, merely by looking at it and tasting it. Yoruba cooks do not, as might occasionally a European housewife, try to keep secret even their favourite recipes for food. While there are countless recipes for medicines, each one the secret property of an individual herbalist, recipes for food are relatively few in number, standardized, and part of common knowledge. Finally, medicines are susceptible to the dangers of revelation. They must be eaten using the left hand of secrecy, and must be kept stored away from the dangerous revelation associated with menstruation. Food, in contrast, must be taken with the right hand, and does not suffer from contact with menstruating women.

The discussion of the social significance of food and medicine will be augmented with a consideration of the role of sexuality and palm-wine in social relationships. Already it has been seen (Chapter 2) that excessive indulgence in palm-wine and sexual activity, like the eating of too much sweet food, are considered to be causes of illness. In addition, sexual intercourse, like menstruation, is harmful to medicines. It has been suggested that palm-wine, like food, is associated with the absence of secrecy (pp. 122 ff.). The hypothesis will be that food, sexuality and palm-wine, may be contrasted with medicine on the basis of a distinction between revelation and secrecy, and that they have a role in social relationships precisely analogous to that which they have in the technology of medicine and illness. By implication this means that society and its central institutions are understood by means of the same paradigm which is used to understand the human body.

(a) The Yoruba lineage and compound

The Yoruba lineage is a staunchly corporate group with a focal point in the family compound, traditionally, though not at all universally, a square courtyard enclosed by walls or buildings, and located in one of the Yoruba towns. As a patrilineal group, practising patrilocal residence, there is an important sense in which the Yoruba lineage and compound may be considered to be male institutions. Those adult lineage members who inhabit the compound are almost exclusively male, and it is they who run the internal affairs of the compound, and determine its corporate relationships with other lineages and with the town as such. Women found in the compound are with few exceptions either members of the resident patrilineage, but too young to be married, or else they are wives of male compound members. This means that adult women are usually outsiders in the male compound.

This situation may be usefully compared with the paradigmatic image of the human body (Image 2). In the body, female (red) menstrual fluid is inherently enclosed within the body of the woman, where it encounters male (white) semen which flows in from outside. In society, the Yoruba family compound is an enclosure containing a male lineage, but the men encounter, coming from the outside, a flow of women. Marriage therefore does not replicate the structure of copulation, it is an inversion of it.

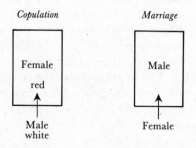

FIGURE. 37. Copulation and marriage

This inversion of that state which, in the body, is both normal and healthy, is perpetuated after marriage, for once married, a woman is not automatically cut off from the outside. On the contrary, she will continue to have deep and lasting emotional attachments to her own patrikinsmen. These links, and especially those which bind her to her own full brothers, will remain with her for the whole of her life. In addition, the woman will strive, probably after the birth of her first child when she is firmly attached to her husband's lineage, to develop trading interests which take her outside her husband's family compound. For many women, trade is not primarily undertaken for the purpose of making money. Rather they seek the relaxed and undisciplined atmosphere of the market away from the control of the husband's lineage. I once made a woman very angry by buying her entire stock of onions (some two dozen) which I needed for a party. She undoubtedly gained financially from the transaction, but she now had to abandon her comfortable stool, and either go to buy some more onions or return home to her husband's compound. For her, trading was little more than an excuse to get away from home and talk to her friends.

This structure of the Yoruba household after marriage is similar to the structure of the new-born healthy child, but in a distorted form. The body of a healthy child combines and conceals red blood and white water, and thus is analogous to the household which combines women (associated with red) and men (associated with white). But in the body, it is the female redness which must remain hidden, and only water may flow in and out (above p. 56). In the household the situation is different; men are firmly and irrevocably attached to their lineage and hence to the compound, and it is women who flow in and out.

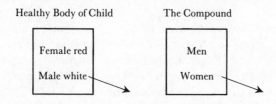

Figure 38. The human body and the household

In this respect the Yoruba household therefore corresponds not to a normal healthy body but to a body racked with illness. As with èelá and ètè, the femininity of the household threatens to come into the open. As with èdà and ọmúròrò, male and female are inverted. The redness overflows the pot.

But in their discussion of the human body informants drew our attention to the idea that disease for them is not merely harmful and negative, but fulfils a positive and beneficial function in the body. So it is also with the inherently 'diseased' state of the Yoruba household. The tendency of men to keep their lineage secrets hidden, to meet with and speak only to their kinsmen, is essential to the good health of the compound. Similarly, it is precisely because the women are outsiders that they are available as wives and it is because of their continuing contacts with their kinsmen that they are able to link the men in their husbands' household to the outside world. By understanding the respective roles of men and women in relation to medicine, food, sexuality, and wine as analogous to diseases in the body, it may be seen why food and wine are the media for social as well as natural openness, and how medicine, even though it is used in social exchange, must be regarded as a secret.

(b) Food, wine, and sex in social relationships

The Yoruba household has been characterized above as an inversion of the normal healthy, paradigmatic structure. Men are inward-looking, women are outward-looking. This tendency of the household to be an inversion of the paradigm is not in itself unhealthy, but, as in a body in which the disease has become 'too much', it can be carried to extremes, leaving the household in disarray.

An extreme inversion of the paradigm would entail two things. First of all, the women of the household would leave their husbands' compound. Their outward tendency would cause them to sever the prime contact which lineage members have with the outside world. The lineage would be devoid of wives and would be unable to perpetuate itself. The household would die. Second, and corresponding precisely to the first, the men would become too inward-looking. The tendency of men to look after and foster their relationships with their own lineage members, could in principle become the sum total of all their relationships. They would cease to marry; their relationships to the town would disintegrate; chieftaincy titles, and the power and influence which the lineage needs to foster its interests, would vanish, and the lineage would become impoverished, childless, and worthless. The household would be an isolated unit of male and female lineage members with no wives, children, power, or wealth.

Clearly, in this extreme form, such a possibility is most unlikely, but in a moderate form it is not a total fantasy. For all that they are concerned to maintain the cohesion of the lineage by retaining their secrets and by giving mutual aid within the lineage, Yoruba men are also preoccupied with avoiding the dangers inherent in their intrinsically isolated and inward-looking situation. Correspondingly, they are anxious that their wives, however much it is necessary that they should maintain close links with their own patrikinsmen, do not carry their outside interests to the extreme.

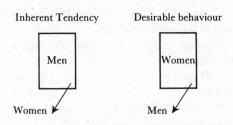

FIGURE 39. Sex-roles

What must be maintained by both men and women is a subtle balance between the inside of the household on the one hand and relationships outside it on the other. Men who are inherently inward-looking must look outward; women who tend to look outside the household must be constrained to look inward. The dangerous but necessary tendencies of the inverted paradigm, the Yoruba lineage, must be themselves inverted to produce a healthy corporate household.

In this inversion of the inversion, on a social as on a technological level, food, sexuality, and wine are crucial.

(i) Sexuality

Sexuality is probably the most important medium through which the men of the Yoruba household have relationships outside the lineage. Yoruba men marry for a variety of reasons, and perhaps the most important of these is so that they may have children. In itself, the birth of male children will ensure the survival of the lineage as a corporate unit, and enhance the political prestige of the father within the lineage. But there are other reasons. The more children a man has, the more land can be farmed, and the more money will he have in old age. He will hope to have many sons to support him politically and economically both within the lineage and externally, but he will not be averse to having daughters as well, since these too will allow him to forge alliances with other lineages in the town. Since Yoruba women abstain from sexual intercourse for the long period before a child is fully weaned, his ambition for many children is best satisfied by the acquisition of as many wives as he is able to afford. A second reason for marriage is that in itself it will provide a man with political and social advancement. A man's relationship to his in-laws is strained and formal, but a father-in-law and a brother-in-law will give the husband political support when he requires it and expect him to reciprocate.

Finally, he will marry in order to have sexual intercourse. The Yoruba highly prize male sexual potency and men deeply resent and dislike the celibacy imposed upon them during the years of pregnancy and weaning. This may be avoided if a man has many wives. Sexual potency is inextricably linked to the desire to have children and to the resulting power and prestige of the man. A man will boast of stupendous feats of sexual athleticism and will hope to remain potent into old age. Indeed, sexual potency in middle and old age is a necessary prerequisite for the acquisition of the many children he desires, for it is only as he grows older that a man is able to amass sufficient wealth to acquire this large number of women. As old age approaches, so fear of impotence grows, for it is only through his sexual potency that a man can hope to fulfil his lifelong dynastic ambitions. Marriage, and also the sexual act itself must be considered not only as vital external relationships which link a man and his lineage to other lineages, but also as a source of wealth, power, and prestige, inside and outside his own household.

For women, the situation is reversed. A woman is expected to enjoy sexual intercourse, but she is not expected to enjoy it as much as a man, for it is admitted that her capacity for sexual enjoyment is inhibited by cliterodectomy. She is expected to confine her attentions to one man, her husband, and even within marriage she will be moderate in her demands. Women who make fun of men for their sexual inadequacy do not thereby imply that their own sexual desires are unfulfilled. Even in Ibadan, where prostitution and marital infidelity are rife, few women would openly boast of their sexual conquests or appetites. The revelation implied by sexuality is appropriate for men but not for women.

(ii) Wine

Similarly with drinking, there is a clear division between the appropriate behaviour of men and that of women. For men, drinking provides a convenient and appropriate opportunity for meeting and conversing with male members of other lineages. The hero of Tutuola's novel *The Palm Wine Drinkard* (1952) is in this only an extreme case of a typical Yoruba man. The Drinkard depends to an absurd degree upon his hospitality in palm wine for social contact with his (extra-lineage) friends. When his 'tapster' dies and the palm wine supply dries up, he is forced to go to extreme lengths to restore it. It is significant, however, that the motivation of the Drinkard in going to 'Deads' Town' to bring back his tapster is not primarily so that he may himself imbibe palm wine. It is so that he may win back the friends who have deserted him (Tutuola 1952, 7–9). In real life, palm wine is scarcely as important as it was for the Palm Wine Drinkard. But it is recognized to have the same function.

In the discussion of the palm-tree (Chapter 6), it was noted that on a natural level, palm wine occupies a similar position in the palm-tree as does semen in the human body. Palm wine is said to have certain undesirable effects on the body, in that, like food, it encourages revelation of disease, and it is also anathema to the god *Ọbàtálá* who forms the child in the womb. Here, on a social level, palm wine provides an opportunity for the inward-looking male members of a Yoruba household to meet with those who live outside. Most commonly, a man will buy a large gourd full of palm wine and outsiders will gather to consume it in his house. Younger men will meet together in bars. Gradually, palm wine is being supplanted by stronger beverages. Beer and gin have greater prestige by virtue of their higher price, but also a locally distilled spirit, *ògògòrò*,[1] is increasingly popular. Despite these innovations, palm wine remains the commonest and the most typical male drink.

In marked contrast to the frequent social drinking of men, is the sobriety of women. Women do not abstain completely from alcohol, but their consumption is much lower. They do not meet together at home to drink, nor, unless they be prostitutes or are simply traders in alcoholic drinks, do they frequent the bars. They refrain from drinking the stronger beverages such as gin, *ògògòrò*, or beer, and they do not generally drink even the fairly mild palm wine. The wine that is consumed by women is that which comes from the raffia-palm (*ògùrò*) which is reputed to be less intoxicating than ordinary palm wine, and even this is drunk in small quantities and usually only on special occasions. Women in general are expected to be sober, and a drunken woman is regarded with disgust.[2]

(iii) Food

There is not the same degree of flexibility in the eating of food to distinguish the sexes as there is in the consumption of alcohol, or in the regulation of sexual intercourse. One may, after all, abstain from wine and from sex, but everyone must eat. Within the limit imposed by physiological necessity, there is nevertheless some differential regulation of eating. Food, like palm wine, is offered to male guests as an almost automatic gesture of hospitality. The visitor is not expected to consume all the food he is offered unless he so desires, but he will always attempt a small portion. Often the meal will be simple: I have been given boiled yam and ground-nut oil, and a minimum token meal is the cola-nut, *obì*. Though the meal will be cooked by women, it is, with few exceptions, offered by men. Women do not participate in the eating of the meal and the occasion is exclusively an exchange of male hospitality. When a woman visits a compound, she too may be offered food, but she will eat with the women in the women's part of the house or compound, and the occasion will lack the ceremoniousness of a male visitation.

The distinction of the men's quarters from the women's is of great significance for an understanding of the issues which are raised here. In the traditional square family compound, seldom nowadays to be seen, men occupied an area at one end of the square. They comprised a number of living rooms where the men could sit and the older men could hold court, and the individual bedrooms where the men slept. At the other end of the square courtyard was a gate, and, in between, around the edge of the area were the wives' sleeping-rooms. All of these rooms opened out into the central courtyard, and to an extent all could be regarded as 'inside' the compound. However, the

men's area was always at the opposite end of the courtyard
from the gate, and was further inside than the women's area.
Cooking was done at an open fire in the courtyard.

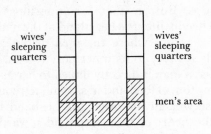

wives'
sleeping
quarters

wives'
sleeping
quarters

men's area

FIGURE 40. The traditional compound

More recently, overcrowding and modern fashion has led to
the replacement of these large square compounds by large
houses, built according to the 'Brazilian' design. Here too the
house is divided into male and female rooms. Men live in the
portion of the house which is most distant from the door.
Commonly, the men's sitting-room is on the first floor. Though
this is sometimes at the front of the house, a visitor nevertheless
has to walk through the whole house in order to reach it.
Women's bedrooms are usually nearest to the front door on the
ground floor. The use of this spatial distinction between male
and female areas, is important to an understanding of the
subtleties of the social interaction of men and women in the
compound and to the conceptual relationships of openness and
hiddenness. In the normal course of daily events, food is cooked
by the women in the relatively open space of the hearth. A wife
will bring a portion of this food to her husband and perhaps also
to his brothers who will eat it in their own area of the house. The
remainder, she will take and share with her children in her own
room, or, if the weather is cool, in the courtyard. She will not
consume it in the presence of her husband, and, although she is
allowed to come and go in the male area of the house, she will
not eat food in this area.

A similar rule applies to sexuality. Adult men have their own
sleeping-rooms, but they will seldom, if ever, sleep with their
wives in these rooms. Instead they will leave their own room

and go and sleep with the wife in the wife's bedroom. A woman, as we have seen, is an outsider in the male compound. By virtue of having sexual intercourse with her husband, by cooking his food, and by bearing his children she establishes herself in the alien enclosure. But in these relationships she may not encroach too deeply into the heartland of the male lineage. She may enter the rooms where the men dispute, but may not regard herself as privy to its innermost secrets. At the crucial moments when a man is directly linked to her as an outsider—in the consumption of food and in sexual intercourse—distance must be preserved; in the other the husband himself moves away from the heart of the compound towards the relative outside where his wife's living quarters are.

I came across an extreme version of this logic when I travelled with a herbalist to a distant town where his wife's lineage was situated. When we arrived, my companion behaved with extreme deference to his in-laws. He prostrated himself before all of his male in-laws, and throughout our stay adopted a general pose of subordination allowing, at first, conversation to be initiated only by them. This, I was told, was the customary behaviour of all men towards their in-laws and the fact that I should remark about it caused some surprise. In addition, though we had to stay the night, my companion was forbidden to stay with his wife in her father's compound. Instead, accommodation was arranged for us all in a neighbouring compound some half mile away. This, it was explained, was because no man may sleep with his wife in the compound of his father-in-law.

The situation seemed to me to be acceptable to both parties for similar reasons. The visitor had already established an extremely close relationship with his in-laws through marriage. He might be offered hospitality in the form of wine and food, but he may not allow the relationship thus created to lose its formality for fear that he himself might become too open in these relationships. Even more so, though he might sleep with his wife in the compound of a stranger or a friend, he might not affirm his sexual relationship to his wife while staying in the house of the very same outsiders to whom he was already so firmly attached.

Similarly, the in-laws themselves, while they had given away their daughter to a stranger, and while they accepted the relationship which the marriage created, had no wish to see their son-in-law ensconced in their household as a permanent fixture, privy to their secrets and exercising claims upon them on behalf of his own lineage.

In this specific instance, of course, there was little chance of such a dangerously close external relationship developing between the two lineages. Here, where the parties resided at a considerable distance from each other, their relationships could be only occasional. The rule was not based upon immediate dangers but was observed as a rule merely of good manners. However, most relationships of affinity are between lineages which inhabit the same town. Here the dangers attached to easy and informal relationships between in-laws are real and the two lineages in their own way will take care to prevent the external relationship of marriage from impinging too closely upon their internal lineage affairs. In the husband's compound they will insist that the wife be subordinate, and she will keep a relative distance from the men at significant moments. In the wife's compound, it is the husband who must be subordinate and respectful, and who must refrain from sexual intercourse with his wife.

(c) Medicine in social relationships

(i) Gifts

Because medicines are secret, it follows that any exchange involving medicine must have one of two forms. Either medicines made of plants, animals, minerals (and incantations) are given, or it is the recipe which is divulged. The most generalized form of exchange (Sahlins 1965, 1974) is the gift. When medicines are given away it is usually to the lineage or compound members in time of need. Within the compound medicines are given freely, but such gifts are most commonly made between close kin. In serious cases, a person will shop around among the different forms of medicine and among different individual healers but he will give due weight to the medicine practised in his own compound and in the compounds of his kinsmen.

Gifts of recipes and information about medicine are given much less freely. Among the Yoruba, as among the Kpelle (Murphy 1980) where the situation is very similar, there is careful control over the transmission of knowledge, and this is especially true of knowledge of medicine. A man will be given recipes freely by his full-siblings, even by his mother (though she will generally know only a little). Occasional recipes will also be given by male kinsmen to whom he is particularly attached and also by his mother's brother. Serious instruction, given free of charge, will generally only come from a man's father. In this way, a man can build up a considerable knowledge of medicine, but if he wishes seriously to know about medicine, and does not have a herbalist for a father, he must become an apprentice. Even here, he will find that knowledge comes slowly, for as I have explained, it is impolite to ask someone for recipes for medicine, and the herbalist will give medicines to his apprentices only when he is certain that the young man is honest and serious in his intentions.

On the occasion to which I have just referred, when I accompanied an Ibadan herbalist to visit his wife's kinsmen in a distant town, one of these in-laws, an elderly herbalist, suggested that we go on a sort of nature ramble so that he could tell the younger man all about medicine. I was for a time puzzled by the behaviour of my friend, for he kept insisting that his main interest in the walk was to collect some rare plants which could not be found in Ibadan. What was so puzzling was the fact that the pieces of wood which he so gleefully discovered, could be found some fifty yards from my office on the Ibadan university campus, and were indeed quite common.

It soon dawned on me what was happening. The old man was indulging in a mildly malicious game which herbalists love to play upon people, particularly on anthropologists. He repeated over and over that he would tell his in-laws about medicine, and he did in fact give him a large number of tit-bits of information about individual ingredients. As the power of medicine does not reside in particular ingredients but in the completed medicine the old man knew that his divulgences would be merely tantalizing. In effect the old man seemed to be saying, 'as my in-law you might be entitled to learn from me some medicines, and in my own good time I might tell you something valuable, but if you want such information you must first suffer a little'. And also, as in the Kpelle situation described by Murphy (1980), he was trying to underline the other's dependence. My companion, it seemed, understood this game before he had even set off on the journey, and so he studiously collected pieces of wood so that he could pretend not to care about the knowledge of the other man.

The giving of recipes is, then, a sign of a close bond between people. It indicates respect and affection, and where these are only tentatively felt, the recipes are given only in part, and with a half-joking but firm indication of the gulf which still separates the people concerned. Such gifts take place predominantly between close kinsmen, but they sometimes take place between outsiders when they are regarded as being 'close friends' (ọ̀rẹ́ ìmùlẹ̀), a term of intense and lifelong endearment. Naturally, the people who are most liberal with their recipes for medicine are those who have least to gain from keeping them secret. Professional herbalists are extremely secretive, while women, who do not normally sell their medicines, are quite willing to tell their meagre secrets to anyone they happen to like.

We have here then, two forms of generalized reciprocity involving medicines, the giving of the recipe and the giving of the medicine itself. In one case, knowledge is imparted; in the other the object which embodies the knowledge is given while the knowledge itself is withheld. This distinction between giving and not giving, between openness and concealment, corresponds precisely to the degree to which men are bound together, or separated by ties of kinship and affection. Even in the most generalized form of exchange however, where recipes for medicine are freely given, the absence of secrecy depends dialectically upon its opposite. Complete openness between friends is only significant because it breaks down the barrier of secrecy which normally separates people. And also the bond created by such openness implies a mutual secrecy against the rest of the world. A man will not thank a friend who publishes his secrets indiscriminately abroad.

(ii) The trading relationship

The other form of exchange involving medicines is the trading relationship. Here, the customer who is ill, or who needs a medicine for some other purpose, perhaps to improve his trade, or to obtain a lover, goes to the herbalist to purchase the medicine. On the face of it, he is buying a piece of private property, a commodity, a 'single-use consumer good'. So he is, but it is not quite as simple as it appears.

Medicine is not the sole prerogative of professional herbalists. A herbalist is merely a man who, having acquired considerable knowledge of medicine, has been able to attract those who need his knowledge. Almost all Yoruba men, outside the 'élite' class, are herbalists to a greater or lesser extent. Nearly everybody has experience and knowledge of at least the simpler medicines, and nearly every compound has at least one man with some degree of expertise. The basic methods of preparation of medicine are simple and well-known. The ingredients too are freely available. The forest is full of medicinal plants and, where it is inconvenient to search for them in the bush, they can be purchased in the market for a few pence. Some ingredients are rare and expensive, but it is not possession of these that distinguishes the herbalist from the customer. What is involved in the trading of medicine is not an exchange based on the private ownership of material objects. It is an exchange based upon the private ownership of ideas.

Marx has argued that man's alienation from nature is derived from the ownership of private property, (1844 133 ff.). The conscious creative activity of man upon nature to satisfy his material needs ceases to be his own when man is divorced from the physical world by private ownership. The physical world is thus transformed into an alien force which confronts man as a task to be done, such that the man becomes a mindless attribute of his work instead of the work being an attribute of man.

In Yoruba medicinal practice, however, a similar but inverted structure presents itself. The patient has physical needs (to cure his illness) and he has the physical means (medicinal plants) with which to satisfy these needs. What he lacks is the knowledge with which he may transform raw nature into a cultural object with which he can satisfy his needs. Such knowledge is denied him in order to create a dependency. The relationship between herbalist and patient is constituted by a dialectic of secrecy and revelation, determined by the fact that medical knowledge is a secret.

(d) The paradigm and symbolism

We may now finally understand why the distinction between secrecy and revelation is so central to Yoruba thought. Secrecy is what distinguishes and divides men, and groups of men, from each other. It is the black skin which conceals the hearts of men from each other; it is the walls of the household which keep the internal affairs of one lineage from the ears of another; it is the boundary which divides one town from its neighbour. Secrecy envelops the rites of every cult, and the dealings of every association. Secrecy distinguishes each individual from every other individual, and defines every relationship from every other relationship. It is the foundation for all social divisions.

But no society is merely divided. If secrecy divides up the society into discrete units, then it is revelation which relates the units into compact wholes. Revelation is at once necessary and dangerous. It is necessary, for without it society would collapse into hostile introspective particularity, but it is dangerous, for it tends to destroy that which gives the discrete units their separate identities. Without secrecy each unit loses its integrity; but without secrecy revelation itself becomes meaningless.

The dichotomy between the hidden and the revealed is of course important to other cultures than the Yoruba—one need think only of the perennial British debate about government intrusion upon privacy. Wilson (1974) regards society as poised between privacy and surveillance. He suggests, appositely enough, that an excess of privacy is what is known as madness, for the madman in his own private world is free from the surveillance of others and therefore constitutes a social threat. It has been shown that in Yoruba thought, the converse is rather the case. Madness is not here thought to be an excess of privacy—but is rather the result of being exposed to a god who destroys and hates both communal and individual secrets. What is important therefore is the way that secrecy fits into overall pattern.

The preoccupation with secrecy in my informants' understanding of the body and its illnesses may thus be regarded as a reflection of a more general preoccupation with secrecy in social life. Douglas (1966, 114–28) has argued that there are

'pressures to create a consonance between the perception of
social and physiological levels of experience', and it would seem
that Yoruba medicinal practice bears this out. Douglas is,
however, sometimes a little ambiguous on one point. At times
she seems to argue that social boundaries are merely homologous to natural boundaries—a point which is reinforced by the
material presented here. But at times, she conveys another
impression. She writes, for example, that 'bodily control is an
expression of social control' (1973, 99), and she quotes as an
example the Hazda, among whom taboos associated with
menstruation are 'a symbolic expression of the tie between
husband and wife' (see Douglas 1966, 137–53). For her, the
body is primarily a symbol of the social order.

Nor is Douglas alone in this orientation. There seems to be a
general desire among many anthropologists to regard everything as a symbol or a metaphor for something else. Beck
(1978b, 84), for example, clearly regards the body as a 'macro'-
metaphor underpinning thought processes. Hudson (1975)
also sees the use of emetics by Cherokee Indians as inherently
symbolic. Because the saliva or food in the belly may, according
to Cherokee ideas, be spoiled by witches and conjurers, then
vomiting 'is a logical course of action for anyone with an illness
diagnosed as having anything to do with saliva or improper
food or certain kinds of witchcraft' (Hudson 1975, 96–7). It is
clear that Hudson regards this sort of healing as 'ritual'. And it
is indeed tempting to ask whether or not even modern medical
practice is not a purely symbolic activity. Perhaps the
administration of an antibiotic or even the removal of a torn
cartilage is a ritual act, or perhaps 'symbolic', or, in the more
current expression, a 'metaphor'.

There are, in fact, those who argue just this. Moerman
(1979) does indeed assert that the giving of medicines and even
surgery in modern medical practice is a metaphorical act. And
his argument is persuasive. He takes his standpoint in the
research of Schapiro (1959), Frank (1963, 1974, 1975) and
others into the placebo effect. Frank argues (1974, 1975) that a
placebo can be between 30 per cent and 60 per cent as effective
as an active medication. He suggests that a medicine 'gains its
potency through being a symbol of the physician's role as a
healer' (Frank 1963, 66).

What is disturbing about all this is the air of unreality with which it cloaks discussion. If the human body is a symbol (or metaphor) for 'society' or for a given social relationship; and if the medicine is a symbol (or metaphor) for a social role, then the act of healing becomes the action of a metaphor for a social role upon a metaphor for society. It is a formula which, apart from being gobbledegook, has lost touch with phenomenological reality. In my experience at least, metaphors for healers' roles are not widely used to heal metaphors for society. Rather healers use medicines to cure the illness of patients.

In the use of such terms as 'symbol', 'metaphor', 'model', 'paradigm', and so forth, it is necessary to be clear about the overall orientation of the argument. Specifically, it is imperative to maintain a clear distinction between an 'emic' approach, which seeks to discover the form and meaning of the informants' own statements, and an 'etic' approach, which strives to place the activity of a specific culture within a framework applicable cross-culturally. In all anthropology, whatever is presented is, of course, the anthropologist's view. In a study of medicine such as this one, in which the overall perspective is emic, the anthropologist strives to present his understanding of the statements and actions of his informants in relation to illness and medicine. In order to do so he may make use of a meta-knowledge in which are to be found such terms as 'symbol' or 'metaphor' or 'proverb', some of which may indeed have corresponding terms in the native language of his informants.

Moerman's approach is avowedly 'etic' in that it is part of the cross-cultural tendency in recent medical anthropology exemplified by the work of Fabrega (1974, 1979), Singer (1975), Kleinman (1977, 1980), Kleinman and Sung (1979), and Nathanson (1975). In such studies, there is, perhaps inevitably, a tendency to see the 'reality' of illness (the writer's etic theory) and the native actor's own theory as somehow in conflict. In Fabrega (1974), for example, the culture's own definition of illness is merely a part of an overall etic definition of embracing medical explanations. Moerman however takes this a stage further. By saying that modern medicine and even modern surgery is metaphorical activity, he is not seeking to

explain or portray the doctors' or patients' understanding of
what they do. He is seeking to criticize it.

The correct use in an emic context of such terms as prose,
metaphor, symbol, proverb, and so on, is to indicate the type of
communication that is going on, or the type of knowledge that
is being expressed. It is to show when Monsieur Jourdain is
speaking prose and when he is speaking verse; when he is being
rational or technical and when he is engaged in ritual. Moerman clearly thinks that because metaphors have a decisive
place both in rational–technical activity and in ritual, it therefore follows that rational–technical activity is ritual. This error
is not generally shared by others (especially Fernandez 1974,
1975; Lakoff and Johnson 1980; Reddy 1979; cf. (ed.) Ortony,
1979) who have shown the importance of metaphor in literal
communication.

It is, of course, perfectly acceptable to build up one's own etic
theory of illness. Medical men do this all the time and by a
process which involves an engagement in just the sort of
dialectical discussion of which Moerman's article forms part.
This sort of enterprise is not appropriate to an emic study. The
task in this volume is to elucidate the ideas of some Yoruba
herbalists on the subject of illness and medicine. It is not to
determine whether or not their views are mistaken. And nor is it
to question whether their rational common sense is 'really'
symbolic.

When Yoruba herbalists construct a medicine, they do so in
order to cure an ailment or for some other specified purpose.
The medicine occasionally has a symbolic content, in the form
of either an incantation or a ritual performance. Much more
usually, however, it is intended to act in a way that will hide,
expel or kill a disease, and, where necessary, repair the damage
that has been done. This is a rational procedure which accords
with the herbalist's common sense. In a similar manner, the
human body is not understood by my Yoruba informants to be
primarily a symbol or metaphor for society or for anything else.
It is an object which they believe to have a certain ideal
structure and which is subject to the ravages of illness. The
nature and causes of these illnesses, and the appropriate
treatment, are for the most part understood according to a
recurring pattern which I have described as a paradigm. These

ideas are not in general symbolic, but form part of the herbalists' encyclopaedic knowledge.

A good example with which to illustrate my argument is the
question of menstrual taboos as raised by Douglas (above
p. 182). It may be that menstruation and the prohibitions
which my Yoruba informants associated with it are, in certain
circumstances, expressive of the social order. I have never
heard them referred to in this way, but it is no part of my
argument to claim that they could not be so used. Sperber,
indeed, has indicated that any item of encyclopaedic knowledge can be placed in quotes and used symbolically. Among my
informants, however, the major menstrual taboo—against having sexual intercourse during the menstrual period—is quite
clearly non-symbolic. In particular it is not a *signifiant* signify-
ing the social order. It is simply a regulation intended to
prevent serious ill-health in young children.

There is a relationship between the image of the society and
that of the human body but this is neither a simple one of
correlation (Montgomery 1974) nor necessarily a symbolic
one. What is true of the human body is true of other images to
be discovered in Yoruba thought. Most obvious of these is the
proverb concerning the cooking-pot in the hearth. It is said that
three stones in the hearth will not spill the soup. As it stands
this statement is indeed nothing more than a simple piece of
sound empirical knowledge. The placing of this knowledge in
quotes by defining it as a proverb, draws the attention beyond
the stories and the pot themselves towards structures to which
they are homologous.

Tonkin has indicated the importance of secrecy as lending
power to that which is hidden (1979), something to which
Murphy (1980) also alludes in a more political context. The
proverb which I was given is not actually very secret, for it is
fairly well known to the public at large. When however it is
placed in giant quotation marks, as it was to me by my
informant who took me aside and whispered it to me in secret, it
becomes evocative of the whole Yoruba cosmos as well as, for
me, many of its component parts.

Douglas once complained (1967a) that Lévi-Strauss's early
attempts at the analysis of myth and those of Leach (especially
1962) provide a remarkably trivial interpretation of the data.

'All the majestic themes which we had previously thought the Oedipus myth was about—destiny, duty, and self-knowledge—have been strained off, and we are left with a worry about how species began. When Edmund Leach applies the same technique to the Book of Genesis, the rich metaphysical themes of salvation and cosmic oneness are replaced by practical rules for the regulation of sex.'

The approach to symbolism which has been followed here by-passes much of this criticism. V. W. Turner has long urged us by the example of his careful work (1953, 1957, 1962, 1963, 1966, 1968, 1969, 1975) to look for the multivocality of symbols and this is given clear definition by Sperber who argues that symbols are not directly comparable to linguistic signs. A symbolic representation, such as a myth, does not exist as a unity of *signifiant* and *signifié* (Barthes 1957, 221–3) but as an item of knowledge similar to other items of knowledge and set apart so as to evoke any number of images to which it is thus related.

Beck (1978b following Fernardez 1974, 1975) argues that metaphors (symbols) are extremely 'shifty'. She would perhaps disagree with much that has been written here on the ground that I have failed to indicate the breadth and scope of metaphorical (symbolic) expression in Yoruba culture. To some extent she would be correct yet my argument is close to her own. She claims a dichotomy between two modes of thought. In one, 'reasoning is by analogy, where thoughts move along paths in a dense network of associations . . .' They may be associations of colour, shape, texture, smell, type of movement, and so forth. At the other pole is the semantic domain—the domain of rational discourse. She argues that metaphors provide a link between these two thought frameworks.

But the problem in presenting Yoruba culture is not at all to demonstrate the diversity of its symbols (metaphors). They crowd in upon any unsuspecting inquirer who listens to any text or watches any ceremony. The problem is not to assert the complexity of Yoruba thought but to reduce it to manageable form. My work here has been to concentrate on a few symbolic and a few non-symbolic images which seem to express the basic 'body based imagery' of which Beck speaks and from which other forms of knowledge are derived (Beck 1978b, 84).

We have in Chapter 6 received an inkling of the variety of symbolic statements derived from the central body-based paradigm. The stories are tales of what the gods did. And for most Yoruba people these stories are as literally true as stories of what human beings have done. It is to be expected that the ancient Greeks thought of the Oedipus story in much the same way. Certainly until the nineteenth century the Genesis version of the Creation was interpreted in Europe as a factual account of events in the beginning. Attempts to suggest (e.g. Richardson 1953) that ancient myths have merely didactic or symbolic import are usually wide of the mark. But this knowledge in the myth is placed in quotes within which it is defined by meta-knowledge as a significant story. Thereby it points beyond itself. The myth has a clear structure, homologous with the structures which people of the culture may discover in other aspects of their lives. Because of this it may evoke an awareness of structure in any one or several of these other aspects of life, depending on the circumstances.

We have seen however that the placing of knowledge in quotes may have an altogether different function. It may allow a piece of knowledge which is not directly compatible with the paradigm of encyclopaedic knowledge to be integrated in the paradigm at another level, the level of meta-knowledge. It is this capacity of 'knowledge in quotes' to be insulated from common sense criteria of belief and disbelief that allows miraculous and downright impossible events to be accepted with equanimity as true when they are recounted in stories. Sometimes, this relative insulation of, say, a story from common sense (cf. Leach 1962) may by a seeming paradox serve to allow it to evoke common sense reality more clearly. This it does by portraying common sense structures as larger than life or by demonstrating impossibly extreme or inverted pictures of ordinary reality. In other cases, and Yoruba medicinal incantation is one of these, the insulation of the knowledge from paradigms of common sense is more complete.

The images which have here been expressed as structures of contrasting pairs are homologous to each other and together constitute a paradigm for Yoruba medicine. In this chapter, it has been suggested that the same paradigm is used in ordinary social relationships. Religious myths seem also to contain the same structures. All of these, however, are structures whereby different aspects of the world are known. They constitute the structure of common sense encyclopaedic knowledge. This knowledge can, and indeed must, be communicated for its existence to continue. But by no means does this knowledge exist *in order to be communicated*. Rather it has usually been developed to cope with specific practical or theoretical problems in understanding and transforming the world.

Folk medicine is not a commentary upon illness; nor is the knowledge which it embodies intended primarily to symbolize society. It is not merely a system of communication. It is an instrumental system of techniques for dealing practically with certain human ills and it embodies a knowledge of plants, animals, and the human body which are used as a means to the achievement of that end. By approaching Yoruba medicine from this instrumentalist perspective an attempt has been made to domesticate the wildly symbolic orientation of cognitive anthropology, to take some of the symbolism out of symbolic classification. Above all, the discussion has focused attention not upon symbolism and metaphor but upon the encyclopaedic knowledge, the common sense and expert knowledge, of Yoruba healers. What has emerged has been a pattern similar to the patterns usually called 'symbolic classification'. It has been argued however that to see this pattern as 'symbolism' is to mistake the plumage for the living bird.

My task has been to demonstrate how different individuals with similar backgrounds and in similar situations confront similar problems in different ways. Within this diversity there is a level at which my informants agree. More properly, there is a shared structure of concepts which is here called a paradigm and which is expressed not only in the homologous 'images' which have been presented, but also in informants' ordinary statements about the nature of illness and misfortune and its treatment.

Beyond the study of Yoruba medicine, my intention has been to show how the study of individuals as men with creative, rational, and independent minds, is not incompatible with a structural approach to anthropology. The fact that men think within a structured framework of related concepts is not incompatible with a wide measure of disagreement and independent thought. I have tried to show that, in any concept of structure where it is applied to human activity, it must be possible to show how people explain and act in an infinity of specific situations each of which is different from any other. The paradigm would seem, on the face of it, to account for most, if not all, of the actions of people who live in the 'traditional' way of life of the Yoruba. But the paradigm is not a narrowly confining dead hand upon the Yoruba. It is the source of spontaneous creative individuality.

Endnotes

[1] *Ogògòrò* is distilled from raffia palm wine (*ògùrò*). Ideally it should taste like Schnapps, but it seldom does. Sometimes it is coloured brown and presented as whisky.

[2] There are exceptions to this: at a meeting of *Ṣòngó* priests which I attended there were women who were outrageously and unashamedly drunk. This exception however seems to prove the rule. *Ṣòngó* priests are notoriously wild and unruly people, and the god himself, the god of lightning and thunderbolts, gives direct and devastating expression to his anger. His symbolic colouring, like that of *Ṣònpònnó*, is red and white, which, when considered with his ferocity, would indicate a dangerous tendency to openness.

APPENDIX A

Medicines for simple illnesses

(a) Oògùn orí fífó (medicine for headache)

Medicines for headache are directed towards the worms in the head. Most of these medicines are either inhaled or deposited in the nose and there is therefore a strong emphasis upon ingredients which have a strong smell.

Oògùn orí fífó ọdẹ orí	Fatoogun
sm. *egbò wówó*	root of an unknown plant
sm. *alùbọ́sà eléwé*	spring onion

Pound and put into a snail's shell or any other container. Find a wrapper that can cover you. Make a hole in the container big enough to put one finger in. The patient will cover himself with the wrapper and open his eyes over the hole to look inside. The heat from the container will go straight to his nostrils and eyes. After twenty minutes the person will be anxious to emerge from the cloth but he should remain a full thirty minutes. When the worms smell the medicine they will run back to the place which God has appointed for them.

FATOOGUN. *Alùbọ́sà* (onion) uses its smell to kill diseases in the body. For example if you find *alùbọ́sà*, you will find that its heat will get into the eyes and it will sting (*ta*) the eyes, so also it uses this power to kill any disease in the body.

BUCKLEY. How does *alùbọ́sà eléwé* (spring onion) differ from *iṣu alùbọ́sà* (onion) in use?

FATOOGUN. It is more powerful than ordinary onion. If you grind spring onion you will find it in your eyes without even facing the place, but the ordinary onion does not affect your eyes nearly so much. This is why it is used in medicine to work immediately against whatever disease it is used for.

BUCKLEY. What is the power of *ewé wówó* to cure *ọdẹ orí*?[1]

FATOOGUN. The smell of this leaf always travels to all parts of the body like smoke to kill any disease in the body. This disease does not like the smell of this leaf. Sometimes the strong-smelling ingredients are combined with a bitter or sour one.

Oògùn orí fífó (orí wájú)	Fatoogun
sm. *ewé rinrin*	peperomia pellucidia (piperaceae)

Grind and mix with *omi oronbó wẹwẹ* (lime-juice). The patient must gaze into the liquid, or it can be dropped into the eyes using the feather of a bird.

BUCKLEY. What is the power of *ewé rinrin* to cure *oríiwájú*?

FATOOGUN. It is the same worm that causes *oríiwájú* that also causes *arọ̀n ojú*. If this worm goes to the head it will cause *orí fífọ́*. If it goes to the eyes it causes *arọ̀n ojú*. If *ewé rinrin* is used in medicine it is the heat of this leaf (i.e. its smell) that will drive the worm out of the eye or head.

Oògùn orí fífọ́ (àgbo)   Fatoogun

sm. *alùbọ́sà*	onion
ewé olójòngbòdú	leaf of *Commelina Vogetii*
sm. *ewé wówó*	leaf of an unknown plant
sm. *ewé àgbásà*	leaf of Cabbage Palm
ewé àrùnjẹrọn	leaf of *Phyllanthus Floribundus (Euphorbiaceae)*

Put into a pot and pour in *omikíkọn* (the 'sour water' from *ẹ̀kọ* production); cook it and drink the liquid and use it to wash with. Use it while it is still warm. The headache will be cured.

To the pungent *alùbọ́sà* and *wówó* is added *ewé àsgbásá*.

BUCKLEY. What is the power of *ewé àgbásá* in *ọdẹ orí*?

FATOOGUN. It uses its smell to kill all the diseases in the body.

The leaf of *àrùnjẹrọn* is similarly used to kill the disease, but it is not apparently used because of its smell or flavour.

BUCKLEY. What is the power of *ewé àrùnjẹrọn* to cure *ọdẹ orí*?

FATOOGUN. This leaf always prevents diseases entering the flesh of the body. It will also remove it from the body. That is why they call it *àrùnjẹrọn* which means '*àrùn kò jẹrọn*' (disease does not eat the flesh).

(Here the name of the leaf reveals its medicinal properties. This use of names is common as is discussed in Chapter Seven.)

(b) Oògùn àkokoro *(medicine for toothache)*

Like other African peoples, Yoruba people clean their teeth each morning using a chewing-stick. Chewing-sticks are selected because of their flavour. This must be bitter, sour, or peppery. Here is a short list of types of wood used as chewing-sticks.

Chewing-sticks

egbò ewúuro	root of *veronia amyglanina*
igi idí	twigs of *microdesmis puberula*
egbò ayín	root of *anogneissus schimperi*
egbò àtako	root of *fagara* genus

When the teeth nevertheless are troubled by toothache the germs which cause it are treated by ingredients which have similar properties to the chewing-stick.

Oògùn àkokoro (àgbo)   Adebawǫ

pep. *Egbò ǫtako (àtako)*	root of Fagara, a tree of the *Rutaceae* genus
pep. *ata*	pepper
pep. *ęęrù*	Ethiopian pepper
pep. *iyèré*	black pepper

Cook and wash the mouth with it.

This medicine is a simple combination of stinging ingredients. The root of *àtako* is used because of its peppery flavour.

Oògùn àkokoro (àgbo)   Fatoogun

b. *Eèpó bǫǫní*	bark of Egyptian Mimosa
eèpo òrà (ìrà)	bark of *Bridelia Ferruginea*
pep. *ata pupa*	red pepper
sr. *omí kǫn*	'sour water' from the production of *ękǫ*
sm. *alùbǫsà*	onion
pep. *ęęrù*	Ethiopian pepper

Cook together and while it is still warm use the *àgbo* to wash the mouth.

BUCKLEY. What power does *eèpo bǫǫní* have to cure *àkokoro*?

FATOOGUN. When cooked, *eèpo bǫǫní* is a very strong medicine which is not liked by the germ (*kòkòrò*) which causes *àkokoro*. When it is taken, it will weaken the power of the germs or kill them in time.

BUCKLEY. What is the power of *eèpo ìrà* (*eèpoòrà*) to cure *àkokoro*?

FATOOGUN. This has the power to adjust the strength of the gums (*idí eyín*) if they are loose. It will also kill the germs.

Of the remaining ingredients only one seemed to me to be problematical.

BUCKLEY. You use red pepper in *oògùn àkokoro*. Does the redness have anything to do with its power,

FATOOGUN. The colour has nothing to do with it. We only use red pepper because the red pepper is ripe enough to sting (*ta*).

Oògùn àkokoro   Fatoogun
b. *ẹyà ọrun dúdú*   blue (lit. black) alum
b. *ẹyà ọrun funfun*   white alum
sr. *omi oronbó*   lime-juice

Grind together (the dry ingredients) and mix with the lime-juice. Rub this on to the base of the teeth.

Ẹyà ọrun (alum) is much used by the Yoruba in its two crystalline forms. As described on page 47, its main purpose is to purify water. It is ground up and put into dirty water and the dirt goes to the bottom. Any germs (*kòkòrò*) remaining in the water will be killed. This means that the water can be drunk. It tastes exceedingly bitter.

BUCKLEY. Is *ẹyà ọrun funfun* stronger than *ẹyà ọrun dúdú*?

FATOOGUN. No. The black one is stronger than the white one. If they are put together in medicine they will become stronger and be able to fight any disease in the body. If other ingredients are not added to *ẹyà ọrun* it can be dangerous because the result is too much defecation.

The lime-juice is once more used as a sour ingredient.

(c) Oògùn arọ̀n àyà (*medicine for worms in the chest*)

Further down the body, medicines which deal with the worms that cause pains in the chest place a greater emphasis on medicines which are taken internally. Adebawọ uses *àsèjẹ* for *arọ̀n àyà* and in these medicines, as previously explained, most of the ingredients, specified or not, are but a medium for the one central medicinal ingredient.

Oògùn arọ̀n àyà (asèjẹ)   Adebawọ
b.   *esò tẹ̀tẹ̀règún*   seed of *amaranthus spinasus*
pep. *ìyèré*   black pepper
sw. *irú*   ground locust-beans
sw. *ẹrọn àgùntòn*   mutton

Cook as *àsèjẹ*.

ADEBAWỌ. If you pound this seed (*èso tẹ̀tẹ̀règún*) and taste its juice you will be able to see that it is just like the flavour of *làpálàpá*, but not as strong as *làpálàpá* (i.e. it tastes bitter).

The next two medicines have a similar but unstated construction—*orógbó* is used because of its bitter flavour, *imí ẹṣú* has a strong, rather unpleasant smell.

Oògùn arọ̀n àyà (asèjẹ)   Adebawọ
b.   *orógbó*   bitter cola
sw. *igbín*   snail
Cut all of it into pieces and cook as *àsèjẹ*.

Oògùn arọ̀n àyà (asèjẹ)   Adebawọ
sm. *ewé imí ẹṣú*   leaf of *Ageratum Conyzoides*
                                       (Compositae)
sw. *igbín*   snail
Cut up the *igbín* and cook as *àsèjẹ*.

Fatoogun gave me two recipes, one of which is *agúnmu*, the
other being neither *àgbo* nor *agúnmu*, but something in between.
In both he is anxious to direct the medicine towards the chest
which is where the pain and the worm is to be found. The
patient therefore must take his medicine lying face down.

Oògùn arọ̀n àyà   Fatoogun
b.   *egbò ifọn*   root of African breadfruit-tree
sm. & sr. *egbò ìpẹ̀ta*   root of violet-tree
sr.   *egbò túdè*   a root
sm.   *alùbọ́sà eléwé*   spring onion
If the person is male, use the intestines of a male duck; if female, use those of a
female duck. Pound together and add *àdín ẹ̀yọn* (a thin type of palm-kernel
oil). He will take two spoonfuls in the morning, afternoon, and evening. When
using the medicine, he must lie flat on his face with a pillow underneath his
belly so that the medicine may flow to his chest. There he must remain for
fifteen minutes before standing up.

BUCKLEY. What is the power of *egbò ifọn* in medicines for *arọ̀n àyà*?
FATOOGUN. Diseases and worms in the belly (*inú*) do not like the smell of *egbò
ifọn*. Most especially (this is true of) the worms in the chest. It is because
this root is very bitter that the worms do not like it. Worms like sweet
things; once the root of *ifọn* is used in medicine, the worms will be
struggling to find their way out and by so doing they will be passed out
together with the faeces.
BUCKLEY. What is the power of *egbò ìpẹ̀ta* in this medicine?
FATOOGUN. This is also strong-smelling with a taste which tends to be sour
(*kọn*). This root stings the worm so much that it will be expelled with the
faeces.

Abraham's (1958) entry *ìpẹ̀ta* describes the flavour more
accurately. 'The root when fresh, has a rank odour with a
sweetish taste, but a numbing after-effect', which Fatoogun

himself expressed on another occasion when speaking more generally.

FATOOGUN. It (*ìpẹ̀ta*) is fairly bitter (*korò*), so people do not like to eat it. Its main function is to bring disease from all over the body to one place. If a person takes the ground-up plant into his mouth, it will remove all the coating from his tongue and from all over the mouth to the extent that cannot immediately take food and be able to distinguish the taste.

BUCKLEY. What is the power of *egbò túdè* in this medicine?

FATOOGUN. This root also has a smell which is easily transmitted to all parts of the body. It also tastes sour (*kọn*).

The use of a duck's intestines seemed to be a curious feature of this medicine.

BUCKLEY. Why is it that you use a male duck for a man and a female duck for a woman in this medicine?

FATOOGUN. This is because the blood of female things is one that can cure the diseases in the blood of a woman. So also the blood of male animals is capable of curing men of their diseases, according to the power of each sex. There are some medicines which would be effective for women and would not be effective for men and vice versa.

BUCKLEY. What, then, is the power of the intestine of duck in this medicine?

FATOOGUN. Its main work is to kill all the diseases in the body when it is used together with the other ingredients.

The palm-kernel oil (*àdín*) is here used to allow the medicine to be eaten with ease.

Oògùn arọ̀n àyà (agúnmu)		Fatoogun
sw. and pep.	*kọnnọ́fùrù*	cloves
b.	*orógbó*	bitter cola
pep.	*ataare*	alligator pepper
	f.óf.ó oló.kun	sea shell
sr.	*ẹ̀tù ìbọn*	gunpowder
sw. and pep.	*kọ́nún*	potash
sm.	*ewé òrokóro*	a leaf
sm.	*ewé ọ̀gọ̀n funfun*	*Combretum Platypterum*

Grind and use this medicine to take hot *ẹ̀kọ* also lying on one's face. This medicine will cause the worms to pass down into the stomach and pass out as faeces.

I asked Fatoogun directly about only a few of these ingredients since I already knew why most of them were employed in this type of medicine.

BUCKLEY. What power does *kǫnnǫ́fùrù* have in this medicine?

FATOOGUN. *Kǫnnǫ́fùrù* has a smell that can easily be transmitted to all parts of the body. This is strong and with all the other ingredients can easily kill the germs in the chest.

However, the curious flavour and smell of cloves clearly does not fit comfortably into a simple classificatory niche and in an earlier discussion Fatoogun had been more subtle.

BUCKLEY. What is *konnǫ́fùrù* used for?

FATOOGUN. It smells very sweet, but if it is tasted it will sting (*ta*) the mouth. The same is true for the disease; it attracts the disease with its smell and kills it with its taste.

The equally curious *f.ǫ́f.ǫ́ olǫ́.kun* or *f.ǫ́f.ǫ́ òkun* was identified by me as a white powdery seashell, long pointed, and somewhat oval in shape. Its cross-section is curved so that it has a concave and a convex surface, the latter being quite hard in contrast to the powdery chalk-like inside surface. Its name, however, *f.ǫ́f.ǫ́ òkun* (foam of the sea) is taken quite literally by my informants who did not seem to associate it with any shellfish.

FATOOGUN. This is the foam of the sea. When it comes to a part of the beach, it becomes solidified. . . . If you taste it, it is different from the taste of *kǫ́nún* (potash) but not completely like *iyǫ̀* (salt) and it works with other ingredients to cure diseases in the blood of the body.

BUCKLEY. What power does *f.ǫ́f.ǫ́ olǫ́.kun* have to cure *ẹ̀dà*? (cf. Chapter Four).

FATOOGUN. *F.ǫ́f.ǫ́ ǫ́ olǫ́.kun* tastes just like salt (*iyò*) and when diseases smell it they will be tempted to taste it. It will cut the diseases into pieces.

BUCKLEY. What power does *ewé òrokóro* have against worms in the chest?

FATOOGUN. The heat from this leaf (i.e. its smell) is one that the worms in the chest do not like. They will run away whenever they smell it.

BUCKLEY. What power does *ǫ̀gǫ̀n funfun* have against worms in the chest?

FATOOGUN. *Ǫgǫ̀n funfun* has the same power as that of *ewé òrokóro*. They have the same smell and heat.

This medicine, like the others, is bitter and hot-smelling; it also contains *kǫ́nún, ẹ̀tù ìbon* and perhaps *f.ǫ́f.ǫ́ olǫ́.kun* to act as a purge. *F.ǫ́f.ǫ́ olǫ́.kun* and *kǫnnǫ́fùrù* have the additional property that they both smell sweet and therefore attract the worm to the medicine so that they may be killed or driven out by their inherent lethal qualities.

(d) Oògùn inú rírun *(medicine for bellyache)*

Inú rírun, bellyache, is a broad term covering all pains in the abdomen. Where it is associated with other symptoms, such as swellings in the body, menstrual abnormalities etc., the *inú rírun* will be treated as part of a separate illness, but where the *inú rírun* is the only identifiable symptom it will be assumed that it is caused by the worm *aròn inú* or perhaps by *jèdíjèdí* and will be treated with the medicine *oògùn inù rírun*.

Bellyache caused by *aròn inú* is not normally taken very seriously.

FATOOGUN. If a person has bellyache (*inú rírun*) the first thing we say is that he should eat alligator pepper (*ataare*) because if the worm that causes the bellyache should taste it or if the *ataare* should touch the body of the worm it will sting (*ta*) the worm and the worm will run away from the place. It can run out of the place to where it can be passed out with the faeces. But if this *inú rírun* is not caused by worms or if this worm is not in the place to which the food we eat goes (i.e. if it is a different kind of worm) the *ataare* cannot cure it. If it is caused by *jèdíjèdí*, *ataare* cannot cure it and only another medicine can cure it.

Pepper, usually *ataare*, is often used in this way as an immediate relief for bellyache. Ex-soldiers who had served abroad in the British army during the Second World War complained to me that there were times when they had to eat European food without pepper. The various digestive troubles from which they suffered at that time were attributed to this. They made a point, I was told, of carrying *ataare* with them to provide protection and relief from these trifling but annoying ailments.

When the bellyache does not respond to such treatment it is taken more seriously. In the following medicine, bellyache is treated in the same way as for *aròn àyà* (worms in the chest) but for the first time we see the systematic addition of purgatives. The first of these is used not only for simple bellyache but also for *kùsínúkùso.de* (see p. 200).

Oògùn inú rírun (agúnmu)   Fatoogun

sw.	*àpólà òbúkò*	a piece of billy-goat meat
b.	*orógbó*	bitter cola
b.	*obì*	cola
pep.	*ewé orógi*	leaf of cactus?

sw. *iyọ̀*   salt
purg. *òbúòtóyọ̀*   saltpetre
pep. *ata*   pepper
Pound and wrap in the (cooked) meat.

FATOOGUN. *Apóla ẹrọn òbúkọ* is the thing that all these ingredients are put
inside and this will prevent their power from getting out before they are
dried up. *Orógbó* and *obí* are both bitter and when their power gets together
they become more powerful. *Ewé ọrógi* has a peppery power. *Obútóyọ̀* can
easily diffuse into the body because it changes immediately into water. It
has the power to remove the disease from the body (i.e. it is a purge). *Iyọ̀* is
to make the medicine taste sweet so that the person will be able to eat it. *Ata*
is to prevent the person vomiting the medicine.

In the next medicine, the power of the two main ingredients is
predominantly purgative, though Fatoogun implies in his
comments that they also taste unpleasant.

Oògùn inú rírun (agúnmu)   Fatoogun
purg. *egbò téy.ọ́*   root
sw.   *ọ̀gẹ̀dẹ̀ wẹẹrẹ*   banana
purg. *bààká*   a type of leek

FATOOGUN. No worm will taste *tẹ́.yọ́* and not die. *Bààká* also kills all diseases
in the body and will gather them together and expel them from the body.
. . . *Bààká* is a strong thing and it can kill any worm that tastes it. *Ọgẹ̀dẹ̀* is
used in this medicine to attract the worms. When the worms are sucking
the *ọ̀gẹ̀dẹ̀ wẹẹrẹ* they will also suck *bààká* with it and this will kill them and
they will be expelled with the faeces.

Both *téy.ọ́* and *bààká* are used as purges.

FATOOGUN. *Tẹ́y.ọ́*, also called *sọ̀nsọ̀nnàgi*, is a type of root which comes from
Tápà (i.e. Nupe country) used to make sponges (for washing the body or
eating utensils). If it is ground up and taken with water, the person will be
defecating within fifteen minutes.

The remaining medicines all have the same general purpose.

Oògùn inú rírun   Fatoogun
sr. *omi orònbó wẹ́wẹ́*   lime-juice
sr. *omi orònbó jàgọnrìn (= orònbó*
làkúègbé)   juice of sour orange
b.   *omi igi tẹ̀tẹ̀règún*   juice of *Namaranthus spinosus*
sw. *omi ìrẹ̀ké*   juice of sugar-cane

purg. *Kọ́nún bíñláñla*   'strong' potash
sr.   *ẹ̀tù*   gunpowder

Grind together the *kọ́nún* and the *ẹ̀tù* and mix with the liquid. This must be drunk.

In this medicine we have a typical collection of sour ingredients. The juice of *tẹ̀tẹ̀rẹ̀gún* is used because it is bitter. Similarly gunpowder 'is readily soluble in water and when tasted it is sour (*ó kọn*). Diseases do not like the flavour, for this sort of flavour kills the disease.'

The two fruits *oròñbó wẹ́wẹ́* and *oròñbó jàgọnrìn* are both sour. Of the former Fatoogun said:

FATOOGUN. It is used in medicines for bellyache (*inú rírun*) or if the stomach is rumbling (*inú kíkùn*). The taste is similar to omikon but it is more powerful. It is used in medicines for *jẹ̀díjẹ̀dí* and also for *kinísà*. It is used for worms. Any medicine used together with *omi oròñbó wẹ́wẹ́* will expel the worms or the disease with the excreta.

The combination of lime-juice with *kọ́nún* (potash) has special interest.

BUCKLEY. Some time ago you suggested that both *kọ́nún* and *oròñbó wẹ́wẹ́* separately were used against diseases, but when put together the lime dissolves the *kọ́nún*. I have found them used together in many medicines.

FATOOGUN. When potash is put into lime-juice it dissolves. What happens is that the power of the potash will be reduced and also the power of the lime-juice. Both of them will change to another type of medicine and this medicine is able to cure *jẹ̀díjẹ̀dí* and *inú kíkun* (groaning stomach).

BUCKLEY. *Is kọ́nún* dissolved by other bitter things or only by lime-juice?

FATOOGUN. There is no other cold liquid that dissolves *kọ́nún* unless the *kọ́nún* is ground up and added to the medicines or if it is added to hot *ẹ̀kọ* it will dissolve also.

This mixture of sour tasting ingredients is made more attractive to the worms and no doubt to the patient, by adding the juice from a sugar-cane.

(e) Oògùn ìgbẹ́ ọ̀rìn; tápà *(medicine for blood in the faeces)*

The commonest manifestation of the worm *jẹ̀díjẹ̀dí* is *tápà* or *ìgbẹ́ ọ̀rìn*—blood in the faeces. Adebawọ relies heavily upon the sour flavour of the two forms of *efinrin* and the similar plant *ìwú arúgbó* to cure this.

Oògùn tápà (àgbo) Adebawọ
sr. *ewé efinrin ńlá* leaf of *Hypotis Suaveolus Labiatae*
  ọṣẹ díẹ̀ a little soap
Squeeze them together in water and drink.

ADEBAWỌ. The sour flavour of *efinrin ńlá* combined with the cleansing power
of the soap will expel the worms with the faeces.

Oògùn ìgbẹ́ ọ̀rìn (asèjẹ) Adebawọ
sr. *èso efinrin ajá* seed of *Hypotis Suaveoleus*
sw. *ẹyin adìẹ* chicken's egg
sr. *èso ìwú arúgbó* seed of a variety of *Hypotis*
Cook and eat.

Fatoogun describes the role of eggs in medicines of this kind.

FATOOGUN. Eggs usually attract diseases. When they smell it they (the
diseases) will like to eat it and when they get it the other ingredients
included in the medicines will kill them and they will be expelled together
with the faeces.
BUCKLEY. I don't know *ìwú arúgbó*.
ADEBAWỌ. This plant is *ìwú arúgbó* is just like *efinrin* with white flowers. That
is why it is called *ìwú arúgbó* (the grey hairs of an old man).

(f) Oògùn kùsínúkùsó.de *(medicine for hernia)*

Fatoogun gave me two versions of this medicine. In the second
version he told me that the medicine would cure *kùsínúkùsó.de*
(hernia) which is caused by the activity of the worm *aròn ìrọ*.

Oògùn kùsínúkùsó.de (aròn ìrọ) (agúnmu) Fatoogun
  àpólà ẹrọn òrúkọ̀ a piece of goat's-meat
b. *orógbó* 11 11 bitter cola-nuts
b. *obì gidi* 11 11 cola-nuts
pep. *ataare* 11 11 pods ? of alligator pepper
purg. *bààká* 11 11 roots of a type of leek
Put all of these into the goat's-meat. Dry this for five years. After this time
pound it in a mortar. Then take:
pep. purg. *ewé ọrọ́gi* a leaf
purg. *obúòtóyọ̀* saltpetre
sw. *iyọ̀* salt
pep. *ata* pepper
Pound this together with the former medicine and use it to take hot *ẹkọ* (sr.).

The curious feature in this medicine is that the ingredients of
the first half of the medicine are stored in a large piece of goat's-

meat for five years before they are used. These ingredients are all extremely common in medicine and might also constitute a *garam masala* suitable for inclusion in any medicine to cure diseases.

(g) Medicines for diseases affecting women

Adebawọ told me that he sometimes prescribed aspirin or codeine to cure *arọ̀n wọ́mọwọ́mo*. I inquired about this when a patient was present.

ADEBAWỌ. Codeine or A.P.C. (proprietary brand) usually makes the body become hot. Any woman affected by this worm—some will take it with Schnapps or some other form of strong liquor (*ọtí*) and this will make their belly become warm and will drive away the worm.

If you notice, when a woman has just given birth, the belly will be as big as it was before until she takes some medicine which will melt the solid blood in the stomach. This belly will reduce itself to a normal size.

Oògùn arọ̀n obìnrin (asèjẹ)   Adebawọ
sm. *egbò wówó*   root of unknown plant
Grind and cook with *ẹja àrò* (mudfish) and eat it. This medicine should not be cooked in the same house where the person affected is present because the worm will smell it. It should be cooked in another house and given to the woman to eat. If this worm should taste it it will be passed out in the faeces.

This medicinal soup (*àsèjẹ*) depends upon the strong smell of the root of *wówó*—Adebawọ's strictures about its construction are intended to prevent the worm being frightened off so that it will avoid tasting the medicine. The root of *wówó* when cooked has a strong smell which is the source of its power to kill disease.

Oògùn arọ̀n obìnrin (àgbo)   Adebawọ
sm. *egbò ataparí obúkọ (= àgbásá)*   root of cabbage-palm
sm. *alùbọ́sà*   onion
purg. *bààká*   a type of leek
purg. *egbò àsùnwọ̀n*   root of *Cassia Podocarpa*
purg. *ewé àsùnwọ̀n*   leaf of *Cassia Podocarpa*
purg. *ewé àsùnwọ̀n òìbó*   leaf of *Cassia Alata*
pep. *odìndi ataare mẹ́ta*   3 white alligator pepper pods
Pound and put into *ọtí òìbó* (Schnapps) Drink a capful every morning.

With this medicine we are in very familiar territory. The root of *agbásá* and the onion are both used because of their smell. *Bààká* is a purge and *àsùnwọ̀n* in its various forms is much used to cure *àtọ̀sí* because of its purgative properties.

Oògùn jàṣẹ́jàṣẹ́ (àgbo)   Adebawọ
purg. *èso páńdọ̀rọ̀ (= amúy.ọ́n)*   sausage fruit
When the woman drinks the *àgbo*, this will drive the worm from the womb.
This woman will pass out the dirty things together with her excreta.

ADEBAWỌ. *Páńdọ̀rọ̀* is a thing that is difficult to eat. We use it in *àgbo*. It is
very bitter; if the worm should taste it, it will run away from the place (he
reaches out and picks a piece from a shelf). This is what is left from a
medicine I made for *jàṣẹ́jàṣẹ́*. A woman came to me complaining that she
had bellyache. During the bellyache she was urinating frequently. I asked
her if she was pregnant and she told me she was about three months
pregnant. I knew then it was *arọ̀n jàṣẹ́jàṣẹ́* that was worrying her. I quickly
prepared this infusion for her and told her to take it before breakfast. She
came back to tell me that the bellyache had stopped and that she had been
defecating. Yesterday she came back to say that she hadn't had any more
bellyache. This is because the worm had tasted the medicine, and this
medicine is just like salt to a snail. She told me yesterday that she had
passed out two worms in her faeces. They were the worms that were
troubling her. It is the juice (*omi*) of *páńdọ̀rọ̀* that brought them down.

(h) Oògùn àtọ̀sí *(medicine for gonorrhoea)*

Medicines for gonorrhoea do not differ essentially from the
other medicines we have considered except that they place
heavy emphasis upon purgatives and diuretics. In the first two
medicines, Fatoogun seeks merely to encourage his patient to
urinate so that the germs which cause *àtọ̀sí* shall be washed
away. These medicines are for the mildest form of *àtọ̀sí*, *àtọ̀sí*
ògbòdò.

Oògùn àtọ̀sí ògbòdò   Fatoogun
iyọ̀   salt
omi   water
Add two handfuls of salt to water and take a little at a time.

Salt is usually added to medicines and food to make it sweet
(*dùn*) but here it would make the water taste sour (*kọn*).

Oògùn àtọ̀sí ògbòdò (àgbo)
Ẹmu   palm wine   Fatoogun
Ewé awọ́n ẹkùn   leaf of thorny plant
Squeeze the leaf in palm wine and drink.

FATOOGUN. We all know that if someone drinks palm wine he will urinate frequently; when the power of this leaf is mixed with the palm wine the person will be able to urinate and sweat the *àtọ̀sí* from his body. The leaf itself (its name means the tongue of a leopard) . . . is called *awọ́n ẹkùn* because, when it grows it has thorns all over its body; so before you can detach it from the plant you must either wear something (protective) or be very careful so that the thorns do not prick you. (Perhaps like taking the tongue from a leopard's mouth).

Adebawọ suggests that its name derives from the fact that it is rough like sandpaper which if the idea is generally accepted would imply its ability to scrape the disease from the body.

ADEBAWỌ. There are many leaves which are used to cure it. The medicine to cure *àtọ̀sí* must include the one that will allow the person to excrete freely. Europeans have some tablets which are swallowed but this will only weaken the power of the disease. If the person does not use the medicine that can make him excrete, the disease will return as soon as he does hard work.

As was suggested earlier, medicines for the diseases affecting the lower part of the body emphasize ingredients that allow the patient to urinate and defecate so that the disease in that part of the body may be expelled. At the same time, we find ingredients being used because of their ability to kill the germs. Such ingredients, as expected, are pungent or bitter or sour in flavour.

Complementary to this emphasis on bitter and sour ingredients, Adebawọ also stresses that the patient should be discouraged from eating sweet food.

ADEBAWỌ. We must not give sweet things to the person affected by *àtọ̀sí*, for example sugar, *ọ̀gẹ̀dẹ̀ omini* (a type of sweet banana) or *dòdò* (ripe plantain fried in ground-nut oil). If the person eats sugar, the penis can be cut by the *àtọ̀sí* or the man may be unable ever to have intercourse with a woman again.

However, sugar can be eaten before taking the medicine for *àtọ̀sí*—say about three or four lumps. This sugar is to attract the *àtọ̀sí* germs. After five minutes the medicine will be taken to meet the germs. These germs will then be expelled together with the faeces.

Oògùn àtọ̀sí (ẹ̀tù)   Adebawọ
purg. *Asùnwọ̀n dúdú*   *Cassia Podocarpus*
purg. *Asùnwọ̀n òìbó*   *Cassia Alata*

purg.	*Téy.ǫ́*	*Cassia Alata*
purg.	*Bàrà*	water melon
b.	*Ṣápó*	*vernonia conferta*
purg. b.	*Egbò páńdǫ̀rǫ̀*	
	(amúny.ǫn)	root of sausage-tree
purg.	*kǫ́nún bíńláńlà*	potash
b.	*òkúsú aró*	refuse from dye-pit
b.	*orógbó*	bitter cola
pep.	*ataare*	alligator pepper
pep.	*iyèré*	black pepper

After burning (*jó*) these leaves and the other ingredients it should be used to eat hot *ẹ̀kǫ* (sr). The person will then be able to urinate freely, and if there is anything that blocks the hole of the penis this will come out together with the urine.

I began to go through the list of ingredients with Adebawǫ beginning with the power of *àsùnwǫ̀n* and *téy.ó* to cure *àtǫ̀sí*. After explaining about *àsùnwǫ̀n* he gave me a list of ingredients that had a similar effect.

ADEBAWǪ. *Asùnwǫ̀n* is just like the medicine that makes you defecate frequently. After the other ingredients have gathered all of the disease together *àsùnwǫ̀n* will then push them out in the form of faeces and urine . . .

This is a list of some of the ingredients that can make a person defecate.

àsùnwǫ̀n	*Cassia*
téy.ǫ́	
bàrà	water-melon
oríkòtóun (called in Yoruba *gbèjẹ̀dì*)	
ǫ̀mùnnún ewé igi arágbá	
àwòròṣo	

But these ingredients cannot cure *àtǫ̀sí* without the help of other ingredients. Each of these ingredients has its own separate ingredients which must be added to it before it will work.

This list, together with our earlier knowledge encompasses almost all of the ingredients in the medicine. Of the others *okúsú aró*, the thick black refuse left over from the process of indigo-dyeing, is included because it is bitter. And *egbò ṣápó* is used because it is bitter and has a diuretic effect. It features in the next recipe, which was given to me by Adebawǫ but explained by Fatoogun.

Oògùn àtǫ̀sí		Adebawǫ
b.	*egbò ṣápó*	root of *vernonia conferta*

purg.	*eèpo amúny.ǫ́n*	bark of sausage-tree
purg.	*bààká*	a type of leek
b.	*ęręsílę̀.és.ín*	a leaf which has fallen to the earth
b.	*bàrà*	melon
purg.	*kǫ́nún*	potash

Cook to make *àgbo* and drink a cupful each day. It will cure *àtǫ̀sí* within a week.

FATOOGUN. This (*àtǫ̀sí*) is a disease that men get from women and it is situated where the sperm (*àtǫ̀*) is. The thing that helps *àtǫ̀sí* is none other than *jèdíjèdí*, and *jèdíjèdí* does not like the bitterness of *bàrà*. The bark of *ṣápó* is also bitter (the recipe in fact used the root rather than the bark) and it will make the person expel the sickness with his excreta. *Egbò ṣápó* can also turn the disease into water. *Atǫ̀sí* is always slippery and *ęręsílę̀.és.ín* will gather the disease together. The other ingredients will help these main ones.

Fatoogun also told me that the shrub *.és.ín* is used to cure *ìgbàló.de* (dirty mouth) which is his own way of saying that it tastes particularly bitter.

Fatoogun's medicines have a similar structure.

Oògùn àtǫ̀sí alájere (àgbo) (medicine for gonorrhoea, 'the owner of colander')

Fatoogun

sr.	*eèbò àràbà*	bark of white silk cotton tree
b.	*egbò làpálàpá funfun*	root of physic nut
purg.	*bààká*	a leek
purg.	*ewé àsùnwǫ̀n*	leaf *Cassia Podocarpa*
pep.	*ę̀ę̀rù*	Ethiopian pepper
b/sw.	*eèpo àwùn*	bark of *alstonia congensis*

Cook thoroughly to make *àgbo*. Drink, a little at a time three times a day.

FATOOGUN. *Atǫ̀sí* does not like bitter or sour things. *Eèpo àhùn* (= *àwùn*) is bitter and that is why we use it to cure *àtǫ̀sí*. *Aràbà* has a sour bark. When all of these are prepared they will cure *àtǫ̀sí* and will enable the person to expel it with faeces and urine.

Aìdǫn is a large seed pot from the tree. Its flavour is ambiguous and rather like cloves (*kǫnnófùrù*). On one occasion Fatoogun emphasized its sweetness.

FATOOGUN. If you taste *aìdǫn* you will find that it is sweet, but it has power inside that sweetness. If it touches a worm it will kill it.

On another he stressed its bitter flavour.

FATOOGUN. *Aìdǫn* is bitter if it is tasted, and the diseases do not like the smell.

Endnote

[1] This question was mistakenly asked about the leaf rather than the root. Usually, however, it seems that the power of a root is considered to be the same as that of the leaf.

Medicines for èelá

I was able to collect only a few medicines for èelá, and none at all for ètè. The medicines for èelá were given to me by Adebawọ. Some of these were of normal concoctions of bitter, sour, and peppery ingredients. Others, however, use black-coloured ingredients to change the red skin of èelá into a healthy black. Whether these are intended to dye the skin or whether the 'power' to turn the skin black is inferred in the manner suggested in Chapter Seven is not completely clear, but nor am I sure whether this distinction is very meaningful.

Oògùn èelá olórontó (àgbo)   Adebawọ
pep. *ẹ̀ẹ̀rù alamọ*   empty seed-pods of Ethiopan pepper
b.   *egbò ọ̀kọn*   root of *Combretum Micranthum*
b.   *eèpo ọgọ́nó*   bark of Benin mahogany tree
The bark of *ọgọ́nó* and the other ingredients will be cooked.

This infusion is simply a mixture of bitter ingredients assisted by the pepperiness of *ẹ̀ẹ̀rú*. The bark of *ọgọ́nó* is a common ingredient in medicine used because of its bitter flavour. *Ọkọn* tastes 'just like *làpálàpá*', i.e. it is very bitter.

Oògùn èelá (ọṣe)   Adebawọ
b.   *eèpo ọ̀bọ̀*   unknown bark
b.   *ọgọ́nó*   Benin mahogany (bark?)
pep. *ẹ̀ẹ̀rù alamọ*   empty seed-pods of Ethiopian pepper
Use in soap. *Eèpo ọ̀bọ̀* will clear up all skin diseases (*àrùn ara*) from the body—it is very bitter.

Oògùn èelá olórontó (ọṣẹ)   Adebawọ
pep. *ẹ̀ẹ̀rù alamọ*   empty seed-pods of Ethiopian pepper
b.   *eèpo ọ̀bọ̀*   unknown bark
sr. *ètù òyìnbó*   gunpowder
Grind these together with some other ingredients and mix with soap. Wash the child with it every three days.

In this next medicine, colour plays a more direct part. The medicine seeks, directly, to make the red skin black.

Oògùn èelá (àgbo)   Adebawọ
b. *ewé ṣayò*   leaf of *Heloptelea Grandis*
   ọgẹ̀dẹ̀ ọ̀mìnì dúdú 4   four green (lit. black) bananas
   ewé òdú   leaf of *Solassum Nodiflornin*
b. *ẹ̀rẹṣílẹ̀.és.ín*   leaf of unknown plant that has fallen
                                        to the ground

These will be cooked in water and the child will drink it and wash with it also. The child will expel the disease from inside his belly with his excreta and he will be well.

Ewé ṣayò is a bitter leaf and so also is *ọgẹ̀dẹ̀ dúdú* . . . The leaf of *ṣayò* can also be used to cure sores if it is squeezed and applied to the sore. The power of these two things is to cure the sores caused by *èelá*.

BUCKLEY. What is the work of *òdú*?

ADEBAWỌ. It does the same work as *ọgẹ̀dẹ̀ ọ̀mìnì* to restore the normal complexion of the child.

In this medicine there is a curious juxtaposition of colours. The fallen leaf of *èés.ín* is bitter, but in response to my question 'How does it cure *èelá*?' Adebawọ pointed to its association with redness.

ADEBAWỌ. If this leaf is cooked it will turn the water red. This leaf can be soaked with other ingredients to wash a sore—it will also kill the germs.

But the medicine is also associated with blackness. The juice of the leaf *ewé òdú* is most commonly used to heal the cuts and as a black dye in tattooing and the medicine as a whole would, despite the redness caused by the *èés.ín*, be a black colour. Perhaps Adebawọ is indicating that, in the same way as this combination of ingredients transforms redness into blackness, so also would the red skin of the child be transformed. At all events the bitterness of *èés.ín* would drive away the disease.

The next medicine, however, uses palm-oil and camwood, both of which are red without any distinctively black ingredients. Care is needed in interpreting it.

Oògùn èelá (when the disease is peeling the body)   Adebawọ
b. *ewé ewúuro*   leaf of *Vernonia*

Grind well and mix with *osùn* (camwood) and *epo* (palm-oil). Rub the child with it after his bath. This will cure all the sores on the body of the child

Camwood is a deep red wood often used to rub upon the skin in order to remove unsightly flecks of dead skin, and palm-oil, which is also red, is used similarly as an embrocation. Although they are both red in colour their redness has an unusual symbolic significance peculiar to them alone. As is implied in Chapter 6, both the red *osùn* and palm-oil have the unusual association of safe, concealed redness. Paradoxically the redness of camwood and palm-oil have the effect of hiding the redness of the *èelá* and restoring a healthy complexion to the child. In this medicine, the main ingredient is significant, because of its bitterness.

The final medicine also combines *ewúuro* with the palm-oil and here the bitterness and blackness of *òdú* is included.

Oògùn èelá		Adebawọ
b. *ewé òdú*	leaf of *Solassum Nodiflorum*	
b. *ewé ewúuro*	leaf of *Vernonia*	
epo	palm-oil	

Grind together and add palm-oil; rub the child after his bath.

Medicines for ẹ̀dà, ṣọmúròrò, and ibà

(a) Medicines for ẹ̀dà and ṣọmúròrò

In all of this discussion of the complex inversions which characterize the syndrome of ẹ̀dà and ṣọmúròrò (Chapter Four) it should not be forgotten that both illnesses belong to Image 1. They are caused by 'germs' which inhabit the body and which need to be expelled before the illness can be cured.

Though they have a similar cause, they are nevertheless always treated as separate illnesses using different medicines. Medicines for ẹ̀dà, like those for àtọ̀sí (gonorrhoea) and for other illnesses of the genital area, are usually taken internally and sometimes contain purgatives. Medicines for ṣọmúròrò are applied directly to the breasts, either in an oil, or in a medicinal soap. As their main purpose is to kill the germs which cause the illness there is a preponderance of ingredients which have bitter, sour, or peppery flavours and which have pungent smells.

Within this familiar general framework, the medicines also take account of the inverted and chaotic state which the diseases have created in the body of the unfortunate woman. The recipes include ingredients which seek to reverse the various harmful processes so that the body may return to a healthy state. Many of these ingredients have the power to perform the required task because, either on their own or in combination, they are perceived to have natural characteristics which are similar to the effect sought for in the body of the patient. The following recipes will be presented with my own and my informants' comments. The issues raised by the symbolic elements in the medicines are discussed in Chapter Seven.

(i) Oògùn ẹ̀dà (medicine for ẹ̀dà)

Oògùn ẹ̀dà obìnrin (women's ẹ̀dà) (asèjẹ)   Fatoogun
sw. ẹyin adìẹ—as many as you can
     afford   chickens' eggs

b. *èso làpálàpá funfun*   physic nut

If the medicine is intended for only one person, use 6 seeds of *làpálàpá* and 2 eggs. Grind the seeds; put into a container and cook using salt and palm-oil and one cupful of water, breaking the eggs into the mixture also. Cook well and give to the woman to eat two or three times so that the germs may be expelled with the faeces.

Oògùn ẹdà (ọṣẹ)   Fatoogun

s. *ewé oronbó wẹẹrẹ*   leaf of lime-tree

  ọṣẹ dúdú àbí ọṣẹ funfun   black or white soap

Pound together; the woman must wash her genitals with the soap.

These two medicines simply use a bitter and a sour ingredient to kill the disease. In the first medicine, eggs are used merely as a sweet ingredient to attract the disease.

FATOOGUN. Eggs usually attract diseases when they are smelled. They (the diseases) will like to eat it. The other ingredients which are included with the egg will kill them and they will be expelled from the body with the faeces.

The next medicines have the same basic formulation, but they have the additional feature that they are concerned to reverse the disruption caused by *ẹdà*. Of the two main illnesses of the *ẹdà-ṣọmúròrò* syndrome, *ẹdà* presents the herbalist with the fewest theoretical difficulties. First of all, his task is merely to kill the germs which are responsible for the illness, and this is attempted in a straightforward way using bitter and sour ingredients. Second, he needs to hide away the semen which is flowing from the woman's body. Finally, he may try to reverse the inversion of blood and water which is implicit in this illness.

In the following medicine all three of these intentions are present.

Oògùn ẹdà (agúnmu)   Fatoogun

    ewé patọnmọ́   *Mimosa pudica*

    owó ẹyọ   cowrie shells

purg. *kọ́nún bínláńlà*   potash

    ẹfun àdó   red-streaked chalk

sm. *eku asín*   a type of rat

Grind and take with hot *ẹ̀kọ*. The woman will expel the disease with her faeces. There should be no sexual intercourse for at least three weeks.

The rat is used with the sour *ẹ̀kọ* (cornstarch gruel) and the purgative *kónún* (potash) for the reasons which were discussed in Chapter Two:

FATOOGUN. God has already given this rat power to cure any type of illness. If you kill this rat, it will smell. And this kind of smell is the one that has power against any disease.

Efun àdó is unlike the normal white chalk in that it contains distinct red streaks. This, it seems, gives it the capacity to separate red and white in the body of the woman.

FATOOGUN. *Efun àdó* is to remove any disease that can change the blood into water. If there is any part of the body that is affected by germs, *efun àdó* can cover the place up, and it usually renews the blood.

Owó ẹyọ, the cowrie shell is, somewhat more obscurely, used for the same purpose.

FATOOGUN. God has given it the power to wash all the diseases from the body when it is used together with other ingredients. *Owó ẹyọ* is not bitter; it will separate water from blood and remove any disease in the blood.

Ewé patọnmọ́ has a different purpose. It is a well known leaf, discoverable, indeed, in British gardens. It has one obvious characteristic. Abraham (1958) gives as his first translation of '*O patọnmọ́n*' the phrase 'she closed her legs'. The peculiarity of this leaf lies in the fact that when it is touched, it shrinks away from the hand as though it is frightened, and informants on various occasions told me that its movements resembled a woman closing her legs. This association may even be implied in the Latin botanical name. In watching the extraordinary movements of this leaf I had no difficulty in seeing the resemblance. Here it is used in medicine to allow the patient to close her legs and thus to stem the flow of semen from her body. The prohibition upon sexual intercourse which the recipe prescribes is merely to discourage the development of the disease which eats and thrives upon semen.

In the following medicine, the shell of the large edible snail (*ìgbín*) is used. This snail is known periodically to seal itself—and also the white fluid *omi ìgbín*—within its shell. I was surprised therefore when Fatoogun did not regard the similarity of the snail shell and the womb as the reason for its use in the medicine.

Oògùn ẹ̀dà obìnrin (medicine for women's *ẹ̀dà*)   Fatoogun
    karawun ìgbín   snail shell
purg. *kọ́nún bínláńlà*   potash

Grind and use it to take hot *ẹ̀kọ*. The germs will come out of the body in the faeces. There should be no sexual intercourse for at least three weeks.

The power of the snail shell is rather similar to that of potash. It is not bitter. Its main work is to wash away any diseases in the body.

In the next medicine it is the water of snail (*omi ìgbín*) which is used. Here again, Fatoogun avoids making a direct parallel between the snail's fluid and the semen.

Oògùn ẹ̀dà fún obìnrin (agúnmu)   Fatoogun
purg. *egbò té.yọ́*   a root
    eèmọ́ àgbò   *Pupalin Lappacea (Amaran Thraceae)*
    kọ́nún bínláńlà   potash
sm. *iṣu alùbọ́sà atápà (= alùbọ́sà*
    funfun)   white variety of onion
    omi ìgbín méjì   fluid from two snails

Grind, and mix with the water from the snails. Use a spoonful to take hot *ẹ̀kọ*, but the medicine should not be taken every day, but rather every five or ten days. The germs will come out in the faeces. The germs are white and visible in the faeces.

Fatoogun had remarked in an earlier interview:

FATOOGUN. *Omi ìgbín* is used to cool down any part of the body which is hot. If you touch *ìgbín* (snail), it is always very cold to the touch.

And certainly *omi ìgbín* is associated very closely with coolness and peace. The snail itself is offered to the god *Ọbàtálá* who is not only 'white' but 'cool' (*tútù*) and pacific. His followers are said to drink the white *omi ìgbín* which in this context is known as *omi ẹ̀rọ̀*, the water of propitiation (Abraham, 1958, *ìgbín*, (1) (a); *ẹ̀rọ̀*). Another remark by Fatoogun emphasizes this aspect of the properties of *omi ìgbín*.

FATOOGUN. I usually relieve the flesh (with *omi ìgbín*) when it has been tied up with diseases. Its main job is to soften any part of the body that is becoming too hard.

The main emphasis of this medicine is upon killing and expelling the disease. *Egbò tẹ́.yọ́* is bitter, but it is also used as a purgative.

FATOOGUN. This has the power to go round the body in the blood, the water and the fat in the body, and it will collect all the diseases together in the body and bring it to the place where they will be expelled.

There seems to have been no particular significance in the choice of the white onion instead of the commoner purple one.

The ingredient *èso eèmó àgbò* is sometimes used because of its sticky quality. According to Abraham, plants called '*eèmón*' are 'distinguished by having burrs which stick to one's clothing'. My initial interpretation of its use was therefore that it would allow the semen to stick (*mó*) in the womb and at first Fatoogun seemed to support this idea.

BUCKLEY. How does *eèmó àgbò* cure *èdà*?

FATOOGUN. It is used to retain the pregnancy in the womb and is used to prevent miscarriage (*àsoògbó*). It is used if a woman is menstruating during pregnancy.

This did not exactly answer my question but it did reinforce my idea. When at a later date I repeated my question, his reply was more confusing.

FATOOGUN. If this is burnt together with other ingredients, it will always wash away (*mó*) diseases in the body. This is why it is called *èso eèmó àgbò*. (Fatoogun here changed the tone of the first 'e' of *eèmó* from mid to low to accommodate his explanation.) These seeds always stick to the body of a ram and that is why we call it *eèmó àgbò* (that which sticks to a ram).

Fatoogun is here savouring the delights of a characteristically Yoruba ambiguity. The syllable *mó*, from which he thinks *eèmó* (or *èèmó*) is derived, has, according to Abraham, five distinct meanings but Fatoogun here is playing with only two. *Eèmó* can mean 'that which cleans' or 'that which sticks'. I had expected its use in this medicine to be the second which corresponds to its most obvious natural characteristic. Fatoogun, rather playfully, has chosen the first.

In the last of these medicines for *èdà* the symbolic nature of the medicine is more explicit.

Oògùn èdà		Adebawo
Ewé eépín	leaf of *Ficus Asperifolia*	
lèwù òpè	hair on top of palm-tree	
èko	cornstarch porridge	
adìe	chicken	

A hen will be sacrificed to the palm-tree, then someone will climb the palm-tree and take from it all the lẹ̀wù ọpẹ that he can find. The intestines (ifun) of the hen will be put on the lẹ̀wù ọpẹ which will have been put together and also the ẹ̀kọ. Then all the feathers of the hen will be added to it. These will be folded in a cap (fìlà) and burnt immediately on returning home. The woman will use the medicine to eat hot ẹ̀kọ, three times a day beginning the second day that the menstruation has stopped flowing.

Adebawọ in this fascinating medicine seemed to feel that he understood the power of each ingredient but he found difficulty in putting his ideas into words.

BUCKLEY. What is the power of ewé eépín in oògùn ẹ̀dà?

ADEBAWỌ. Eépín is not the only thing that is used in this medicine (i.e. do not think that we can understand it in isolation). It is when the womb turns upside down that the semen usually flows out of it. We should not use the leaf that is turned upside down but only the one that is the proper way up. We use the leaf so that the womb will turn upward into its normal position. For example, we use àpáàdí that faces the wall [broken pots (apáàdí) are sometimes built into the walls of houses] for medicines of love (oògùn olúufẹ́) and also we use the same àpáàdí of which the back has stuck to the wall for émèrè (abíkú) because the àpáàdí with its back to the wall cannot see the wall. Thus we use the leaf of eépín that faces upward. We also use lẹ̀wù ọppẹ and ẹ̀kọ for this. It is always stored in a cap and the woman will start to use it five days after menstruation.

There is here, of course, a slight variation in the detail—the second day has changed to five days after menstruation. More interesting is his emphasis that the leaf should face upward so that the womb should not spill its load. Though he does not state it in so many words the analogy is here being drawn between the woman's belly and a pot or calabash. Given this analogy, the use of ewé eépín in this medicine is not surprising. Eépín is a tough sandpapery leaf ideally suited and commonly used as a scourer for cleaning out pots and calabashes.

But we have scarcely begun: This, together with lẹ̀wù ọpẹ, the guts of the chicken, and a lump of ẹ̀kọ are burnt in a cap.

BUCKLEY. Why do they tie this medicine in a cap?

ADEBAWỌ. When a man puts on a cap (fìlà) it is impossible for anyone to see his hair. When we are going to prepare this medicine the ẹ̀kọ must be tied in the cap. We do not always understand why our grandfathers did these things in medicine and we can only explain some of it that we understand. There are some medicines which must not see light.

We shall take this ẹ̀kọ and climb a palm-tree where we shall cover the ẹ̀kọ with *lẹ̀wù ọ̀pe*. The hen that is going to be used in the medicine must be the one with eggs inside. It will be cut open and the guts (*ifun*) and the eggs will be put into the *ẹ̀ko*. This will be covered with *lẹ̀wù ọ̀pẹ* before it is put into the cap. This can be burned together with the cap so that the *ẹ̀dà* will not affect the woman again.

We still have the problem of understanding the chicken's guts and the *lẹ̀wù ọ̀pẹ* but we can attempt an interpretation so far. *Eépín* cleans the womb of diseases as it normally cleans a calabash or pot, but care is taken in the selection of the leaf that it will not induce the womb to spill what is inside it. *Ẹ̀ko* is white, like the semen which must be kept inside the womb, and it is to this that Adebawọ refers when he explains the significance of the cap. The cap is what hides the hair; it hides the white *ẹ̀kọ* in the medicine; and it serves to hide the semen inside the woman. So much is clear enough.

But why is a cap appropriate? An answer has already been suggested where we indicated the possibility that hair had strong associations with whiteness. The analogy may thus be stated in Figure 41.

white hair ⟶ body in white cloth ⟶ hidden in earth
white hair ⟶ hidden in cap
white *ẹ̀kọ* ⟶ hidden in cap
white semen ⟶ hidden in womb
white semen ⟶ hidden as though in a calabash or pot

FIGURE 41. A medicine for *ẹ̀dà*

The analysis is however not complete, for the significance of the chicken and of *lẹ̀wù ọ̀pẹ* has still to be discovered. In his first statement of the medicine, only the guts of the chicken are mentioned and Adebawọ seems to state that the *lẹ̀wù ọ̀pẹ* is placed first into the cap. His account improves with repetition however. Adebawọ told me that the guts, together with the unlaid eggs of the chicken, are used, and that they are all covered with the *lẹ̀wù ọ̀pẹ* before being put into the cap.

The use of the chicken is therefore clearly to express the womb-like quality of the cap, for it is the *interior* of the chicken and specifically its unlaid eggs which are thus concealed. The eggs are of course not merely white, but are themselves an encased mixture of red and white, for ultimately, though the medicine emphasizes the hiding of whiteness, it is pregnancy which is desired.

Lẹ̀wù ọ̀pẹ (the hair at the top of a palm-tree) is more problematical but its significance is clear enough when we understand that it is akin not to the other contents of the cap so much as to the cap itself. Lẹ̀wù ọ̀pẹ is the hairy substance found in the stem of the palm-tree and also in the male inflorescence (àrọn) on the palm-tree (see pp. 124 ff.) where it is like a woven mat. According to Mr Ayandokun it can be used as kindling and can even be ignited relatively easily by striking two stones together near it. Abraham shares this opinion (1958, lẹ̀wù, B).

Here however we have a different side to its character. The stem (igi) of the palm-tree and àrọn are both directly connected with white palm wine. The stem is known to be the place where the palm wine is found and it is tapped from the inflorescence at the top of the tree àrọn. To reach the wine the tapper must cut his way through the lẹ̀wù ọ̀pẹ in the àrọn. When he has finished his work the lẹ̀wù will be used to stop the flow of the wine.

I asked Adebawọ about this.

BUCKLEY. Lẹ̀wù ọ̀pẹ is used in many types of medicine to stop liquids flowing, for example in oògùn ẹ̀dà and to stop the flow of blood. What is its power to do this?

This was, of course, a 'leading question', but Adebawọ was not easily led and his answer, while vague, seems to reinforce my point of view.

ADEBAWỌ. Lẹ̀wù ọ̀pẹ is not the only ingredient used. I have told you how we use lẹ̀wù ọ̀pẹ to wrap ẹkọ and put it into a cap. (Similarly) if blood is rushing out of a wound and lẹ̀wù ọ̀pẹ is put on to it the blood will stop. It usually works together with other ingredients such as ewé eépín and ẹkọ. In this medicine it is difficult to know the specific power of lẹ̀wù ọ̀pẹ. Lẹ̀wù ọ̀pẹ can also be burnt with other ingredients which are given to a woman to put into the cloth she uses for menstruation. Immediately the menstruation touches this, the blood will stop.

In a general discussion of the power of lẹ̀wù ọ̀pẹ Fatoogun seemed to share this opinion.

FATOOGUN. It is used so that women can conceive and also to cure all types of ẹ̀dà and all types of àṣẹ, àṣẹ dúdú and àṣẹ funfun. It is able to clear all the dirt in the vagina and also to close it together.

Lẹ̀wù ọ̀pẹ, then, like the cap, the womb, the calabash and the black earth has the capacity to hide. Normally it hides white palm wine inside the palm-tree; here it combines with the other ingredients to hide the semen inside the body of a woman. This medicine is not totally divorced from Image 1, for the leaf of *eépín* is included in it to counteract the germs which cause the illness. Nevertheless, we have here a complex structure of symbols which evokes the bodily state which the herbalist seeks to induce in his patient.

(ii) *Oògun ṣọmúròrò* (medicine for *ṣọmúròrò*)

Medicines for *ṣọmúròrò* are distinct from medicines for *ẹ̀dà* but are founded on similar principles. They are applied directly to the breasts and have the intention of killing the germs which cause the illness.

Oògùn ṣọmúròrò (ọ̀ṣẹ)   Fatoogun
sr. *èso efinrin*   seeds of *Ocimun viride*
sr. *ewé efinrin*   leaves of *Ocimum viride*
Pound together with soap to wash the breast that has germs.

Oògùn ṣọmúròrò   Adebawọ
sr. *ọsọ̀n jàgọnyìn*   sour orange
This is cut and put into a pot together with something whose name I have forgotten. This is cooked with *epo* (palm-oil) and is rubbed on the breast.

These medicines are construed according to the simplest principles of Yoruba medicine, and raise no difficulties.

I had discovered however in my first source of medicinal recipes, the book by Agosu, that medicines for *ṣọmúròrò* were sometimes rather more complicated and I asked Fatoogun about one of them.

BUCKLEY. I have found medicines in which a woman suffering from this disease divides the medicine into two parts, and, using two sponges, washes each breast separately into a separate hole in the ground using one sponge and a portion of medicine for each breast.

FATOOGUN. I know a medicine which involves these two holes. And one must use two pegs to knock the holes in the ground. The pegs are removed and the woman washes the breasts, the left one into the left hole, the right one into the right hole. After this the two pegs are hammered into the holes to prevent the disease from returning. The germs that cause this disease live in the air (*inú atẹ́gun ni wọ́n gbé*). So when the breasts are washed and the peg has been knocked into the hole or covered with sand, the germs will not be able to come up again.

Adebawọ volunteered similar information:

ADEBAWỌ. *Ṣọmúròrò* can be cured with soap medicine together with two different sponges. We must not use the sponge that is used to wash the left breast to wash the right breast. So also the calabashes that the breasts will be washed into. Two holes will be dug and the left sponge will be put into the left hole. The right sponge will be put into the right hole.

   There is a type of medicine that will be prepared which the woman will rub on her breasts (like ointment). If the breasts are washed with soap we will be able to see the germs in the calabash.

Here is one such medicine.

Oògùn ṣọmúròrò   Adebawọ
sr.   *efinrin wẹ́wẹ́*   *Ocimun.viride (labiatae)*
pep. *ẹ̀ẹ̀rù alamọ*   empty seed pod of Ethiopian pepper
Pound with soap and use to wash the breasts.

BUCKLEY. What is the power of *efinrin wẹ́wẹ́* and *ẹ̀ẹ̀rù alamọ* to cure *ṣọmúròrò?*
ADEBAWỌ. These are pounded together with *ọṣẹ* to wash the breasts and it will kill the germs in the breast.

This is in essence a simple medicinal soap to kill germs.

BUCKLEY. What is the purpose of using one sponge for the left breast and another for the right?
ADEBAWỌ. This is because the germs in one breast may be more than in the other, and that is why we do not use the sponge of the left for the right breast. It is just like the doctors who always dip the thing that they use in the hospital in hot water before they use it. This is to prevent a disease from one breast affecting another. These sponges will be buried, the left one in the left hole and the right one in the right hole.

Medicines of this sort have an explicit aim, which is to hide the germs away in the earth where they may not cause reinfection and to avoid contaminating one breast with the germs that afflict the other.

   This explanation is, of course, sufficient in itself, but I do feel that there is room for a little more sophistication than either man allows for. In the first place, burying germs in the earth requires presumably only one hole, not two. Second, neither Adebawọ nor Fatoogun refers to these holes simply as 'two separate holes'. They are 'the left hole' and 'the right hole'. But no two holes in the ground can be identified as 'left' and 'right' without a conscious effort of will.

In the illness *ṣọmúròrò*, as in *ẹ̀dà*, there is a complex destruction of the order of the female body. In both illnesses it may be considered sufficient merely to expel the germs which cause the disruption for this in itself will serve to separate the red and white fluids and restore the body to health. But if the illnesses are considered separately it will be seen that there are two sets of problems.

In *ẹ̀dà* the medicine has the relatively clear task of stemming the flow of semen from the womb, and this can be undertaken using specific procedures. In *ṣọmúròrò*, the disruption is more diffuse and is dealt with by a more radical emphasis upon orderliness. By making an extreme distinction between left and right, the medicine seeks to restore the correct relationship between the upper and lower, inside and outside, and red and white features of the female body, all of which are in disarray.

(b) Medicines for ibà (fever)

Medicines for *ibà* are so very well known in Yorubaland, that my informants were ill-disposed to discuss them at any great length. Here are a few recipes which indicate the general nature of medicines for *ibà*. They have the same principle of construction as other simple recipes.

The first of these uses a leaf which is nowadays widely used in medicines for *ibà*.

Oògùn ibà àbí ibà pọ́njúpọ́njú (àgbo)   Adebawọ
b. *ewé dongóyárò*   a leaf
Cook and drink the water.

ADEBAWỌ. This tree was called *ẹ̀kẹ* in the olden days, and we did not know that it could work on *ibà*. There are three types of *dóngóyárò*: one is used in the roofing of a house; the other one grows a finger-like fruit; the third one grows round fruit. This tree is bitter and this is the power it has to cure *ibà*. I can remember about two and a half years ago when I was affected by *ibà*, one of the sons of my landlord told me to go and cook *dóngóyárò* but he warned me that it was too bitter. I cooked this *dóngóyárò* with other ingredients for *ibà* that I know, for when I tasted it I found that it was too bitter. So I had to cook it alone so as to know its power. *Ibà* does not like sweet things. There are some people who use saccharine and they think that this cannot bring about *ibà*. *Ibà* does not do any good to the body except to kill a person. Using sweet things in (medicine for) *ibà* can kill a person.

Fatoogun also knows this tree.

BUCKLEY. Do you know the tree called *igi ẹkẹ* also called *dóńgóyárò*?
FATOOGUN. (After some thought) This is called *ẹkẹ òyìnbó* (European *ẹkẹ*).
BUCKLEY. Is it to be found in your area?
FATOOGUN. This has been in my area for a long time. This tree was used to cure *ibà*, but I cannot say whether it was the Europeans who brought the tree to this country because I do not find this tree in the *Ifá* stories (*itọ̀n ifá*), because each tree has its own story in *Ifá*. It was the Europeans that brought this tree because of *ibà*—so that we could be using it to cure *ibà*. If this tree is cooked, it is always bitter and that is why it can cure *ibà*. If it is drunk when it is hot it will make the person perspire. We all know that *ibà* prevents a person from perspiring.

The next medicine contains the ingredients from the *orúwọ̀* tree, also much used in medicines for *ibà*.

Oògùn ibà (àgbo)   Adebawọ
b. *egbò orúwọ̀*   root of the brimstone tree
b. *eèpo ọgọ́no*   bark of Benin mahogany
b. *ewé orúwọ̀*   leaf of the brimstone tree
Cook with some other leaves and give to the patient to drink. He will perspire and pass a lot of urine.

The tree *orúwọ̀* here combined with the bark of the bitter *ọgọ́nó* is well known as an ingredient in medicines for *ibà* and *ibà pọ́njúpọ́njú*. It has a bright yellow wood and, when I still knew little about Yoruba medicine, I was told by Europeans and others with a little knowledge of traditional medicine that the reason it was used was because the colour of the wood was that of jaundice (*ibà pọ́njúpọ́njú*).

Fatoogun once seemed to indicate that the 'redness' of the trees was relevant.

FATOOGUN. This is used to purify the blood, for example black blood. This is a very bitter root, more bitter than many other things. It turns black blood into red.

But then I suggested that the redness of *orúwọ̀* might account for its use in medicines for *ibà*. This Fatoogun denied.

FATOOGUN. *Orúwọ̀* is not used because it is red. It is used because of its bitterness, which *ibà* does not like.

Discussing this with several herbalists and market traders selling ingredients I found that everyone concurred.

The following medicine too contains merely bitter ingredients:

Oògùn ibà (àgbo)   Adebawọ
b. *ewé ìyèrèpè*   unknown leaf
b. *ejìnrìn wẹẹrẹ*   leaf of *Mormorchia*

These leaves will be squeezed in water. Then all the dirt will be removed from the liquid.

ADEBAWỌ. This medicine was given to me by my master who taught me to be a tailor who was called I. M. Odus. He taught me it in 1932. My master was frequently affected by *ibà*. I can remember when we went to a farm called Egùdú there was nothing wrong with my master before we left home, but when we got to the farm he was shaking. So my master called to me that I should collect *ewé ìyèrèpè* and *ewé ejìnrìn*. As we all know that *ìyèrèpè* does not grow in the farm, but mainly in the refuse tip in the town, I had to go back to a town called Ilara about three miles from the farm to fetch the leaves. I squeezed them in water and he drank it twice. He also gave some of it to me, but I found it so bitter that I went to throw it away. At that time all I liked to eat was sugar. I could use about ten cubes of sugar in making *gàrí*. About two hours after my master had taken this medicine he was well, and we went to the farm to do our work.

The remaining medicines have a slightly different construction in that they include smelling ingredients, but in this they merely exhibit features inherent in Image 1. As the illness affects the temperature of the body they are also applied directly to the body.

Oògùn ibà pọ́njúpọ́njú (àgbo)   Fatoogun
b. *ewé ejìnrìn wẹẹwẹ*   leaf of *Mormordica*
b. *ewé ejìnrìn ajá*   leaf of *Mormordica*
sr. *ewé orònbó*   leaf of lime-tree
sm. *ewé kọ́lé ọrọ́gbà*   leaf of *Pergalasa Extensa*
pep. *àwọ̀nká ẹẹrù*   Ethiopian pepper without the seeds.

Put the *àwọ̀nká ẹẹrù* first into the pot and then the other ingredients. Cook. The person must cover himself with a wrapper. When the thing is well cooked and the water is as red as the urine, the person must drink it and he may also wash with it.

We find here the leaves of two types of *ejìnrìn*, both of them bitter in flavour, combined with the sour leaf of the lime, the curious smelling kọlé ọrọ́gbà and a pepper to increase the power of the other ingredients.

Oògùn ara gbígbónọ́ wórawóra (àgbo)		Adebawọ
b.	ifọn	African breadfruit
b.	ìpẹ̀ta	the violet-tree
swb.	àìdọn	fruit of *Tetrapleura Tetraptera* (*Mimosiaceae*)
pep.	ẹ̀ẹru alamọ	seeds and pods of Ethiopian pepper
sm.	ewé alùbọ́sà	leaf of onion
pep.	ẹ̀ẹrùjù	wild Ethiopean black pepper
	ìdàrọ́	iron dross

Put the ìdàrọ́ first into the pot, then cook and use it to wash with.

This medicine includes only two ingredients which we have not encountered before. Ẹ̀ẹrùjù is wild ẹ̀ẹrù and differs not at all in its function from the more commonly encountered ẹ̀ẹrù. I was unable to persuade Adebawọ to venture an opinion on the purpose of putting iron dross into this medicine.

Oògùn ibà		Awotunde
sm.	isẹ́ẹtà	musk gland from civet cat (ẹtà)
sm.	eku asín	a type of rat
sm.+b.)	ọ̀gà	chameleon
	àdín ẹyọn	liquid palm-kernel oil

Pound these together (not the oil) and add to the palm-kernel oil. The person who is sick will be licking it and rubbing it on his body.

Fatoogun told me 'The taste (of isẹ́ẹtà) is rather like that of làpálàpá (which is bitter). Its taste however is not bitter. The smell is very distinctive and strong.'

Fatoogun also spoke of ọ̀gà the chameleon.

FATOOGUN. Ọgà is not edible, and if it is added to medicine it will kill the disease. The meat is not bitter, but it is not good to eat. But the disease does not like the taste of this either so it is used in medicine.

He contradicted himself however on a later occasion.

FATOOGUN. Ọgà is a bitter thing and that is why we do not cook it in soup. This bitterness, together with the other ingredients, can kill any disease living in the body. It can also remove any disease.

It has been shown that eku asín is a rat whose dead body has a strong smell.

APPENDIX D

Medicines for black blood

As with so many other medicines, those to cure black blood are intended primarily to hide, drive out, or kill the diseases which caused the illness. They therefore contain ingredients which are bitter, sour, and peppery. In addition, in some of these medicines there are ingredients which are themselves red in colour and whose purpose is to turn the blood red.

The first of these recipes are constructed entirely according to the familiar principles of Image 1. Although some of the ingredients, for example *òrúwọ* or *eèpo òórá*, may be considered as specifically red, this is not the main emphasis of the medicines.

Oògùn àṣẹ́ dúdú (caused by làkúègbé (agúnmu))   Fatoogun

b.	*eèpo òórá*	bark of a type of fig-tree
pep.	*ata wẹ́wẹ́*	a type of pepper
pep.	*egbò àta*	root of Fagara-tree (various)
b.	*eèpo ọ̀gọ́nó*	bark of Benin mahogany
b.	*orógbó*	bitter cola
b.	*eèpo àfọn*	bark of African breadfruit-tree
b.	*eèpo ìgbá*	bark of locust bean-tree
sm.	*eku asín*	a type of rat
purg.	*f.óf.ó òkun*	a sea shell (foam of the sea)
	(f.óf.ó oló.kun)	
purg.	*ẹtù ibọn*	gunpowder
sw.	*iyọ̀*	salt
b.	*ọ̀gà*	chameleon

Pound, and take with *ẹ̀ko gbígbónó* (hot cornstarch gruel).

Here we have medicine concerned almost exclusively with the process of driving out the disease. There is one ingredient that might be connected with the power to make things red. Ayandokun, my field assistant, told me that when he was a boy, the juice from this peeled root of *asoféyẹjẹ* (a similar tree to *òórà*) was used by him and his friends to make their eyes turn red so that they could frighten people. This is not however the part of the tree that is used here. According to Adebawọ, the bark is used to cure *ibá* (fever) and it would seem to have a general use as a bitter ingredient to attack diseases as indeed do the other main ingredients here.

FATOOGUN. *Eèpo òórà* is used to cure serious diseases—for example, if diseases have been worrying the person for a long time, *eèpo òórà* can remove the diseases from the blood.

Ata wẹ́wẹ́ (pepper) is here used as might be expected as a general aid to the medicine's power.

FATOOGUN. *Ata wẹ́wẹ́* has no power on its own to cure *àṣẹ́ dúdú* but it works together with the other ingredients to cure it. It enables the medicine to work effectively by moving them to different parts of the body.

Here it is used in conjunction with the similarly flavoured root of the tree *igi àta* (Fagara tree).

FATOOGUN. This is a powerful root. It stings like pepper. If anyone tastes it, it will sting any part of the mouth where the saliva (*itọ́*) carries it.[1] It uses its power to kill any diseases in the body, whether they be in the flesh, the blood, or the water of the body.

If the bark (of *ọgọ́nó*) is cooked or soaked in water and one tastes the water it will be very bitter. This bitterness is disliked by many diseases.

The bitter qualities of the *orógbó* have been discussed. The barks of *ìgbá* and *àfọn* are similarly bitter, and the chameleon (*ọ̀gà*) is used for similar reasons (above p. 223).

This recipe contains rather a long list of ingredients, but their purpose is simple enough: through their bitterness, smell, or simply their inedibility, they have the ability to kill and to drive out the disease.

Oògùn àṣẹ́ (àgbo)	Fatoogun
b. *eèpo àhùn*	bark of the *Alstonia Congensis*
sm. *ewé alùbọ́sà*	onion-leaf
b. *esò àìdọn*	fruit of *Tetra Pleura Tetraptera*
pep. *ẹ̀ẹ̀rù púpọ̀ àwọnká àbí alamọ*	Ethiopian pepper. Plenty of either the one with seeds or without.
b. *ewé eépín*	leaf of *Ficus sperifolia*
b. *egbò eépín*	root of *Ficus sperifolia*

Put in a pot and add a lot of water to it, and cook it very well until the liquid is reduced by half. Take the medicine when it is warm, two cups in the morning, in the middle of the day, and in the evening. Some of the medicine should be used to wash in. It should be used for three months.

Here we have a familiar type of medicine. The first three
ingredients are bitter and present no difficulty, *ẹ̀ẹ̀rù* here
fulfilling the role of pepper. The only slightly unusual feature of
this medicine is in the use of the leaf and the root of *eépín*. In one
sense, the ingredients are normal, since they have a pronounced bitter flavour.

FATOOGUN. These are strong ingredients and when the juice of these leaves
and roots mix with the blood, it will purify the menstruation.

Further to this, as we saw in Appendix C, the leaf *eépín* is often
found in medicines for the cleansing of the womb for it has an
abrasive surface much like sandpaper and is in common daily
use for the cleansing of soiled calabashes.

Oògùn àṣẹ́ dúdú caused by làkúègbé (àgbo)   *Fatoogun*
b.   *èso tẹ̀tẹ̀règún*   seed of prickly spinach
                                          Collect many of these; pound a little;
                                          add
b.   *ìtọ̀ màlúù*   cow's urine
Pour into separate bottle and give to the woman to drink.

FATTOGUN: If we pound *èso tẹ̀tẹ̀règún* and taste its juice, we will be able to see
that it tastes just like the sap of *làpálàpá*, but it is not as strong as *làpálàpá*.[2.]

It is perhaps significant that the seed of the *tẹ̀tẹ̀règún* plant which
is a type of spinach is a deep red colour.

FATOOGUN. If the mouth is slimy and the person is suffering from *ahọ́n dúdú*
(lit. black tongue) the taste of the cow's urine will remove all of these things.

Fatoogun occasionally used the example of *ahón dúdú* as a way of
referring to bitterness of certain ingredients.

Oògùn àṣẹ́ tó ńrùn (aṣẹ́ dúdú) (àgbo)   Fatoogun
(Medicine for menstruation which smells)
sm. *Egbò wówó*   root of *wówó*
b.   *èso orí tẹ̀tẹ̀règún*   seed at the top of prickly spinach
Pound together and add the urine of cow (*ìtọ̀*). Leave until the second day
when the liquid is poured into a bottle. The woman will take the medicine,
three spoonfuls in the morning, three in the middle of the day and three in the
evening. After this the menstruation will cease to smell.

Wówó is a smelly leaf whose smell 'diseases do not like' and
which he adds to the ingredients of the last medicine.

Oògùn àṣẹ́ dúdú (agúnmu)	Fatoogun
pep. *Egbò àtako (= àta)*	root of Fagara
sm. *egbò ifọ̀n*	root of African breadfruit
b. *egbò ìpẹ̀ta*	root of the violet-tree
b. *egbò òrúwọ*	root of the brimstone-tree
pep. *ẹ̀ẹ̀rù*	Ethiopian black pepper
Grind, add to *àdín àgbo*	coconut oil
or *àdín*	palm-kernel oil
or *ìsèlé epo*	refined palm-oil

This medicine is constructed similarly according to the basic principles of Image 1.

Oògùn àsé dúdú (agúnmu)	Awotunde
b. *orógbó*	bitter cola
b. *obí*	cola
pep. *ataare*	alligator pepper
red *ewé ákẹ́sẹ*	leaf of the cotton-tree

Pound together and take with hot *ẹ̀kọ*, and in the evening the woman will take a little lime-juice. The menstruation will turn to red from the third day after she has taken the medicine. *Orógbó* will wash the womb, while *ákẹ́sẹ* will turn the blood red.

Awotunde's remark at the end of the recipe sums the medicine up completely. *Obì* is here used in conjunction with bitter cola because of its bitterness; the leaf of the cotton-tree contains a red-staining juice; and the pepper reinforces the action of the other ingredients.

Oògùn àṣẹ́ dúdú (agúnmu)	Fatoogun
b. *eèpo igi àhùn (= àwùn)*	bark of the *Alstonia Congensia*
b. *eèpo egbò ewúuro*	bark of the root of *Veronica*
b. *orógbó*	bitter cola
pep. *ataare*	alligator pepper
sm. *iyọ̀*	salt
pep. *ata*	pepper
sm. *alùbọ́sà*	onion

Pound together, and the person must take it with hot *ẹ̀kọ* or any *ọtí alágbára* (strong drink).

In addition to those ingredients with which we are familiar, we have the following:

FATOOGUN. The power of *awùn* resembles that of *eépín*. They work in the same way. *Awùn* is bitter and that is why we use it to cure *àṣẹ́ dúdú*.

The leaf *ewúuro* is a common ingredient in soup as well as in medicine. In Nigerian English, it is often referred to simply as 'bitter leaf' and as Mr Ayandokun indicated to me:

AYANDOKUN. The water in which the leaf is squeezed is very bitter, but after drinking it the mouth will be very sweet. (Here it is bark of the shrub which is being used.)

In the remaining recipe for *àṣẹ́ dúdú*, we find an additional principle being used for the selection of ingredients. This is found in the use of red ingredients. It seems that redness in an ingredient, either the redness found in the natural object itself, or a redness which emerges when the ingredient is cooked, gives the medicine the power to change black blood back to its correct colour.

	Oògùn àṣẹ́ dúdú	Fatoogun
	lẹ̀wù ọ̀pẹ	hair at the top of a palm-tree
purg.	*kọ́nún bínláńlà*	potash
b.	*egbò òrúwọ*	root of *Veronica*
red	*osùn*	camwood
red	*ìkóódẹ*	tail feather of parrot
red	*ìyẹ́ àlùkò*	feather of a type of bird
red	*egbò l.áli*	root of Egyptian privet (henna)
red	*ọkà bàbà*	guinea-corn

Grind together and mix with *oje eépín* (the sap of *eépín*, *Ficus Asperifolia*) and mould together in the form of *ayò* (seeds shaped like marbles and used in a number of games). It should be taken with hot *ẹ̀kọ*, one ball in the morning, one in the evening. It should be used immediately the menstruation starts until the end, and started again five days before menstruation is due. The menstruation will be nice and red (*pupa dáadáa*).

In this medicine we have Fatoogun using the same principles that he suggests are used in the medicines found in the book by Agosu. Of the eight ingredients here, no fewer than six of them are noticeably 'red' in colour. *Osùn* is camwood, the soft, deep red wood used in the past for rubbing the skin. *Ikóódẹ* are the magnificently bright red tail feathers of the African grey parrot. The bird *àlùkò* is often used in medicine and usually with the bird *agbe*. It has reddish brown feathers and is sometimes referred to as *olósùn* (the owner of camwood). *Ọkà bàbà* (guinea corn) is a deep red colour. *L.áli* is the Egyptian privet whose essential oil is the red dye henna.

The sixth of these 'red' ingredients should however be treated with caution. The root of the tree *òrúwọ* is indeed a spectacularly bright yellow (*pupa*), but it is not primarily used because of this 'red' colour.

There was an apparent paradox in finding *òrúwọ* as an ingredient in medicines for the treatment for *ibà pọ́njú-pọ́njú*, where the patient suffering from jaundice was already the colour of the yellow root. I put the paradox to Fatoogun:

BUCKLEY. How is it that in medicines for black menstruation red things are used to make the black blood red, while in this medicine for *ibà pọ́njú-pọ́njú* where the patient's eyes are already 'red' you still use red things?

FATOOGUN. *Orúwọ* is not used because of its redness, it is used because of its bitterness which *ibà* does not like.

Here Fatoogun is talking about *ibà* and quite clearly not about *àṣẹ́ dúdú*, despite my question. Nevertheless it does indicate one of the dangers which one can fall into in interpreting one's data. *Orúwọ* might well be used in the medicine for black menstruation because of its colour, but its other well-known property, that of a violently bitter taste, could be the reason for its being included here.

Two other ingredients remain. *Kọ́nún* is potash which is commonly used as a purge. *Lẹ̀wù ọ̀pẹ* however is more problematical. In a medicine discussed above (pp. 214–18) it was indicated that *lẹ̀wù ọ̀pẹ* has the power to keep fluids in the womb. If this is the case Fatoogun's use of the same ingredient here would seem incorrect! Unfortunately I did not notice this until I had left the field.

Oògùn *àṣẹ́ dúdú* caused by *làkúègbé*   Fatoogun
red *ewé ọgbọ́ pupa*   European flax

Collect many of these; pound or squeeze, add cold water if this comes to a bottleful, take 3 spoonfuls in the morning, 4 in the afternoon and 4 in the evening.

Ọgbọ́, according to Bascom[3] (1966, 185 n.) is the name for European flax and also for *Omphalogonus nigritanus*, whose fibres are used for making cord. Adebawọ tells me that the leaf turns red when it is squeezed, this property of redness being used to turn the menstruation red.

Oògùn àṣẹ́ dúdú   Awotunde
Ewé ákẹ́ṣẹ́   leaf of the yellow flowering cotton
                                          tree
sr.   *omi oronbó*   lime-juice
purg. *kọ́nún bínláńlà*   potash
Squeeze the leaf in water, add lime-juice and *kọ́nún*, and the woman will be
drinking it.

I came across this medicine by asking the question:

BUCKLEY. What is *òwú akẹ́sẹ́*?

AWOTUNDE. It is a red leaf used in medicine to cure *àṣẹ́ dúdú* (he gave me the
above recipe) . . . This leaf will change the *àṣẹ́* to red.

BUCKLEY. What power has this leaf to cure *àṣẹ́ dúdú*?

AWOTUNDE. If this leaf is squeezed in water the water will be red; this
together with other ingredients will clear the womb and *ewé akẹ́sẹ́* will turn
the black menstruation red.

Endnotes

[1] It is used according to Abraham, (1958) *àta* B (1) as a chewing-stick.

[2] *Làpálàpá* epitomises bitter plants (above p. 47).

[3] In Bascom's account however the shrub is associated with whiteness—this
may be due to the white latex which emerges from the branches of both
varieties.

Medicines for Ṣọ̀npọ̀nnọ́

It is sometimes said that in principle there are no medicines to cure the illnesses caused by Ṣọ̀npọ̀nnọ́. Medicine is one of the things which makes Ṣọ̀npọ̀nnọ́ angry, and to use medicine is to invite his wrath. Presumably, if the analysis in Chapter Six is correct, this is because medicine is a secret, cultural phenomenon. This does not however prevent people from using herbal remedies to counteract Ṣọ̀npọ̀nnọ́, but they are not called 'medicines' (oògùn). They are called propitiations (ẹ̀rọ̀).

I discovered, when I had collected a number of ẹ̀rọ̀ Ṣọ̀npọ̀nnọ́, that it was extremely difficult to discuss their construction with the owners. Whereas my informants could tell me why they included ingredients in ordinary medicines, they seemed to find great difficulty in explaining the ẹ̀rọ̀. One principle seems to be clear however. Any natural object which has markings similar to those caused by smallpox, seems to be a suitable ingredient for ẹ̀rọ̀. It seems that just as someone who has smallpox scars on his face and has therefore recovered from the illness, is henceforth immune, and also a follower of the god, so a natural object which has affinity with Ṣọ̀npọ̀nnọ́ is able to transmit to the patient its power to pacify Ṣọ̀npọ̀nnọ́. It must be admitted however, that these principles do not, or at least do not seem to, provide an explanation of all recipes fore ẹ̀rọ̀ Ṣọ̀npọ̀nnọ́. I have here undertaken to try to explain a few such recipes.

The first two medicines contain the skin of crocodile and may be considered together.

Ẹ̀rọ̀ Ṣọ̀npọ̀nnọ́	Adebawọ
Awọ ọ̀nì	Skin of crocodile

ADEBAWỌ. If a piece of *awọ ọ̀nì* is put in a pot of drinking-water from which the household usually drinks *Egbónọ́* will not kill anyone in the house. It is a bad incantation which I must not tell you because it is dangerous to tell people. *Ọ̀nì* was the first thing that *Egbónọ́* affected. He was first living on the land, but *Egbónọ́* troubled him too much, and that is why he went to live inside the river. It was when he entered the river he was relieved.

Egbónọ́ set fire to him as we heard it in a certain book. He was cured by
Oluweri. Then he said, '*Tó àbàìwọ́n, iye ọmọ òun tó bá ti bọ́ sínú omi tọ òun lọ;
Egbónọ́ ò tún gbọ́dọ̀ mú mọ́.*' It is forbidden, all his children that follow him to
the river; *Egbónọ́* must not affect them again.

Ẹrọ̀ Ṣ ʼonpọ̀nnọ́   Adebawọ
Awọ ọnì   skin of crocodile
ewé oló.de (= ewé akòko)   leaf of *Newboldia, Laevis Bigoniacea*
Pound together with soap and wash with cold water. We must not roast the
awọ ọnì before pounding it, because *ọnì* does not live in fire but in the river.

In this use of the skin of the crocodile, there is a series of
contrasting concepts which may relate to patterns already
established.

First of all, the crocodile, when on the land, was set on fire by
Ṣọ̀npọ̀nnọ́—he developed smallpox. In contrast, when he
retreated to the water, he was cured. In the second of these
medicines the contrast is similarly drawn between a more
normal use of the crocodile skin in medicine, where it would be
burned or roasted, and the way it is here used—placed in water.

Hot	Cool
Earth	Water
On fire	Fire quenched
Roasted	In water
Smallpox	Cured of smallpox

FIGURE 42. The crocodile on land and in water

This pattern of contrasts coincides precisely with the structure which was discussed in Chapter 6 (pp. 129 ff.) when
Ọrúnmìlà first tried to cool himself from the effects of *Ṣ ʼonpọ̀nnọ́*'s
wrath by drinking all of the water of *Ifẹ*. It may also be
significant that the crocodile skin, in the first recipe is not
merely used in medicine, but is put into the pot containing the
household's drinking-water.

Already some significance was attributed in Chapter 6 to
pots and containers, and it was suggested that the earth (*ilẹ̀*)
itself is regarded by some people in certain contexts, as a
container embracing the world (*ayé*) in which we live. In this
medicine, these may be an image of the earth as a container for
the water which provides a refuge for the crocodile.

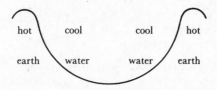

FIGURE 43. The crocodile on land and in water

In these two medicines, the use of the crocodile skin is typical of the two elements in èrò Ṣònpònnó. First there is the suggestion that has just been made, that the marks on the skin of the crocodile were caused by smallpox and that this skin has the power to resist the illness. But second there is the explicit remark, that because of this affinity with the god, it is dangerous to roast the crocodile skin. I have found that it is considered dangerous to roast other objects, and also that these same objects may be used to prevent or cure ègbónó.

The analysis of the second medicine, may be completed by looking at the leaf of the tree oló.de, more commonly called akòko. Akòko is an important tree whose significance differs from town to town. Abraham (Ogún 12 f), and Idowu (1962, 124) agree that the tree is sacred to Ogún, but in Ilẹ Oluji near Ondo where there is a large cult of Ogún it is symbolic of the god Ọlófin.

I cannot pretend to understand its full significance, for this would require investigation of the relevant cults, but Abraham's description of its ritual uses (akòko 1. and 2.) is reinforced by my own informants.

FATOOGUN. It is an important and a strange tree. It is one of the trees which the spirits (ẹbọra) first saw when they first reached the earth. It does not shed its leaves and it is a 'live' tree (igi íyè). It is used as a symbol for a god, and is also used in medicine. It was known even before the tree called ọdón. Akòko will never die unless it is cut down or burnt.

ADEBAWỌ. Ewé akòko is a famous leaf among all other leaves. It is the first in sacrifice (ètùtù), when they install a king or chief; ewé akòko must be used and hence the incantation:

> A fèmi lagbé fi ńṣaró
> A fèmi làkùkò fi ńṣosùn
> A fèmi lodídẹrẹ fi ńba wọn déwó, modò ọba
> Ọmọ ọba tó di wèrè

A kìí foló.de sílę
ká faba joyè
Itòn rere kìí se lórí awun

They use me so that *agbe*[1] can make dye
They use me so that *àlùkò* can make camwood
They use me so that *odídęré* accompany them
to Iwó on the river *Ǫbà*
Child of the king who became mad
They will not put *Oló.de* (= *Ṣònpònnó*) on the earth
So that they should invest the king with a title
Good stories do not miss the head of tortoise

These associations have a bearing on kingship and on cults
which lie far beyond the scope of the present work. For our
purposes we must sidestep the wider issues involved in the tree
and look only at the connection which our informants describe
between *akòko* and *Ṣònpònnó*.

Fatoogun was not particularly helpful in this:

FATOOGUN. It is used against *Ṣònpònnó*. The young leaves are mixed with
other ingredients and used to rub the body so that *Ṣ`onpònnó* cannot affect
the person. If *Ṣònpònnó* has already attacked the person the medicine will
weaken his power.

Adebawǫ on the other hand told me a medicine and explained
it with a story. This is for *ęgbęsì*, a skin condition attributed to
Ṣònpònnó.

Oògùn ęgbęsì   Adebawǫ
ewé oló.de (= *akòko*)   leaf of *Newboldia*
ewé tàngírì   a leaf
Pound together and the person will lick it.

Here the leaves of the *akòko tree* are mixed with those of the
climbing plant *tàngírì*[2] which has a round or ovoid fruit some
five or six inches in diameter which is striped in elegant green
and white stripes. Adebawǫ explains his medicine thus:

ADEBAWǪ. *Akòko* is also called *oló.de*. This is where we hear the story of
tàngírì. *Tàngírì* was servant to *akòko* and one day he sent *tàngírì* on an errand.
Tàngírì passed through the place where *Oló.de* (*Ṣònpònnó*) was and *Ṣònpònnó*
shot him with an arrow. When *akòko* heard this he was angry and wanted to
fight against *Ṣònpònnó*, but *Ṣònpònnó* pleaded with him and turned the spots
of *tàngírì* into beauty.

This is why we usually mark some *Ifá* (i.e. make an appropriate *odù* mark) on the body of *tàǹgírì* and hang it in the doorway during *ègbònnó*. This will prevent *Ṣòǹpọ̀nnọ́* from entering the house. *Ewé ìròsùn* is also a servant of *akòko* and that is why we use it in medicine for *Ṣ`ọnpọ̀nnọ́* and *èyí* and *ègbẹ̀sì*.

This explanation of the medicine is perfectly adequate in itself, but clearly further research is required to explore the direct relationship between *akòko* and *Ṣòǹpọ̀nnọ́*. It may be that, for example, *akòko* is associated with white *òrìṣà* who could therefore occupy the same place as *Ọbàtálá* does in my earlier account (above, pp. 105–9). The draping of a tree with a white cloth noted by Abraham (*akòko* 2.) and which I have seen in the town of Ilẹ Oluji would reinforce this interpretation, but such an idea is contradicted by the association of *akòko* with *Ogún*, (Idowu 1962, 126; and Abraham 1958 *Ogún* 12 (f)). What little work I did on the important *Ogún* cult in Ilẹ Oluji would suggest that *akòko* and *Ogún* are closely related, but that this relationship is an indirect one, being in that form at least, a reflection of the relationship between *Ogún* (a black god) and *Ọlọ́fin* (a white god), whose symbol *akòko* is. An exploration of such symbolism must of necessity await much more detailed investigation of the cults themselves.

Endnotes

[1] *Agbe*, the blue turaco bird; *àlùkò*, a similar but red bird; *odídẹ́rẹ́*, the West African grey parrot.

[2] Abraham (1958) identifies a similar plant as *tàgúrì* but I found no one who used this name.

APPENDIX F

Awúre

In Chapter 7 medicines for *àwúre* were presented as illustrative material to demonstrate the several ways in which incantation is used to show the power of ingredients. In the process the precise nature of *àwúre* itself has not been fully considered and this may here be rectified.

Oògùn àwúre are, as has been shown, those medicines which are intended to bring good fortune to the user, by bringing him popularity, prestige, and wealth. But more fundamentally, these medicines are intended to change a person's destiny. Before a person is born he, or more precisely his head (*orí*), must kneel and choose his destiny.[1] According to Idowu (1962, 173–4) this destiny is chosen freely by the individual, but once chosen it is conferred upon him for ever. Within the broad limits set by this choice, the individual is free to improve his lot in the world through his own efforts, but in general he may not hope to contradict the destiny which he has chosen for himself. Should he have omitted to choose wealth, honour, or general good fortune before he entered the world, then, in principle at least, no effort on his part can affect his fortunes.[2] Though he is at first ignorant of his pre-natal choice, a man may discover from experience or divination that his original choice of destiny was inadequate. He may then, nevertheless try to modify his fortune. One means of doing this is simply to worship the head, for it is generally accepted that the head which is in heaven (above pp. 63–4) may go to God and petition on his owner's behalf.[3]

Awúre is another way of trying to change a person's destiny. Idowu does not mention *àwúre* in his full discussion of destiny and indeed argues to the contrary; '*orí burúku kò gbọ́ ọṣẹ́*', 'A bad *orí* cannot be rectified with soap (by washing)' (Idowu 1962, 171–2). But while the evidence of Chapter 7 would appear to suggest that not everyone agrees with his assertion, Idowu is not incorrect in his emphasis. *Awúre* can change a person's

destiny, but any radical change is of major significance to him,
and it can be dangerous.

Here are two versions of a medicine for *àwúre*, given to me by
Adebawọ on different occasions. They illustrate the inherent
difficulty involved in overcoming one's destiny.

Oògùn Awúre (ọṣẹ)   Adebawọ
Ewé dásá 201   201 leaves of *dásá*
Tegbò àtewé igi pegúnrun   root and leaves of *pegúnrun-tree*
Pound with soap. The person will wash with it in the river if he has been
working without yield.

Incantation
  i. *Dásá awo olú igbó;*
      Wẹ̀sìdànù awo ẹlùjù ọd.ọ́n
      Dá fuń Ọrúnmìlà.
      Ifá tí kọlé ọrun bọ̀ ní kọlé ayé.
  v. *Wọ́n ní àmúbó nIfá ó. lọ máa mu.*
      Wọ́n ní aṣẹ̀ẹrí nIfá ó. máa ṣe.
      Ifá ló.un ó. ni mà mú bọ̀
      O ló.un ò ní sàṣéerí
      O ní bó ṣe bí tèmi ọmọ òun,
  x. *Ni ó ni ìì ní má mú bọ̀*
      Ìì ní sàseèrí
      Wọ́n ní, ìwọ Ọrúnmìlà, wọ́n ti gé.gun fún lọ́.run
      Ọrúnmìl.á ní wọn gé.gun lọ́.run
      O ní ló.un jáwé pegúnrun
  xv. *O lo.un yẹ egbò ìdíìẹ̀*
      O ní akòko ni ó.kó ibi tó nbẹ láraàmi kúrò.

  i. *Dásá* the diviner of the lord of the forest,
      He who washes hardship away, the diviner of the savannah
      Cast *Ifá* for *Ọrúnmìla.*
      Ifá had turned to come from heaven towards the world.
  v. They said, that what he grasps will slip is how *Ifá* shall go and
      grasp things.
      They said, it is work without gain that *Ifá* shall go and do.
      Ifá said he would indeed catch anything that slipped
      He said he would not work without gain.
      He said if it is like me his child,
  x. He said he will not grasp anything that will slip.
      He will not work without gain.
      They said, addressing *Ọrúnmìlà*, that they have made a declaration
      in heaven.[4]

Ọrúnmìla said, they made a declaration in heaven.
He said he plucks the leaf of the *pegúnrun*
xv. He said he dug the root of its base.
He said it is *akòko* that will carry off the evil that is in my body.

At this point Adebawọ broke off the incantation. He gave me this at a fairly early stage in our discussions when he was unwilling to divulge more than incomplete recipes. Indeed in the last line he indicates that some part of the tree *akòko* (*Newboldia Laevis*) formed part of the medicine. He concluded with the words: '*Dásá* is used in that way too'.

Oògùn Awúre   Adebawọ
Ewé dásá   leaf of *dásá*
Egbò igi pegúnrun   root of *pegúnrun*
Pound with soap and the person will wash with it in the river, if he has been working without yield.

Incantation
i. *Dásá awo olúugbó*
Wẹ̀sì dànù awo èlùjù ọ̀dọ̀n
Wẹ̀sì dànù awo èlùjù ọ̀dọ̀n
Wàseèrí dànù awo èlùjù ọ̀dọ̀n
v. *O dá fún Ọrúnmìlà*
Lójọ́ tó ti kọlé ọ̀run bọ̀ níkolé ayé
Tí wọ́n ibi gbogbo tèlẹ́ léhin
Wọ́n ní bó ṣẹṣẹ́ owó,
Kò ní ní lọ́wọ́
x. *Wọ́n ní bó ṣẹṣẹ ọmọ,*
Kò ní rọmọ bí.
Ọrúnmìl.á ní tó bá ṣe pé tèmi ọmọ òun ni
O ní tí nbá délé ayé
O ní maá jáwé pegúnrun;
xv. *Maá yẹgbò ìdíìẹ̀.*
Akòko ni ó.kóbi tó ńbẹ láraàmi lọ.
Njẹ́ ibi oṣó tó ńbẹ láraàmi
Gbogbo ibi.
Ibi a kò ṣàì bẹ́ri a ṣọ̀n
xx. *Ibi ajẹ́ tó ńbẹ láraàmi*
Gbogbo ibi
Ibi a kà sàì bẹ́ri a ṣọn
Gbogbo ibi.

i. *Dásá* the diviner of the Lord of the Forest
He who washes hardship away, the diviner of the savannah

He who washes poverty away, the diviner of the savannah
He who washes work-without-reward away, the diviner of the
savannah.

v. He cast *Ifá* for *Ọrúnmìlà*
On the day that he was coming from heaven to the world
And that they sent all kinds of evil to follow him
They said that if he did the work of money
He would not have it in his hand.

x. They said if he did the work of having children
He would not bear children
Ọrúnmìlà said if it is my own child,
If I arrive in the world
He said that I shall pluck the leaf of *pegúnrun*

xv. I shall dig the root at its base
It is *akòko* that will take away all the evil in my body,
Therefore the evil of wizards that is in my body,
All evil,

xx. The evil of witches that is in my body
All evil
The evil of witches that is in my body
All evil.

In these medicines, *Ọrúnmìlà*'s destiny is stated by the *Ifá* oracle to be evil. In the first, he is told that he will be unable to grasp whatever he tries to hold, and that he would work without gain; in the second he is to be followed by evil, and be unsuccessful in his work, and be able to have neither children nor money. Despite this dire prediction, *Ọrúnmìlà* was able to transform his destiny. As the archetypal diviner, *Ọrúnmìlà* is the one who instituted the *Ifá* divination procedure of which the central feature is grasping palm-nuts so that they will not slip. Similarly, it is obvious to any Yoruba, that of all their mythical figures, *Ọrúnmìlà* is the most successful, having many children (the 256 *odù*) and, like any good diviner, a modest, but not inconsiderable, prosperity.

What the verse states is most unusual. It is that, by using this specific medicine, *Ọrúnmìlà* has been able to overcome the predictions of the *Ifá* oracle. Nowhere else, in any of the vast number of *Ifá* verses which I have encountered, have the predictions of diviners been stated as invalid. Yet, in *àwúre*, it is precisely this destiny which can be revealed by *Ifá* divination, which is to be overturned, by medicine.

Oògùn Awúre	Adebawọ
Ewé ìsẹ́pẹ́ agbe	leaf of *Psychotria Warneckii*
Ewé alúkèrèsé	a leaf
ìgbín 2	two snails
ìyèrè díẹ̀	a little West African black pepper

A knife must not be used to cut the snails. (Here he showed me a piece of wood cut from a palm-tree which was shaped as a knife, and which he used for the purpose.) When cooked it is pincers (*ẹ̀mú*) that are used to eat the snail. The snail must be cut into nine pieces (I presume this would be seven pieces if it were being prepared for a woman) and it is all cooked as *àsèjẹ àwúure* to obtain money. *Ogúda bèdè*⁵ will be marked in the divining dust (*ìyèròsùn*) in an *Ifá* tray (*ọpọ́n Ifá*).

Incantation

i.   *Abẹ́ ṣẹ́rẹ́ṣẹ́rẹ́ wọlú,*
       Asọ̀n mìmì;
       Asọ̀n rẹrẹ ròkun;
       Erelú agámọ̀;

v.   *Ifá ọmọ bíbí inú ni o fi mí se*
       Má. fi.mi ṣẹru
       Má. fi.mi ṣewọ̀fà
       Má. fi.mi salásasìn lásọ̀n
       Ọmọ bíbí inú ni lówó mọ́wó

x.   *Ọmọ bíbí inú ni bímọmọmọ*
       Ọmọ bíbí inú ni ńkólémọlé
       Ọmọ bíbí inú ralẹ̀mọlẹ̀
       Ifá, tó gẹ́gẹ́ ó wá fi.mi ṣòlùkuùrẹ
       Iṣẹ́pẹ́ agbe ni ńsòlùkù agbe

xv.   *Alúkèrèsè niísòlùku ilẹ̀*
       Tí ìgbín bá dẹnu délẹ̀, ilé à ta lọ́re
       Ti ẹ̀mú bá tẹnu bọnọ́ irin ńláńlá níí gbé já.de,
       Owó ńláńlá ni kí wọn máa mu wá fún.mi.

i.   He that cut his way into the town
       He that flows,
       He that flows to the sea⁶
       Erelú agámọ̀ (a title)

v.   *Ifá*, it is the child of the womb that you should make me.
       Do not make me a slave,
       Do not make me a bondsman.⁷
       Do not make me into a person who works for nothing.
       It is the child of the womb who has money upon money.

x.   It is the child of the womb who has child after child.
       It is the child of the womb who builds house after house.

It is the child of the womb who buys plot after plot of land.
Ifá it is time for you to make me your friend.
Iṣ́ẹ́ṕ́[8] is the friend of *agbe* (the blue turaco bird)

xv. *Alúkèrèsé* is the friend of the earth
If the snail puts its mouth on the earth, the earth will give it a gift,
If pincers (those of the blacksmith) puts its mouth into the fire, it is
huge iron that it brings out.
It is big money that they will bring for me.

In this medicine, two types of person are contrasted. On the
one hand is the slave, the pawn or bondsman, the man who
works for no return; on the other is the owner of money and
children, who builds houses and owns land. To achieve the
fortunate position of the second type of person, the supplicant
begs *Ifá* to become his friend, just as, in the incantation, *iṣ́ẹ́ṕ́*
agbe is the friend of the blue turaco (*agbe*), and *Alúkèrèsé* is the
friend of the earth. In addition he takes his medicine using the
rather unwieldy pincers of the forge, which are successful in
bringing out huge pieces of iron from the fire. But the supplicant also wishes to become 'the child of the womb' (*ọmọ bíbí inú*)
for it is thus that the second, fortunate type of person is
characterized. In addition, the person who eats the medicine
must cut the snail into nine pieces using, not a metal knife, but a
wooden imitation cut from palm-wood. Where is the
connection?

It has been suggested elsewhere (p. 121) that the significance
of nine in a medicine is to associate it with the masculinity of the
patient (it would be seven for a woman). Perhaps this is to
identify the medicine with the patient? The difference between
a 'child of the womb' and one who is a little older is that the
former has not been circumcised nor cut in any other way with
an iron knife. As circumcision and other markings are performed by the followers of *Ogún*, the god of iron, the difference
between being cut by iron and cut in some other way is of
considerable significance. If in some way the supplicant is
becoming identified with the snail which has not been cut with
a knife, he may be considered to be once more a 'child of the
womb'. The medicine, in short, constitutes a miniature *rite de
passage* in which the supplicant is symbolically born again.

Adebawọ was most concerned with medicines for money. In
Ibadan Ijẹbu people such as he are believed to know much

about such medicines, and indeed their reputed prosperity is said to derive from it. I asked him if there were medicines to bring people money.

ADEBAWỌ. Yes. But this doesn't mean you should waylay people who have been to the bank to collect money. There is one thing that is compulsory in this type of medicine. It can only be prepared for a person who is working. The person for whom this medicine can be prepared, must have a shop or something of this sort—it cannot be prepared for a lazy man who just sleeps in his house.

Awúre can be divided into three types: one is oṣó inú (the wizard inside), oṣólẹ̀ (the wizard of the earth), the other is called àwúre, but if we should meet a person who says he is looking for àfẹ́ẹ̀rí, also called ìbojú (lit. blindfold or veil), or ìṣújú (that which darkens the eyes), this is not àwúre.

He is here drawing a contrast between àwúre, the legitimate medical aid by which a hardworking man gains a just reward for his labours, and the dishonest 'bad' medicine, àfẹ́ẹ̀rí, which is used to 'blind' traders or customers, so that they fall victim to commercial sharp practice.

Most medicines to bring good fortune are considered to be relatively harmless, with the intention of bringing about a minor change in the person's destiny. There are, however, a number of medicines which are intended to bring about a major change, and these are dangerous for they elicit the help of powerful agencies.

The following medicine, like the last, contains elements of a *rite de passage* but in addition it calls upon the assistance of a god (òrìṣà).

Oògùn àwúre (ẹ̀tù)   Adebawọ
There are some people who work very hard, but despite this they may not have any money. We have a different way of preparing àwúre for them. There is an òrìṣà (god) which I must not say.

Oògùn àwúre (ẹ̀tù)	Adebawọ
ìwọ́rọ́n oló.kun	a shell?
owó ẹyọ 201	201 cowries
yọ́nrin òkun	(varieties of wild
yọ́nrin ọ̀sà	lettuce)
ewé egbèé	*Trachyphrinium*
ewé irọ́njé	a creeper

This is an ẹ̀tù and it is usually prepared on a white plate. We must sacrifice a he-goat (òrúkọ̀) to it. If you prepare this medicine, the medicine will come to

you at midday in the form of a human being. You will only know that it was
the medicine that came after he has gone. This is one way that we can show
that there is medicine (i.e. that Yoruba medicine really works). The medicine
will be put on a plate and an old he-goat that is already smelling will be
sacrificed. This medicine can be used every eight, fifteen, or thirty days. You
must not have any sexual intercourse the night before you use the medicine,
and you must wash the body before using the medicine. You have to sew a
white cap, white wrapper, and white trousers, and when you put the medicine
down you must prostrate yourself before it. Then you sacrifice he-goat to it
from time to time. It will be placed in a container with *ẹyin adìẹ* (chicken's egg)
and *omi ìgbín* (the fluid from snail).

Incantation

i. *Akógi lépá fìraarẹ̀ sogidọn*
   Apàntèté ẹ kíyè sẹ́ru
   Oyìngbó òyìngbà òkùku bẹ̀lẹ̀jẹ̀ ni ńsọmọ yèyé ajé
   Wọ́n ńbọ̀rìṣà.kọn ló.de ìtólú

v. *Orûmi, ìwọ ni wọ́n ńbọ̀ ńbẹ̀*
   Orûmi gbígbe ni o
   Gbè mí oo
   Igba lewé erégbèé é (= egbèé)
   Orûmi gbígbè ni o

x. *Gbè mi oo*
   ggba lewé erégbèé e
   Orûmi gbígbè ni o
   Gbè mí oo
   Igba lewé erégbèé é

xv. *Ojú kìí pọ́nrọnjé ẹlùjù kò má. lè sogba okùn*
   Ojú kìí pọ́nrọnjé ẹlùjù kó má. lè sogba idẹ
   Ojú kìí pọ́nrọnjé ẹlùjù kó má. le sodindi abá owó sùrùnù
   Oòsà gbígbè ni ó gbè mí oo
   Igba lewé erégbè

xx. *Ọkùnrin, obìnrin*
   Wọ́n kìí mọ bi ti ẹyin díẹ korí kọ̀dí si
   Kí wọ́n má. mo ibi tí àṣírûmi ti ńbọ̀.

i. He who carries wood on his shoulder turns himself into a rope.
   He who skilfully balances things on his head, watch out for the
   load.
   Oyìngbò òyìngbà òkùkù bẹ̀lẹ̀jẹ̀ is the son of the mother of money.
   They are worshipping a god in Itolu

v. My head, you are the one they are worshipping there.
   It is my head that is my protection.
   Protect me oh!

Two hundred are the leaves of *erégbèé* oh!
It is my head that is my protection
x.   Protect me oh!
Two hundred are the leaves of *erégbèé* oh!
It is my head that is my protection
Protect me oh!
Two hundred are the leaves of *erégbèé* oh!
xv.   Eyes are not red for *ìrọnjẹ́ ẹlùjù* for being unable to tie 200 ropes.
Eyes are not red for *ìrọnjẹ́ ẹlùjù* for being unable to tie 200 brasses.
Eyes are not red for *ìrọnjẹ́ ẹlùjù* for being unable to tie a whole bag of money.
Òrìṣà, you are my protection
Two hundred are the leaves of *erégbèé*.
xx.   Men and women
They do not know where the egg's head or bottom is,
Let them not know where my secrets are hidden.

In this incantation we have a whole series of deliberate ambiguities. The simplest is the punning relationship between the leaf, *egbèé*, and the protection, *gbigbe*, sought by the person taking the medicine. Slightly more complicated is the word '*so*' in the fifteenth, sixteenth, and seventeenth lines. There are two distinct meanings to the syllable '*so*'; one is 'to tie', the other is 'to bear fruit'. *Irọnjẹ́* is a creeper which bears 'ropes' which are useful as the incantation suggests in the tying of brasses, and bags of money. The first line is somewhat difficult to interpret but seems to refer to the plant *iwọ́rọ́n oló.kun* (lit. the firewood of the owner of the sea).

This medicine is obviously more complicated than most of the others. In it the power of the medicine is personified as a god (*òrìṣà*). Adebawọ was reluctant to name the *òrìṣà*, but it would seem likely from the emphasis upon white clothes, the white plate, and the white fluid from the snail, that the *òrìṣà* is one of a group of gods associated with whiteness, of which *Ọbàtálá* is the most important. By taking the medicine, the client commits himself to the service of the *òrìṣà*, who will in return provide him with a more favourable destiny. His commitment, and the radical break that this implies with his former destiny, is signified by his change of clothing and his need to make frequent sacrifices of the he-goat to the *òrìṣà*.

A more common method of soliciting help is to gain the

support of a wizard (*oṣó*), and here the dangers were stated more explicitly.

BUCKLEY. What is *oṣó*?

FATOOGUN. It is a male witch (*akọ àjẹ́*). Men are the only ones who own this *oṣó*. They have no separate society, but move together with the *àjẹ́* (witches). A *babaláwo* will never tell you that a person is affected by wizards (*oṣó*). Wizards do not fight against people. *Oṣó* is used mainly for having money, but they can send witches against anyone.

BUCKLEY. How does *oṣó* give you money?

FATOOGUN. God does not create anybody with *oṣó* from heaven. *Oṣó* is made by medicine. You mention what you want to use the *oṣó* for when you prepare it . . . whether for money or for anything else. It can also be used to allow a person to become old, or to bear children.

BUCKLEY. What is *oògùn oṣó*?

A HERBALIST. This medicine will remain in the belly, but it can cut short the life of the person. This does not change the person into a wizard (*oṣó*) but it will enable the person to have money by any means. It is the spirit of the *oṣó* that will be helping him. If he is a trader, he will be selling his goods in no time.

ADEBAWỌ. There are some people who, no matter how hard they work, they will have no money. We usually say that it is these people's destiny (*kádàrá*). Some people, because of their destiny will make a strong medicine called *oṣó*. This medicine will work badly and the person will die after three years because their destiny is not with them.

As with the last medicine, the particular danger involved is that the client who takes it will neglect to make proper sacrifice to it. Taking *oògùn oṣó* is not a once-for-all transformation of one's destiny, it is a lifetime's commitment. The first of the two medicines given here requires a regular sacrifice of guinea-fowl. The second is more expensive, and demands a sheep.

Oògùn àwúre (oṣó) (ẹtù)	Adebawọ
orí èjímèrè	head of the brown pataguenon monkey
orí ẹkùn	head of leopard
orí ọnì	head of crocodile

(There are two types of *ọnì*, the one called *ọnì*, and the one called *ègùngun*.)

orí gbígbẹ.kọn	human skull

Incantation
    i. *Ejímèrè ọmọ inú igbó.*
      Ọnì ọmọ odò

Enìòn ọmọ ìlú
Enìòn ẹ mówó èní wá fun mi
v. *Ẹkùn kìí jẹron ìkàsìn*
Owó ọnọ́ dìkàsìn
Owó tuntun tòní ni ẹ wá fún mi
Ojúmó kìí mọ kẹkùn má. fọwọ́ bẹ̀jẹ̀
Mo jí tèmi ló.ní;
x. *Kí ńmáa tẹ́wọ́ gbówó.*

i. Brown monkey, child within the forest.
Crocodile, child of the river.
Human being, child of the town.
Human being bring money, bring the money of today for me
v. Leopard does not eat stale food.
The money of yesterday has become stale.
It is the new money of today that you should bring me
Daybreak does not dawn such that the leopard does not touch blood with his hand.
I awake on my own today,
x. Let me be spreading my hands to get money.

Guinea fowl (*awó*) is always sacrificed to this *àwúre*. The ingredients will be burnt and *èjì ogbè* will be marked on it. The incantation will be said. It is put into a calabash (*ṣẹ́rẹ́* is a calabash with a long neck). This *ètù* is very powerful in that, if you are the only person sleeping in the house where it is, it will always wake you to tell you when it is going out, and if you dream, you will always dream that you are working on rivers. Some people call this *ètù oṣó*.

The next medicine is also for *àwúre*, and, as the incantation suggests, it is powerful, and will provide a wide range of good things for the person who uses it. The medicine is *oṣó*, and it resides in the belly doing the recipient good as long as he continues to make sacrifice to it.

Adebawọ gave me two incomplete versions of this medicine. I have conflated his two versions here to give what I consider to be one virtually complete medicine. I shall indicate which version is which by calling them 1. and 2.

Oògùn oṣó (ètù)   Adebawọ
1. *ajá*   dog
   àgùntọ̀n   sheep
   orí ọ̀sìn   head of fish eagle
   many other birds' heads

Kill the dog and put the head and the blood into a container. The sheep also will be killed and the head put into a container with the blood. The rest of the dog can be thrown into the forest, but we can eat the sheep. The medicine will be burnt and the *odù* marked upon it. This medicine is *oṣó* (wizard) and we usually sacrifice a sheep to it.

In the second version, the list of birds' heads is much longer; the dog's head is replaced by dog's meat, and the role of the sheep's blood is made more clear. It is a sacrifice made to the medicine in the stomach.

2. *Ẹran ajá* — meat of the dog

orí igún—3	3 vultures' heads
orí àkàlà—3	3 ground hornbills' heads
orí ẹyẹ ọ̀sìn—3	3 fish eagles' heads
orí agbe—3	3 blue turacos' heads
orí àlùkò—3	3 heads of *àlùkò*
orí odídẹrẹ́ (= .ódẹ)—3	3 grey parrots' heads
alá.pàndẹ̀rẹ̀ (= alá.pàndẹ̀dẹ̀)	Ethiopian swallow
ewé Ifá	leaf of *Ifá*

We must sacrifice a sheep to this medicine every three months.

Incantation 1 and 2

i.   *ayé rí mi nọ́ọ̀, ọmọ Ogún*
       Ijàami kòì rọlè, awo Akárángbàdú
       Kíntà awo àlákẹtu
       Odídẹrẹ́ awo alú.dọ̀dún

v.   *Alùkò awo abẹrín ṣẹ̀sẹ*
       Alá.pàndẹ̀rẹ̀ awo abisínnogọ̀go
       Awọn la súré kunkun dáfá
       Awọn lokùnkùnrumì takùntakùn
       Awon labẹ̀rúkúṣẹṣẹ lórí abọṣẹ

x.   *Akàlàọ̀ṣẹ̀ẹ̀rẹ̀màgbò ni ó.jẹ́ kí ǹrífà nílé Ọlọ́fin*
       Owó tó nbe ló.de ìlú,
       Ẹ mu wá fún mi.
       Akàlààmi rà
       Awúreèmi àkàlà.

xv.   *Ẹj.ó jòwèrè*
       Ire owó ẹ jòwèrè wá bá mi.
       Ẹj.ó jòwèrè
       Alákọn tibẹ̀sè dé
       Ire owó ẹ tibẹ̀ṣẹ̀ wá bá mi

xx.   *Alákọn tibẹ̀ṣẹ̀*
       Agùnt.ọ́n ṣièrè dé
       Ire owó ẹ sièrè wá bá mi
       Agùntọ̀nọ́ ṣièrè
       Ajá jare owó tèmi wá fún mi

xxv. *Awàlà kóré ajá òo*
      Awàlà
2. only *Ilèkè kí.lèkè kìí bórí iyùn*
        Ilèkè kí.Ièkè kìí bórí sègin
        Ilèkè kí.lèkè kìí bórí erinlá
xxx.   *E má. je kí tókùnrin borí tèmi*
       E má. je kí tóbìnrin borí tèmi
       Kí ñlówó lówó
       Kí ñlómo
       Ki ñláso
xxxv. *Kí ñfi gbogbo ire sanípé*

i.   The world sees me, child of *Ogún*[9]
       'My flight is not yet finished', the diviner of *Akáràngbàdú*,
       Kintà, the diviner of *Aketu*,
v.   *Alùkò*, the diviner who laughs all the time,
       Alá.pandèrè the diviner of *abisíñogògò*
       These are the people who quickly cast *Ifá*
       These are the entangling darkness
       These are the onces who use *èrúkúsèse* on the heads
       of the worshippers of soap.
x.   It is *Akàlàosèèrèmàgbò*[10] that will let me see again in the
       house of *Olófin*[11]
       The money that is inside the town
       Bring it to me
       My hornbill is hovering
       My àwúre of the hornbill
xv.   Snake comes wriggling
       Goodness of money, come wriggling to me
       Snake comes wriggling
       Crab come from the place of sin
       Goodness of money, come to me from the place of sin.
xx.   Crab came from the place of sin.
       Sheep will become mad and arrive
       Good of money, become mad and come and meet me.
       Sheep will be mad
       Dog, bite off the good of my money, and come for me.
xxxv. Dog that carries wealth oh!
       Carrier of wealth.
2. only There is no type of bead more popular than *iyùn*.
        There is no type of bead more popular than *sègin*.
        There is no type of bead more popular than *erinlá*.
xxx.   Do not let the one of men be more popular than mine.
       Do not let the one of women be more popular than mine.

Let me have money in my hand.
Let me have children.
Let me have cloth.

xxxv.   Let me have all good things.

This is a medicine for *oṣó*, and it is therefore dangerous if
sacrifice is not made to it regularly. As the medicine resides in
the belly, the sacrifice takes the form of drinking the blood of the
sheep. In addition, Adebawọ prepares the belly for the recep-
tion of its new inhabitant.

ADEBAWỌ. Before we prepare this *oògùn oṣó*, we must first of all give the
person *àjẹsára*[12] because about two months after he has begun to lick the *oṣó*
or powder (*ẹ̀tù*), he will have fearful dreams—that is why some people say
that *oṣó* can kill people; *oṣó* can kill people if there is no *àjẹsára*. If there is no
sacrifice, it can kill a person.

This discussion of *oṣó* concludes the description of the principles
underlying *àwúre*.

Endnotes

[1] *Ayọ̀nmọ, kádàrá, àkúnlẹ̀yọn, àkúnlègbà*, and *kàdarà* may each be translated as
'destiny'.

[2] Abimbọla (1976, 113 ff.) and Idowu (1962, 169–85) deal with this in greater
detail.

[3] Drewal (1977) argues that the head in Yoruba symbolism has a general
symbolic association of a point of contact between man and the gods or
God. This argument is, I believe, broadly correct.

[4] *Ọrúnmìlà*'s destiny has already been settled in heaven before his birth.

[5] One of the *odù Ifá*.

[6] The words *ṣ́ẹ́rẹ́ṣ́ẹ́rẹ́* and *mìmì* indicate the motion of cutting and flowing
respectively and are virtually untranslatable.

[7] *Iwọ̀fà* is a bondsman or pawn who works for a creditor until repayment of the
debt.

[8] The name *iṣ́ẹ́pẹ́ agbe* literally means, 'the firewood of the blue turaco'.
Fatoogun suggested that its name comes from the fact that it looks like the
bird's leg.

[9] *Ogún*, god of iron.

[10] A name for *àkàlà*—the hornbill.

[11] *Ọlọ́fin* could refer to *Ọlọ́.run, Ọbàtálá*, to the chief of Lagos, or perhaps to
someone else.

[12] *Ajẹsára* is a medicine to be taken before another that is much stronger.

Bibliography

ABIMBỌLA, W. (1964). 'The Odù of Ifá'. *African Notes*. 2, 1.

—— (1965a). 'The Ẹsẹ of Ifá', *African Notes*, 2, 3.

—— (1965b). 'The place of Ifá in Yoruba traditional religion'. *African Notes*. 2, 2.

—— (1968). *Ijìnlẹ̀ ohùn ẹnu ifá—apá kìíni*. Collins, Glasgow.

—— (1973a). 'The Yoruba concept of the human personality'. *La Notion de Personne en Afrique Noire*, CNRS, Paris.

—— (1973b). 'The literature of the Ifá cult'. In (ed.) Biobaku (1973).

—— (1976). *Ifá: an exposition of Ifá literary corpus*. Ibadan.

ABRAHAM, R. C. (1958). *Dictionary of modern Yoruba*. University of London Press, London.

ACKERKNECHT, E. H. (1942). 'Problems of primitive medicine'. In Ackerknecht (1971).

—— (1965). *History and geography of the most important diseases*. Hafner publishing Co., New York and London.

—— (1971). *Medicine and ethnology, selected essays*. Ed. H. H. Walser and H. M. Koelbing, Johns Hopkins Press, Baltimore.

ADENIRAN, A. (1969). 'The intrinsic vital force of words—a sociological case study of "ọfọ" or "aṣẹ" in Yorubaland', unpublished dissertation B.Sc. Sociology, University of Ibadan, Ibadan.

ADETUGBA, A. (1973). 'The Yoruba language in Yoruba history'. In (ed.) Biobaku (1973).

AINA, J. A. c. (1932). *The present-day prophets and the principles upon which they work*, reprinted with an introduction by H. W. Turner. Crowther College of Religion, University of Nigeria, Nsukka, 1964.

AJIBOLA, J. O. (1947). *Owe Yoruba*. OUP, London.

AJOSE, O. A. (1957). 'Preventive medicine and superstition in Nigeria'. *Africa*. 28, 268–76.

AKIGA (1939). *Akiga's story—the Tiv tribe as seen by one of its members*, translated by Rupert East. OUP, London.

AKINRINSOLA, F. (1965). 'Ogun festival'. *Nigeria Magazine*. 85, June.

ARDENER, E. (1970). 'Witchcraft, economics and the continuity of belief'. In (ed.) Douglas (1970).

—— (1971). 'The new anthropology and its critics'. *Man*. 6, 449–67.

—— (1973). ' "Behaviour", a social anthropological criticism'. *Journal of the Anthropological Society of Oxford*. 4, 152–5.

—— (1978). 'Some outstanding problems in the analysis of events'. In (ed.) Schwimmer (1978).

ARMSTRONG, R. G. (1964). 'The use of linguistic and ethnographic data in

the study of Idoma and Yoruba history'. In Mauney, Thomas, and
Vansina (1964).

ARMSTRONG, R. P. (1971). *The affecting presence—an essay in humanistic
anthropology.* University of Illinois Press, Urbana, Chicago, London.

ASUNI, T. (1962). 'Suicide in Western Nigeria'. *British Medical Journal.* 2,
1091.

—— (1979). 'The dilemma of traditional healing with special reference to
Nigeria'. *Social Science and Medicine.* 13B, 33–9.

AWE, B. (1974). 'Praise poems as historical data: the example of the Yoruba
oriki'. *Africa.* 44, 331–49.

AWOLALU, J. O. (1970). 'The Yoruba philosophy of life'. *Presence Africaine*
(NS). 73, 20–38.

—— (1973). 'Yoruba sacrificial practice'. *Journal of religion in Africa.* 5,
81–93.

—— (1979). *Yoruba beliefs and sacrificial rites.* Longman, London.

AYORINDE, J. A. (1973). 'Oriki'. In (ed.) Biobaku (1973).

BALFOUR, H. (1929). 'Concerning thunderbolts'. *Folklore.* 40, 37–49.

BAMGBOOSE, T. A. (1965). *Yoruba orthography, A linguistic appraisal with
suggestions for reform.* Ibadan University Press, Ibadan.

—— (1966a). *A grammar of Yoruba.* CUP, London.

——(1966b). 'The assimilated low tone in Yoruba'. *Lingua.* 16, 1–13.

—— (1968). 'The form of Yoruba proberbs'. *Odù.* 4, 74–86.

—— (1972). 'The meaning of Olódùmarè'. *African Notes.* 7, 25–32.

BAMISAIYE, A. (1974). 'Begging in Ibadan, Southern Nigeria'. *Human
Organization.* 33, 197–202.

BANTON, M. P. (ed.) (1965). *The relevance of models for social anthropology.*
Tavistock Publications, London.

—— (1966). *Anthropological approaches to the study of religion.* Tavistock Publications, London.

BARBER, K. (1981). 'How man makes God in West Africa: Yoruba attitudes
towards the òrìṣà'. *Africa.* 51, 724–45.

BARNES, S. B. (1969). 'Paradigms—scientific and social'. *Man.* (NS) 4,
94–102.

BARTH, K. (1957). *An introductory essay.* In Feuerbach (1843).

BARTHES, R. (1957). *Mythologies.* Editions du Seuil, Paris.

BASCOM, W. R. (1941). 'The sanctions of Ifá divination'. *Journal of the Royal
Anthropological Institute.* 71, 43–51.

—— (1942). 'The principle of seniority in the social structure of the Yoruba'.
American Anthropologist. 44, 37–46.

—— (1943). 'The relationships of Yoruba folklore to divining'. *Journal of
American Folklore.* 56.

—— (1944). 'The sociological role of the Yoruba cult group'. *American
Anthropologist Memoir.* 63.

—— (1951a). 'Yoruba food'. *Africa.* 21, 41–53.

—— (1951b). 'Yoruba cooking'. *Africa.* 21, 125–37.

—— (1951c). 'Social status, wealth and individual differences among the
Yoruba'. *American Anthropologist.* 53, 490–505.

—— (1952). 'The esusu, a credit institution of the Yoruba'. *Journal of the Royal Anthropological Institute*. 82, 63–70.

—— (1959). 'Urbanism as a traditional African pattern'. *Sociological review*. 7, 29–43.

—— (1960). 'Yoruba concepts of the soul'. In (ed.) Wallace (1960).

—— (1961). 'The order of the figures of Ifa'. *Bulletin de l'IFAN*. 23, 676–82.

—— (1966). 'Odu Ifa: the names of the signs'. *Africa*. 36, 408–21.

—— (1969a). *The Yoruba of South Western Nigeria*. Holt, Rinehart and Winston, New York.

——(1969b). *Ifa divination: communication between gods and men in West Africa*. Indiana University Press, Bloomington and London.

——(1980). *Sixteen cowries: Yoruba divination from Africa to the New World*. Indiana University Press, Bloomington and London.

BATESON, G. (1973). *Steps to an ecology of mind: collected essays in anthropology, psychiatry, evolution and epistemology*. Paladin, Bungay.

BEALS, A. R. (1976). 'Strategies of resort to curers in south India'. In (ed.) Leslie (1976).

BEATTIE, J. (1963). 'Sorcery in Bunyoro'. In (ed.) Middleton and Winter (1963).

BECK, B. E. F. (1978a). 'The right-left division of South Indian society'. *Journal of Asian studies*. 29, 779–97.

—— (1978b). 'The metaphor as a mediator between semantic and analogic modes of thought'. *Current Anthropology*. 19, 83–97.

BEIDELMAN, T. O. (1973). 'Naguru symbolic classification'. In (ed.) Needham (1973).

BEIER, H. U. (1956). 'Quack doctors in a Yoruba village'. *Dokita*. 1, 57.

——(1958). 'Gelede masks'. *Odu*. 6, 5–23.

—— (1963). 'Three Igbin drums from Igbomiru'. *Nigeria Magazine*. 78.

—— (1964). 'The Agbegijo masqueraders'. *Nigeria Magazine*. 82, 188–99.

—— (1970). *Yoruba poetry—An anthology of traditional poems*, compiled by H. U. Beier, illustrated by Suzanne Wenger, CUP.

BERGER, P. L. (1967). *The sacred canopy—elements in a sociological theory of religion*. Doubleday, New York.

BERLIN, B., and KAY, P. (1969). *Basic color terms*. University of California Press, Berkeley and Los Angeles.

BIOBAKU, S. O. (ed.) (1973). *Sources of Yoruba history*. Clarendon Press, Oxford.

BIRD, M. E. C. (1958). 'Social change and marriage among the Yoruba of Western Nigeria', unpublished Ph.D. thesis, Department of Social Anthropology, Edinburgh.

BISILLIAT, J. (1976). 'Village diseases and bush diseases in Songhay: an essay in description and classification with a view to a typology', translated J. B. Loudon. In (ed.) Loudon (1976).

BLACK, M. (1969). 'Eliciting folk taxonomy in Ojibwa'. In (ed.) Tyler, (1969).

BOSTON, J. S. (1974). 'Ifa divination in Igala'. *Africa*, 44, 350–60.

BRADBURY, R. E. (1973). *Benin Studies*, ed. P. Morton Williams. OUP, Oxford.

BREIDENBACH, P. G. (1976). 'Colour symbolism and ideology in a Ghanaian healing movement'. *Africa.* 46, 137–45.

BRIL, B. (1979). 'Analyse des nombres associés à l'homme et à la femme en Afrique de l'ouest'. *Africa.* 49, 4 1979, 367–76.

BUCKLEY, A. D. (1976). 'The secret, an idea in Yoruba medicinal thought'. In (ed.) Loudon (1976).

—— (1982). *A gentle people: a study of a peaceful community in Northern Ireland.* Ulster Folk and Transport Museum, Cultra, Holywood, Co. Down.

—— (1983a). 'Neighbourliness: myth and history'. *Oral History.* 11, 44–57.

—— (1983b). 'Playful rebellion: social control and the framing of experience in an Ulster community'. *Man.* (NS) 18, 383–95.

—— (1984). 'Walls within walls: religion and rough behaviour in an Ulster community'. *Sociology* 18, 19–32.

BURRIDGE, K. O. L. (1967). 'Lévi-Strauss and myth'. In (ed.) Leach (1967).

BUXTON, J. (1973). *Religion and healing in Mandari.* Clarendon Press, Oxford.

CALDWELL, J. C., and CALDWELL, P. (1977). 'The role of marital sexual abstinence in determining fertility: a study of the Yoruba of Nigeria'. *Population Studies.* 31, 193.

CARROLL, K. F. (1973). 'Art in wood'. In (ed.) Biobaku (1973).

CHAPPEL, T. J. H. (1972). 'Critical carvers: a case study'. *Man.* (NS), 7, 296–307.

CHELHOD, J. (1964). 'A contribution to the problem of the preeminence of the right hand based upon Arabic evidence'. In (ed.) Needham (1973).

CLARKE, J. D. (1939). 'Ifa divination'. *Journal of the Royal Anthropological Institute.* 69, 235–56.

COLSON, A. B. (1976). 'Binary opposition and the treatment of sickness among the Akawaio'. In (ed.) Loudon (1976).

COSMINSKY, S. (1977). 'Alimento and fresco: nutritional concepts and their implications for health care'. *Human Organization.* 36, 203–7.

DELANO, S. O. (1973). 'Proverbs, songs and poems'. In (ed.) Biobaku (1973).

DE NEGRI, E. (1962). 'Yoruba men's costume'. *Nigeria Magazine.* 73, 4–12.

DENNETT, R. E. (1906). *At the back of the black man's mind.* Macmillan, London.

—— (1910). *Nigerian Studies—or the religious and political system of the Yoruba.* Cass, London, 1968.

DOS SANTOS, J. E., and DOS SANTOS, D. M. (1973). 'Eṣu Bara: principle of individual life in the Nago system'. *La Notion de Personne en Afrique Noire.* CNRS, Paris.

DOUGLAS, M. M. (1963). 'Techniques of sorcery control in central Africa'. In (ed.) Middleton and Winter (1963).

—— (1966). *Purity and danger, an analysis of concepts of pollution and taboo.* Routledge and Kegan Paul, London.

—— (1967a). 'The meaning of myth: with special reference to "La geste d'Asdiwal"'. In (ed.) Leach (1967).

——(1967b). 'Witch beliefs in central Africa'. *Africa.* 37, 72–80.

—— (ed.) (1970). *Witchcraft confession and accusations*. Tavistock publications, London.

—— (1970). 'Introduction: thirty years after "Witchcraft Oracles and Magic" '. In (ed.) Douglas (1970).

—— (1973). *Natural symbols—explorations in cosmology*. Penguin Books, Harmondsworth.

DOW, T. E. (1977). 'Breast feeding and abstinence among the Yoruba'. *Studies in Family Planning*. 8, 208–14.

DOWNIE, R. A. (1970). *Frazer and the Golden Bough*. Gollancz, London.

DREWAL, M. T. (1977). 'Projections from the top in Yoruba art', *African Arts*. 3, 43–91.

DUNDES, A. (1964). 'Some Yoruba wellerisms, dialogue, proverbs and tongue twisters'. *Folklore*. 75, 113–20.

EICHINGER FERRO-LUZZI, G. (1978). 'More on salt taboos'. *Current Anthropology*. 19, 413–15.

ELINSON, J., and GUTTMACHER, S. (1971). 'Ethno-religious variations in perception of illness: At the use of illness as an explanation for deviant behaviour', *Social Science and Medicine*. 5, 117–25.

ELLIS, A. B. (1894). *The Yoruba speaking peoples of the Slave Coast of West Africa*. Anthropological publications, Oosterhout, N. B., The Netherlands, 1966.

ENGELS, F. (1876). 'The part played by labour in the transition from ape to man'. In Engels and Marx (1962).

—— and MARX, K. (1962). *Selected works Vol. II*, Foreign languages publishing house, Moscow.

EPSTEIN, A. L. (1967). *The craft of social anthropology*. Social Science Paperbacks in association with Tavistock Publications, London.

EVANS PRITCHARD, E. E. (1937). *Witchcraft oracles and magic among the Azande*. OUP, London.

—— (1956). *Nuer religion*. OUP, London.

—— (1965). *Theories of primitive religion*. OUP, London.

FABREGA, H. (1974). *Disease and social behavior*. MIT Press, Cambridge, Mass., and London.

—— (1979). 'The ethnography of illness'. *Social Science and Medicine*. 13A, 565–76.

—— and MANNING, P. K. (1972). 'Health maintenance among Peruvian peasants'. *Human Organization*. 31, 243–56.

—— METZGER, D., and WILLIAMS, G. (1970). 'Psychiatric implications of health and illness in a Mayo Indian group—a preliminary statement'. *Social Science and Medicine*. 3, 609–26.

FAGG, W. (1959). 'On a stone head of variant style at Esie, Nigeria'. *Man*. 59, 60.

FEIERMAN, S. (1979). 'Change in African pluralistic societies'. *Social Science and Medicine*. 13B, 277–84.

FERNANDEZ, J. W. (1974). 'The mission of metaphor in expressive culture'. *Current Anthropology*. 15, 119–33.

—— (1975). 'On the concept of the symbol'. *Current Anthropology*. 16, 652–4.

FEUERBACH, L. (1843). *The essence of Christianity*. Translated by George Eliot with an introductory essay by Karl Barth and a foreword by H. Richard Niebuhr. Harper Torchbooks, Harper and Row, New York, Evanston and London.

FORDE, D., and KABERRY, P. M. (ed.) (1967). *West African kingdoms in the nineteenth century*. OUP, London.

FORGE, A. (1970). 'Prestige, influence and sorcery—a New Guinea example'. In (ed.) Douglas (1970).

FOSTER, G. M. (1979). 'Methodological problems in the study of intracultural variation—the hot/cold dichotomy in Tzintzuntzan'. *Human Organization*. 38, 179–85.

FOX, J. J. (1973). 'On bad death and the left hand—the study of Rotisese symbolic inversions'. In (ed.) Needham (1973).

FRAKE, C. O. (1961). 'The diagnosis of disease among the Subanun of Mindaneo'. *American Anthropologist*. 63, 113–32.

FRANK, J. D. (1963). *Persuasion and healing*. Schocken, New York.

—— (1974). 'Therapeutic components of psychotherapy'. *Journal of Nervous and Mental Diseases*. 159, 325–42.

——(1975). 'Physiotherapy of bodily diseases: an overview'. *Physiotherapy and Psychosomatics*. 26, 192–202.

FRANKENBERG, R., and LEESON, J. (1976). 'Disease, illness and sickness: social aspects of the choice of healer in a Lusaka suburb'. In (ed.) Loudon, (1976).

FROBENIUS, L. (1913). *The voice of Africa*. Translated by L. Blind, Benjamin Blom, Bronx, New York, 1968.

FUJA, A. (1967). *Fourteen hundred cowries, traditional stories of the Yoruba*. OUP, Ibadan.

GIAPASSI, J., and KURTZ, R. F. (1975). 'Medical and social work students' perceptions of deviant conditions and sick role incumbency'. *Social Science and Medicine*. 9, 249–55.

GLICK, L. B. (1967). 'Medicine as an ethnographic category: the Gimi of the New Guinea Highlands'. *Ethnology*. 6, 122–5.

GODDARD, S. (1965). 'Town-farm relationships in Yorubaland—a case study, from Ọyọ'. *Africa*. 35, 21–9.

GOFFMAN, E. (1974). *Frame analysis: an essay on the organization of experience*. Penguin Books, Harmondsworth.

GOLDMANN, L. (1967). 'The sociology of literature: status and problems of method'. *International Social Science Journal*. 19, 493–516.

GRAY, R. F. (1963). 'Some structural aspects of Mbugwe witchcraft'. In (ed.) Middleton and Winter (1963).

GRIAULE, M. (1965). *Conversations with Ogotemmeli, an introduction to Dogon religious ideas*. OUP, London.

HARWOOD, A. (1971). 'The hot-cold theory of disease—implications for the treatment of Puerto Rican patients'. *Journal of the American Medical Association*. 216, 1153–8.

HEGEL, G. W. F. (1970). *The philosophy of nature*. Edited and translated with an introduction and explanatory notes by M. J. Petry, George Allen and Unwin, London. Humanities Press Inc., New York, 3 vols.

HERTZ, R. (1909). 'The preeminence of the right hand—a study in religious polarity'. Translated by R. Needham. In (ed.) Needham (1973).

HILL, C. E. (ed.) (1975). *Symbols and society.* University of Georgia Press, Athens, Ga.

HOLY, L. (ed.) (1976). *Knowledge and behaviour.* Department of Anthropology, Queen's University of Belfast, Belfast.

—— (1976). 'Sorcery and social tensions: the Lewu case'. In (ed.) Holy (1976).

HOMANS, G. C. (1941). 'Anxiety and ritual—the theories of Malinowski and Radcliffe Brown'. *American Anthropologist.* 43, 164–72.

HORTON, R. (1967). 'African traditional thought and western science'. *Africa.* 37, 50–71 and 155–87.

—— (1968). 'Neo-Tylorianism—sound sense or sinister prejudice'. *Man.* (NS) 3, 625–34.

HUDSON, C. (1975). 'Vomiting for purity: ritual emesis in the aboriginal southeastern United States'. In (ed.) Hill (1975).

HUNTINGFORD, G. W. B. (1963). 'Nandi witchcraft'. In (ed.) Middleton and Winter (1963).

IDOWU, E. B. (1962). *Olodumare, God in Yoruba belief.* Longmans, London.

IGUN, U. A. (1979). 'Stages in health—seeking: a descriptive model'. *Social Science and Medicine.* 13A, 445–56.

JAHODA, G. (1966). 'Social aspirations, magic and witchcraft in Ghana—a social psychological interpretation'. In (ed.) Lloyd (1966).

JOHNSON, S. (1921). *The history of the Yoruba,* Routledge and Kegan Paul, 1966.

JONES, G. J. (1970). 'A boundary to accusation'. In (ed.) Douglas (1970).

KENNEDY, J. G. (1967). 'Nubian Zar ceremonies as psychotherapy'. *Human Organization.* 26, 185–94.

KIEV, A. (ed.) (1964). *Magic faith and healing.* Free Press, New York.

KLEINMAN, A. M. (1977). 'Depression somatization and the new cross cultural psychiatry'. *Social Science and Medicine.* 11, 3–11.

—— (1980). *Patients and healers in the context of culture—an exploration of the borderland between anthropology, medicine and psychiatry.* University of California Press, Berkeley, Los Angeles, London.

—— and SUNG, L. H. (1979). 'Why do indigenous practitioners successfully heal?' *Social Science and Medicine.* 13B, 7–26.

KRUYT, A. C. (1941). 'Right and left in Central Celebes'. Translated by R. Needham. In (ed.) Needham (1973).

KUHN, T. S. (1962). *The structure of scientific revolutions.* University of Chicago Press, 1962.

LADIPO, D. (1966). *Ọba kò so, the king did not hang.* Transcription by R. L. Awujọọla and R. G. Armstrong, translated R. G. Armstrong from recording by Carl Witlig, Ibadan Institute of African Studies, University of Ibadan.

LA FLESCHE, F. (1916). 'Left and right in Osage ceremonies'. In (ed.) Needham (1973).

LAKOFF, G., and JOHNSON, M. (1980). *Metaphors we live by*. University of Chicago Press, Chicago and London.

LAMBO, T. A. (1956). 'Neuropsychiatric observation in the Western Region of Nigeria'. *British Medical Journal*. ii, 1386–96.

—— (1965). 'Akufo and Ibarapa'. *Lancet*. 1965, 307–8.

'LAOYE, I. J. A. (1956). *The story of my installation*. Afin Tìmì, Ẹdẹ, Nigeria, published by the author.

LASEBIKAN, E. L. (1956). 'The tonal structure of Yoruba poetry'. *Presence Africaine*. 8, 10.

LAWAL, B. (1977). 'The living dead: art and immortality among the Yoruba of Nigeria'. *Africa*. 47, 50–61.

LEACH, E. R. (1958). 'Magical hair'. In (ed.) Middleton (1967).

—— (1961). 'Lévi-Strauss in the Garden of Eden—an examination of some recent developments in the analysis of myth'. *Transactions of the New York Academy of Sciences*. II, 23, 386–96.

—— (1962). 'Genesis as myth'. In (ed.) Middleton (1967).

—— (ed.) (1967). *The structural study of myth and totemism*. Tavistock Press, London.

LEIGHTON, A. H., LAMBO, T. A., HUGHES, C. C., LEIGHTON, D. C., MURPHEY, J. M., MACKLIN, D. B. (1963). *Psychiatric disorder among the Yoruba: a report from the Cornell-Aro mental health research project in the Western Region, Nigeria*. Cornell University Press, Ithaca, New York.

LESLIE, C. (ed.) (1976). *Asian medical systems: a comparative study*. University of California, Berkeley, London.

LEVINE, R. A. (1963). 'Witchcraft and sorcery in a Gusii community'. In (ed.) Middleton and Winter (1963).

LÉVI-STRAUSS, C. (1949). 'L'efficacité symbolique (1)'. In Lévi-Strauss (1958).

—— (1955). 'The structural study of myth'. *Journal of American Folklore*. 68, 428–44.

—— (1958). *Anthropologie structurale*. Plon, Paris.

—— (1964–71). *Mythologiques:– I Le cru et le cuit* (1964); *II Du miel au cendres* (1966); *III L'origine des manières de table* (1968); *L'homme nu* (1971), Plon, Paris.

—— (1967). 'The story of Asdiwal'. In (ed.) Leach (1967).

—— (1977). *Myth and meaning*. Routledge and Kegan Paul, London.

LEWIS, I. M. (1970). 'A structural approach to witchcraft and spirit possession', in (ed.) Douglas (1970).

LIENHARDT, G. (1961). *Divinity and experience, the religion of the Dinka*. OUP, London, 1967.

LITTLEJOHN, J. (1967). 'Temne right and left: an essay in the choreography of everyday life'. *New Society*. 9 Feb. 1967, 198–9.

LLOYD, G. (1962). 'Right and left in Greek philosophy'. In (ed.) Needham (1973).

LLOYD, P. C. (1953). 'Craft organization in Yoruba towns'. *Africa.* 23, 30–44.

—— (1962). *Yoruba land law.* OUP, London.

—— (ed.) (1966). *The new elites of tropical Africa.* OUP, London.

LOGAN, M. (1973). 'Humoral medicine in Guatemala and peasant acceptance of modern medicine'. *Human Organization,* 72, 385–95.

LOUDON, J. B. (ed.) (1976). *Social anthropology and medicine.* Academic Press. London, New York.

LUCAS, J. O. (1948). *The religion of the Yorubas, being an account of the religious beliefs and practices of the Yoruba peoples of southern Nigeria, especially in relation to the religions of ancient Egypt.* Church Missionary Society Bookshop, Lagos, 1948.

MACLEAN, C. M. U. (1964). 'Attitudes and beliefs relating to health and disease in an urban West African community'. Dissertation for diploma in public health. Edinburgh University, 1963–4.

—— (1965a). 'Traditional medicine and its practitioners in Ibadan. Nigeria'. *Journal of Tropical Medicine and Hygiene.* 68, 237.

—— (1965b). 'Tradition in transition: a health opinion survey in Ibadan'. *British Journal of Preventive and Social Medicine.* 19, 192–7.

—— (1971). *Magical medicine, a Nigerian case study.* Allen Lane, The Penguin Press, Harmondsworth.

—— (1976). 'Some aspects of sickness behaviour among the Yoruba'. In (ed.) Loudon (1976).

—— (1978a). 'Yoruba mothers, a study of changing methods of child rearing in urban and rural Nigeria'. *Journal of Tropical Medicine and Hygiene.* 69, 253–63.

—— (1978b). 'Choices of treatment among the Yoruba'. In (ed.) Moreley and Wallis (1978).

MCCLELLAND, D. (ed.) (1972) *Karl Marx: Early texts.* Blackwell, Oxford.

MCCLELLAND, F. M. (1966). 'The significance of number in the odu of Ifa'. *Africa.* 36, 421–30.

MADSEN, W. (1955). 'Hot and cold in the universe of San Francisco. Tecospa'. *Journal of American Folklore.* 68, 123–40.

MARGETTS, E. L. (1965). 'Traditional Yoruba healers in Nigeria' *Man.* 65, 102.

MARWICK, M. G. (1967). 'The study of witchcraft'. In (ed.) A. L. Epstein (1967).

MARX, K. (1844). 'Economic and Philosophical manuscripts'. In (ed.) McClelland (1972).

MATTHEWS, D. S. (1956). 'A preliminary note on the ethnological and medical significance of breast feeding among the Yoruba'. *Report du conférence international des Africanistes de l'ouest IFAN'.* Dakar, 1956, 269–79.

MAUNEY, R., THOMAS, L. V., and VANSINA, J. (1964). *The historian in tropical Africa,* OUP, London.

MAZES, R. B. (1968). 'Hot-cold food beliefs among Andean peasants'. *Journal of the American Dietetic Association.* 53, 109–13.

MIDDLETON, J. F. M. (1960). *Lugbara religion—ritual and authority among an East African people.* OUP, London.

—— (1963). 'Witchcraft and sorcery in Lugbara'. In (ed.) Middleton and Winter (1963).

—— (ed.) (1967). *Myth and cosmos: readings in mythology and symbolism.* New York, Natural History Press for the American Museum of Natural History.

—— and WINTER, E. H. (ed.) (1963). *Witchcraft and sorcery in East Africa.* Routledge and Kegan Paul, London.

MITCHELL, R. C. (1963). 'The aladura movement among the Yoruba'. Revised edition of paper to the African Studies Association Annual Meeting, San Francisco, October 1963.

—— (1965). 'Witchcraft, sin, divine power and healing: the aladura churches and the attainment of life's destiny among the Yoruba'. In *The traditional background to medical practice in Nigeria.* University of Ibadan, 1965.

—— (1968). 'Religious protest and social change—the origins of the aladura movement in Western Nigeria'. Unpublished manuscript.

—— (1970). 'Towards the sociology of religious independency'. *Journal of Religion in Africa.* 3, 2–21.

—— and TURNER, H. W. (ed.) (1968). *A comprehensive bibliography of modern African religious movements.* Northwestern University Press, Evanston.

MOERMAN, D. E. (1979). 'Anthropology of symbolic healing'. *Current Anthropology.* 20, 59–80.

MONTGOMERY, R. C. (1974). 'A cross-cultural study of menstruation, menstrual taboos and related social variables'. *Ethos.* 2, 136–70.

MORELEY, P., and WALLIS, R. (ed.) (1978). *Culture and curing—anthropological perspectives on traditional medical beliefs and practices.* Peter Owen, London.

MORTON WILLIAMS, P. (1956a). 'The Atinga cult among the South Western Yoruba, a sociological analysis of a witch finding cult'. *Bulletin de l'IFAN.* XVIII, ser B, 3–4.

—— (1956b). 'The egungun cult in southwestern Yoruba kingdoms'. *WAISER conference proceedings,* 1954, Ibadan West African Institute of Social and Economic Research.

—— (1960a). 'Yoruba responses to the fear of death'. *Africa.* 30, 1, 34–40.

—— (1960b). 'The Yoruba Ogboni cult in Ọyọ'. *Africa.* 30, 362–74.

—— (1964). 'An outline of the cosmology and cult organization of the Ọyọ Yoruba'. *Africa.* 34, 243–61.

—— (1967). 'The Yoruba kingdom of Ọyọ'. In (ed.) Forde and Kaberry (1967).

—— and WESTCOTT, J. (1962). 'The symbolism and ritual context of the Yoruba laba Shango', *Journal of the Royal Anthropological Institute,* 92, 23–38.

MURPHY, W. P. (1980). 'Secret knowledge as property and power in Kpelle society elders versus youth'. *Africa.* 50, 192–207.

NADEL, S. F. (1954). *Nupe religion.* Routledge and Kegan Paul, London.

NASH, J. (1967). 'The logic of sickness behaviour: curing in a Maya Indian town'. *Human Organization.* 26, 132–40.

NATHANSON, C. A. (1975). 'Illness and the feminine role—a theoretical review'. *Social science and medicine.* 9, 57–62.

NEEDHAM, R. (1960). 'The left hand of the Mugwe—an analytical note on the structure of Meru symbolism'. In (ed.) Needham, (1973).

—— (1967a). 'Percussion and transition'. *Man.* 2, 606–14.

—— (1967b). 'Right and left in Nyoro symbolic classification'. *Africa.* 37, 425–51.

—— (1972). *Belief, language and experience.* Blackwell, Oxford.

—— (ed.) (1973). *Right and left: essays on dual symbolic classification.* University of Chicago Press, London and Chicago.

NEUMANN, T. W. (1978). 'Reply to Eichinger Ferro-Luzzi. 1978'. *Current Anthropology.* 19, 413–15.

NGUBANE, H. (1976). 'Some aspects of treatment among the Zulu'. In (ed.) Loudon (1976).

NGUBANE, H. (1977). *Body and mind in Zulu medicine: an ethnography of health and disease in Nguswa—Zulu thought and practice,* Academic Press, London.

NICOLAS, G. (1968). 'Un système symbolique: le quatre, le trois et le sept dans la cosmologie d'une société hausa (valée du Marad.)'. *Cahiers d'études Africaines.* 8, 566–616.

ODUYOYE, M. (1971). *The vocabulary of Yoruba religious discourse.* Daystar Press, Ibadan.

OGDEN, C. K. and RICHARDS, I. A. (1923). *The meaning of meaning: a study of the influence of language upon thought and of the science of symbolism.* Kegan Paul, Trench, Trubner, London.

OGUNBA, O. (1973). 'Ceremonies'. In (ed.) Biobaku (1973).

OJO, J. R. O. (1968). 'Some Ifa divination apparatus'. *Odu.* 4, 52 ff.

—— and OLAJUBU, CHIEF O. (1977). 'Some aspects of Ọyọ Yoruba masquerades'. *Africa.* 47, 253–75.

ORTONY, A. (ed.) (1979). *Metaphor and thought.* CUP, Cambridge.

ORUBULOYE, I. O. (1979). 'Sexual abstinence patterns in rural Western Nigeria: evidence from a survey of Yoruba women'. *Social science and medicine.* 13A, 667–72.

OTTO, R. (1917). *The idea of the Holy.* Translated by J. W. Harvey. Penguin Books, Harmondsworth, 1959.

OYEBỌ LA, D. D. O. (1980a). 'Traditional medicine and its practitioners among the Yoruba of Nigeria: a classification'. *Social Science and Medicine.* 14A, 23–9.

—— (1980b). 'The method of training healers and midwives among the Yoruba of Nigeria'. *Social Science and Medicine.* 14A, 31–7.

—— (1981). 'Professional associates, ethics and discipline among Yoruba traditional healers of Nigeria'. *Social Science and Medicine.* 15b, 87–92.

PARK, G. K. (1963). 'Divination and its social contexts'. *Journal of the Royal Anthropological Institute.* 93, 195–209.

PARRINDER, E. G. S. (1949). *West African religion: a study of the beliefs and practices of Akan Ewe, Yoruba, Ibo and kindred peoples.* Epworth Press, London, 1961.

—— (1950). 'Theistic beliefs of the Yoruba and Ewe peoples of West Africa'. *African ideas of God: a symposium.* Edinburgh House, London, 224–41.

—— (1951). 'Ibadan annual festival'. *Africa*. 21, 54–8.

—— (1953). *Religion in an African city*. OUP, London.

—— (1958). *Witchcraft, European and African*. Faber and Faber, London, 1963.

PEEL, J. D. Y. (1965). 'Two aladura churches of Yorubaland'. Paper read to seminar, University of Ibadan, Ibadan.

—— (1966). 'A sociological study of two independent churches among the Yoruba'. Ph.D. thesis, University of London, 1966.

—— (1967). 'Religious change in Yorubaland'. *Africa*. 37, 292–306.

PIERCE, T. O. (1980). 'Political and economic changes in Nigeria and the organization of medical care'. *Social Science and Medicine*. 14B, 91–8.

PRINCE, R. H. (1959). 'Psychotherapy with herb medicines and magic. "Curse" as a possible precipitating factor for neurosis and psychosis'. *Review and Newsletter: transcultural research problems in mental health*. McGill University, Montreal, 1959, 42–4.

—— (1960). 'The use of rauwolfia for the treatment of psychoses by Nigerian native doctors'. *American journal of psychiatry*. 117, 147–9.

—— (1961). 'The Yoruba image of the witch'. *Journal of Mental Science*. 107, 795–805.

—— (1962). 'Western psychiatry and the Yoruba—the problems of insight psychiatry'. *Proceedings of the 8th conference of the Nigerian Institute for Social and Economic Research*. 8.

—— (1964a). 'Indigenous Yoruba psychiatry'. In (ed.) A, Kiev (1964).

—— (1964b). *Ifa: Yoruba divination and sacrifice*. Ibadan University Press, Ibadan.

—— (1966). 'Pellagra: its recognition and treatment by the Yoruba healers of West Africa'. *Verhandlungen des XX Internationalen kongresses für Geschichte der Medizin Berlin, August 1966*, Georg Olms Verlagsbuchhandlung, Hildesheiln, 1968

REDDY, M. (1979). 'The conduit metaphor: a case of frame conflict in our language about language'. In (ed.) Ortony (1979).

RICHARDSON, A. (1953). *Genesis I–XI Introduction and commentary*, Student Christian Movement Press, London.

RIGBY, P. (1966). 'Dual symbolic classification among the Gogo of Central Tanzania', *Africa*. 36, 1–16.

RILEY, J. N. (1980). 'Client choice among osteopaths and ordinary physicians in a Michigan community', *Social Science and Medicine*. 14b.

RUBEL, A. J. (1960). 'Concepts of disease in Mexican American culture'. *American Anthropologist*. 62, 795–814.

SAHLINS, M. D. (1965). 'On the sociology of primitive exchange'. In (ed.) Banton (1965).

—— (1974). *Stone age economics*. Tavistock Publications, London.

SAUSSURE, F. DE (1915). *A course in general linguistics*. Ed. Charles Bully and Albert Sechohaye in collaboration with Albert Reidlinger, translated from the French by Wale Baskin. Peter Owen, London, 1960.

SCHAPIRO, A. K. (1959). 'The placebo effect in the history of medical treatment—implications for psychiatry'. *American journal of psychiatry*. 116, 298–304.

SCHWAB, W. B. (1952). 'The growth and conflicts of religion in a modern Yoruba community'. *Zaïre*. VI. 829–35.

—— (1955). Kinship and lineage among the Yoruba'. *Africa* 25, 352–74.

SCHWIMMER, E. (ed.) (1978). *The yearbook of symbolic anthropology*. C. Hurst and Company, London.

SIMPSON, G. E. (1980). *Yoruba religion and medicine in Ibadan*. Ibadan University Press, Ibadan.

SINGER, K. (1975). 'Depressive disorders from a transcultural perspective'. *Social Science and Medicine*. 9, 289–301.

SMITH, R. G. (1969). *Kingdoms of the Yoruba*. Methuen, London.

SOWANDE, F. (n.d.) *Ifa*. Forward Press, Yaba.

SPERBER, D. (1974). *Rethinking symbolism*. Translated by Alice C. Morton, CUP, Cambridge, 1975.

—— (1975). 'Pourquoi les animaux parfaits, les hybrides et les monstres sont-ils bons à penser symboliquement?' *L'homme*. 15, 5–34.

—— (1976). 'Dirt, danger and pangolins'. *Times Literary Supplement*. 3868, 30 April 1976, 502–3.

SPIER, L. (ed.) (1941). *Language, culture and personality, essays in memory of Edward Sapir*. University of Utah Press, Salt Lake City.

STEVENS, P. (1965). 'The festival of the images at Esie', *Nigeria Magazine*. 87, 237–45.

STRICKLAND, D. A., and SCHLESINGER, L. E. (1969). ' "Lurking" as a reasearch method'. *Human Organization*, 28, 248–50.

STUCHLIK, M. (1976). 'Whose knowledge?' In (ed.) Holy (1976).

TAMBIAH, S. J. (1968). 'The magical power of words'. *Man*. (NS) 3, 175–208.

TONKIN, E. (1979). 'Masks and power'. *Man*. 14, 237–48.

TURNBULL, T. N. (1959). *What God hath wrought—a short history of the Apostolic Church*. Puritan Press, Bradford.

TURNER, H. W. (1965). 'Prophet and politics—a Nigerian test case', *Bulletin of the Society for African Church History*, 2.

—— (1967a). 'Religious and political independence in Africa: the place of independent religious movements in the modernization of Africa', *Istanbul Round Table meeting of the International Political Science Association*.

—— (1967b). *History of an African independent church: The Church of the Lord (Aladura)*, (2 volumes). OUP, London.

—— (1967c). 'A typology for African religious movements'. *Journal of Religion in Africa*. 1.

—— (1969). 'The place of independent religious movements in the modernization of Africa'. *Journal of Religion in Africa*. 2, 43–63.

—— (ed.) (1970). 'Bibliography of religious movements supplement II', *Journal of religion in Africa*. 3, 161–208.

—— (1977). *Bibliography of new religious movements in primal societies. Volume I, Black Africa*, Boston, G. K. Hall.

TURNER, T. (n.d.). 'Myth as model: the Kayapo myth of the origins of cooking fire'. Unpublished, Department of Anthropology, University of Chicago.

TURNER, V. W. (1953). *Lunda rites and ceremonies*. Rhodes Livingstone Museum, occasional papers 25, Livingstone, Northern Rhodesia.

—— (1957). *Schism and continuity in an African society—a study of Ndembu village life*. Manchester University Press, Manchester.

—— (1962). 'Themes in the symbolism of Ndembu hunting ritual'. *Anthropological Quarterly*. 35, 37–58.

—— (1963). *Lunda medicine and the treatment of disease*. Rhodes Livingstone Museum, occasional paper 25, Livingstone, Northern Rhodesia.

—— (1966). 'Color classification in Ndembu ritual: a problem in primitive classification'. In (ed.) Banton (1966).

—— (1968). *The drums of affliction: A study of religious processes among the Ndembu of Zambia*. Clarendon Press, Oxford.

—— (1969). *The ritual process: structure and anti-structure*. Routledge and Kegan Paul, London.

—— (1975). 'Ritual as communication and potency—an Ndembu case study'. In (ed.) Hill (1975).

TUTUOLA, A. (1952). *The palm-wine drinkard and his dead palm-wine tapster in the Deads' Town*. Faber and Faber, 1963.

TYLER, S. A. (ed.) (1969). *Cognitive anthropology*. Holt, Rinehart and Winston, New York.

TYLER, S. A. (1969). Introduction to (ed.) Tyler (1969).

UYANGA, J. (1979). 'The characteristics of patients of spiritual healing homes and traditional doctors in Southeastern Nigeria'. *Social Science and Medicine*. 13A, 323–9.

VERGER, P. F. (1957). *Notes sur le culte des oriṣa et vodun Saints, au Brazil, et à l'ancienne Côte des Esclaves en Afrique*. Mémoires d'IFAN, 51, Dakar.

—— (1966). 'Tranquillizers and stimulants in Yoruba herbal treatment'. Presented at special seminar, *The traditional background to medical practice in Nigeria*. University of Ibadan, Ibadan.

—— (1967). *Awǫn ewe Ǫsanyin, Yoruba medicinal leaves*. Institute of African Studies, University of Ifẹ.

—— (1973). 'Notion de personne et ligne familiale chez les Yoruba'. *La notion de personne en Afrique Noire*, CNRS, Paris.

WALLACE, A. F. C. (1958). 'Dreams and the wishes of the soul—a type of psychological theory among the seventeenth century Iroquois'. *American Anthropologist*. 60, 234–48.

—— (ed.) (1960). *Men and cultures*. University of Pennsylvania Press, Phil.

WEISCHOFF, H. A. (1938). 'Concepts of left and right in African cultures'. In (ed.) Needham (1973).

WESTCOTT, J. (1962). 'The sculpture and myths of Eshu—Elegba, the Yoruba trickster; definition and interpretation in Yoruba iconography'. *Africa*. 32, 336–54.

WHORF, B. L. (1941). 'The relation of habitual thought and behaviour to language'. In (ed.) Spier (1941).

WILLIAMS, D. (1964). 'The iconography of the Yoruba Ẹdan Ogboni'. *Africa.* 32, 139–66.

—— (1965). 'Lost-wax brass-casting in Ibadan'. *Nigeria Magazine,* 85, 69–100.

—— (1973). 'Art in metal'. In (ed.) Biobaku (1973).

WILLIS, R. G. (1967). 'The head and the loins: Lévi-Strauss and beyond'. *Man.* 2, 519–34.

—— (1972). 'Pollutions and paradigms'. *Man.* 7, 369–86.

—— (1978). 'Magic and "medicine" in Ufipa'. In (eds.) Moreley and Wallis (1978).

WILSON, P. J. (1974). 'Oscar—an inquiry into madness'. *Natural History.* 83, 43–50.

Index

Alphabetical order. In this index, a double vowel in a Yoruba word is treated as though it were a single vowel. Thus *èelá* succeeds *èkùrọ́* rather than *eburú*. The letters 'gb' are treated as two separate letters and not, as is sometimes the case in Yoruba dictionaries, etc., as a single letter.